LITERACY TEACHER EDUCATION

LITERACY TEACHER EDUCATION

Principles and Effective Practices

Deborah G. Litt
Susan D. Martin
Nancy A. Place

Foreword by Victoria J. Risko

THE GUILFORD PRESS
New York   London

© 2015 The Guilford Press
A Division of Guilford Publications, Inc.
72 Spring Street, New York, NY 10012
www.guilford.com

Printed in the United States of America

This book is printed on acid-free paper.

Last digit is print number: 9   8   7   6   5   4   3   2   1

Library of Congress Cataloging-in-Publication Data

Litt, Deborah G.
    Literacy teacher education : principles and effective practices / Deborah G. Litt,
Susan D. Martin, Nancy A. Place.
        pages cm
    Includes bibliographical references and index.
    ISBN 978-1-4625-1832-6 (pbk.) — ISBN 978-1-4625-1841-8 (hardcover)
    1. Reading teachers—Training of.   2. Literacy.   I. Martin, Susan Duell
II. Place, Nancy A.   III. Title.
    LB2844.1.R4L57   2015
    428.4071′2—dc23
                                                                  2014038052

About the Authors

Deborah G. Litt, PhD, is Associate Professor of Education at Trinity (Washington) University in Washington, DC, where she directs the Reading Program and teaches courses in literacy learning, instruction, and assessment to preservice and inservice teachers. She previously worked as an independent consultant introducing Writer's Workshop to schools in the DC metropolitan area, and then for 10 years as a Reading Recovery teacher and reading specialist in Title I schools. Her current research interests include emergent and early reading, reading difficulties, and literacy teacher education.

Susan D. Martin, PhD, is Professor in the Department of Literacy, Language, and Culture at Boise State University. She has taught a range of literacy courses, including courses dedicated to writing/writing instruction at undergraduate and graduate levels. She was an elementary classroom teacher for 18 years and still spends 1 day a week in a partner school, working with teacher candidates, mentor teachers, and others. Her research interests include writing teacher education, classroom writing instruction, and self-study of her teacher education practices.

Nancy A. Place, PhD, recently retired as Associate Professor of Education and Associate Director of the Education Program at the University of Washington Bothell. Over the course of nearly 30 years she was a classroom teacher, Reading Recovery teacher, coach, and district curriculum specialist. She taught courses on literacy development, instruction and assessment, and facilitated groups of candidates seeking National Board certification. Her research interests include preservice and inservice teacher education and emergent literacy.

Contributors

Erica Bowers, EdD, Department of Reading, California State University, Fullerton, Fullterton, California

Mary Ann Cahill, EdD, Department of Literacy, Language, and Culture, Boise State University, Boise, Idaho

Maggie Chase, PhD, Department of Literacy, Language, and Culture, Boise State University, Boise, Idaho

Tricia DeGraff, MS, Department of Curriculum and Instructional Leadership, University of Missouri–Kansas City, Kansas City, Missouri

Sherry Dismuke, PhD, Department of Curriculum, Instruction, and Foundational Studies, Boise State University, Boise, Idaho

Elizabeth Dobler, PhD, Department of Elementary Education, Early Childhood, and Special Education, Emporia State University, Emporia, Kansas

Joanne Durham, MEd, literacy consultant, Kure Beach, North Carolina

Elizabeth Dutro, PhD, Department of Literacy Studies, University of Colorado Boulder, Boulder, Colorado

Kathy Ganske, PhD, Department of Teaching and Learning, Peabody College of Education, Vanderbilt University, Nashville, Tennessee

Anne Gregory, PhD, Department of Literacy, Language, and Culture, Boise State University, Boise, Idaho

Karen Kindle, EdD, Department of Curriculum and Instruction, University of South Dakota, Vermillion, South Dakota

Lotta Larson, PhD, Department of Curriculum and Instruction, Kansas State University, Manhattan, Kansas

Cynthia Schmidt, PhD, Department of Curriculum and Instructional Leadership, University of Missouri–Kansas City, Kansas City, Missouri

Antony Smith, PhD, Department of Education, University of Washington Bothell, Bothell, Washington

Eun Hye Son, PhD, Department of Literacy, Language, and Culture, Boise State University, Boise, Idaho

Lee Ann Tysseling, PhD, Department of Literacy, Language, and Culture, Boise State University, Boise, Idaho

Foreword

When we think about the learning of children and adolescents in school, nothing matters more than teacher education. The teacher is the single most important contributor to student learning, and high-quality teacher preparation and professional development are catalysts for promoting excellence in teaching. Those teachers who graduate from rigorous teacher education programs and continue to be involved in sustained professional development are most likely to be associated with students' gains in learning and achievement. They are also likely to stay in the profession longer.

Teacher education and professional development programs face tremendous pressure, however, with calls for reforms from policymakers, legislators, and education leaders. While questioning the merit and quality of teacher education, some reform efforts are advancing noncertification accelerated programs or arguing for a reduced set of teacher education courses. In some regions in the United States, teachers are receiving no credit (traditionally associated with merit recognition or salary benefits) for completing advanced college course work or professional development across multiple sites.

With these calls for change, little attention is given to a growing and substantive body of teacher education research, especially in the area of literacy teacher education. For at least three decades, teacher education researchers have focused specifically on questions that affect teacher educators worldwide: *What should teachers learn? What conditions*

enable such learning? Will high-quality teacher education have a posi-
tive impact on teacher performance and student learning? Overall, these
researchers have established a credible research base addressing the first
two questions; the third question, however, has been less addressed by
research. Yet the impact of teacher education on teacher learning and
performance is receiving increased attention. One effort comes from
the consortia involving Stanford University, the American Association of
Colleges of Teacher Education, and universities in 34 states that are col-
laborating to conduct a rigorous assessment of the teaching performance
of graduating and first-year teachers across multiple sites.

The question of how best to prepare teachers brought the authors of
this book together, and they answer it with well-documented, thoughtful, and compelling recommendations. They have pursued this question
of teacher preparation for several years, through an analysis of their own
teaching and their collaborations with each other. Some of this work has
been presented at annual conferences of the Literacy Research Association. As a reactor to their paper presentations, I had the opportunity to
join in rich discussions of their concerns, their choice of instructional
strategies, and what they were learning from their teaching. The wealth
of information that came from those sessions and the authors' additional
work is an important contribution to the field, helping other teacher educators take a giant leap forward in making sense of their own teaching
dilemmas and decisions.

Deborah Litt, Susan Martin, and Nancy Place represent so many
of us in teacher education. We entered the profession with years of
PreK–12 teaching experience and well-established theoretical, content,
and pedagogical knowledge. Yet we have questions about our role as
teacher educators and how to translate our knowledge into particular
teaching strategies that will enhance teachers' professional development.
Our questions about what teachers need to know, and how to apply that
knowledge to their teaching, pose a constant challenge.

For the authors of this book, these questions seeded investigations of
their own practices and culminated in a comprehensive examination of
literacy teacher preparation. Drawing on a wide theoretical and research
base related to how children and adolescents develop as literate beings,
they explain what teachers of literacy need to know and why this learning is important. They also illustrate and provide a rationale for specific
activities that engage teachers' critical thinking and innovation.

I had two immediate reactions to this book. First, I was drawn into
the power of the activities described and found myself visualizing how

my students would respond to and apply what they were learning. Second—and this happened almost immediately—I began to draw mental associations between the authors' discussions of rationale and instructional activity and a wide body of research that supports high-quality teacher education and is extremely relevant to the potential success of the activities described by these authors.

It is readily apparent that the authors have a keen understanding of the research on how to develop teachers' content and pedagogical knowledge, and they represent this research well. For example, there is widespread agreement that highly qualified teachers should know the content they are teaching (content knowledge), know how students learn that content (knowledge of student development), and know instructional strategies (pedagogical knowledge) that enable students to learn. And there is evidence that particular conditions, such as sustained reflection and guided mentoring of teacher decision making, have a positive impact on teacher development and students' learning.

The recommendations advanced in this book align well with the substantive research on literacy teacher education. For example, the teaching practices recommended here correspond to findings presented in a synthesis of the International Reading Association's research on reading teacher preparation, available at: *www.reading.org/Libraries/reports-and-standards/teaching_reading_well.pdf.*

Across a number of these studies, including those I conducted with my colleagues (Risko et al., 2008; Hathaway & Risko, 2013), there is consensus around specific characteristics of teacher education programs that contribute to preparing highly qualified teachers. For example, personal narratives, patterned after multicultural young adult novels that draw teachers' attention to attitudes and beliefs about differences, were found to be highly effective in sensitizing teachers to issues of racial and ethnic discrimination and to changing their knowledge and beliefs about cultural diversity. Relevant to existing research, Elizabeth Dutro describes a teaching activity in this book that illustrates the power of cultural narratives for developing teachers' understandings of cultural differences and of how texts can privilege and silence particular perspectives on diversity.

Throughout the book, similar associations can be made with the research on how and what teachers learn and the conditions fostering such learning. The authors' emphasis on critical thinking and critical literacy activities aligns well with the finding that teachers' deep beliefs about the ability of their students and the effectiveness of their own teaching (especially when teaching struggling readers) can be changed in positive ways. These changes occur most frequently when teachers' instruction is informed by student data they are collecting and by extensive and prolonged involvement with pupils in field-based settings. A prelude to the analysis of student data might be the activity in which teachers collect and analyze their own oral reading data, as suggested by the authors.

Learning by doing is another characteristic of the recommendations in this book. This approach is a strong predictor of prospective teacher learning, especially when teachers are engaged in applying pedagogical knowledge to authentic teaching situations. Typically, effective models supporting teachers' application of newly formed knowledge are framed with explicit teaching moves: use of examples, explicit explanations and demonstrations, frequent practice with pupils in field settings, and specific feedback for teacher planning and instruction.

In our study of the research, we identified several instructional tools for advancing teacher learning. Various activities throughout this book demonstrate the power of these tools. For example, teachers have a higher regard for the text comprehension strategies they are expected to teach when they first have examined how these strategies supported their own reading actions. Other powerful tools we identified include those that help teachers identify their students' histories and interests so that personal relationships among teachers and students can be formed; explicitness of models and demonstrations of teaching activities that can be applied in the classroom; and the use of logs and journals for self-reflections. Many of the researchers identified in our literature review commented on the power of teacher reflection, especially when engaged in dialogic exchanges with teaching peers and teacher educators. Forums for dialogic exchanges are embedded in the teaching activities recommended throughout this book.

Taken together, the multiple investigations published by literacy teacher educators provide a robust and substantive knowledge about why and how teacher education matters, and in some instances how teacher education impacts student learning. Similarly, the teacher educators represented in this book, who come to their work grounded in teacher education research, provide a compelling argument for the practices they recommend.

Teacher educators who examine their own practices, collaborate with others to refine and deepen their thinking about these practices, and share what they are learning provide a fertile grounding for identifying the best possible practices for teacher preparation and professional learning. Indeed, practices such as those described in this book have the capacity for advancing future research and establishing a set of practices that can deepen teachers' knowledge and their students' learning. And the recommended activities hold potential for demonstrating the power of teacher reflection and critique of one's own teaching practices. Thoughtful teacher educators beget thoughtful teachers.

Today, with multiple teacher education reform efforts in play, it is important that teacher educators, through their own research and self-study, lead by being vocal about what matters most for teacher development. *Who better to direct the future of teacher education than teacher educators?*

VICTORIA J. RISKO, EdD
Professor Emerita, Vanderbilt University
2011–2012 President, International Reading Association

REFERENCES

Hathaway, J. I., & Risko, V. J. (2013). On becoming teachers: Knowing and believing. In K. Hall, T. Cremin, B. Comber, & L. Moll (Eds.), *International handbook of research on children's literacy, learning, and culture* (pp. 427–439). West Sussex, UK: Wiley-Blackwell.

Risko, V. J., Roller, C., Cummins, C., Bean, R., Block, C. C., Anders, P., et al. (2008). A critical analysis of the research on reading teacher education. *Reading Research Quarterly, 43*(3), 252–288.

Preface

When we were newly minted PhDs, each of us was excited to take on a new role as teacher educator. We were thrilled to be sharing knowledge that we had gained in our doctoral programs, along with that garnered from many years of K–8 classroom experience. We felt we had a lot to contribute to our teacher candidates' development. However, the task of crafting our knowledge and experience to meet the needs of our adult students was challenging. We found few resources to help in the process and lamented the lack of practice-based resources that we found so abundant in our K–8 teaching. Just like novice K–12 classroom teachers, we were "making it up" on a daily basis.

In 2008, Debby attended a discussion at the National Reading Conference/Literacy Research Association (NRC/LRA), during which several people described assignments and instructional activities they used with literacy teacher candidates. As Debby listened to these ideas (and wrote furiously to capture them), she found herself wishing that she had known about them when she had first started her university job. This led her to develop two highly successful conference sessions in which literacy teacher educators shared instructional strategies that they found successful with their own candidates. Nancy and Susan were presenters in these sessions. A book focused on teacher education practices had long been a gleam in their eyes. As novice teacher educators, they shared instructional strategies they were developing for their courses with each other, and discussed the idea that a book describing successful literacy instructional activities would be helpful to new (and perhaps even experienced) literacy teacher educators. When they first talked about the session that Debby organized at NRC/LRA, Susan exclaimed, "There's our book!" They partnered up with Debby—and here it is.

THE PURPOSE OF THIS BOOK

In this book we share instructional activities and assignments that have worked for us over our careers as teacher educators. We have invited other teacher educators to share as well. We hope to provide literacy teacher educators with instructional strategies that will help them support and develop excellent K–12 teachers. We recognize that a good teacher is key to a child's success as a learner, and that teaching children to read and write is an increasingly complex task occurring in increasingly complex situations. Excellent literacy teachers must be knowledgeable about subject matter, their students, and the contexts within which they are teaching—and then they must be able to use this knowledge to create literacy instruction responsive to particular students in unique contexts.

As literacy teacher educators we hope to provide prospective and experienced teachers with opportunities to develop a deep knowledge base, and a repertoire of pedagogical tools so that they can meet the needs of a wide range of learners. At the same time, because of the complexity of literacy instruction, we promote a stance of openness and inquiry, and a disposition toward thoughtful reflection and continuous growth. We feel that these habits of mind and heart are especially important for teacher candidates because many of them come to the profession with strong preconceptions about teaching and learning, based on their own experiences as students. These preconceptions may or may not apply to the teaching context or the students with whom they find themselves working. We are also aware of the enormous challenge of helping novices become sufficiently capable in a short period of time to be effective teachers during their first few years of teaching. Reflection on practice, the ability to learn from the teaching activity, is crucial to the ongoing development of all teachers and something we explicitly model in our own practice and in this volume.

We created this book to provide a resource to literacy teacher educators—whether they are called professors or professional developers. We envision it as a book of high-quality exemplar lessons, assignments, and instructional activities that have been found by experienced literacy teacher educators—many of whom also conduct research on teacher preparation—to be especially powerful in developing the knowledge, skills, and dispositions that make for highly effective teachers of children. We hope it will be helpful to those who do the important work of preparing the future teachers of our children.

SHARED ASSUMPTIONS AND UNDERSTANDINGS

In planning this book, we grappled with the assumptions we bring to our teaching practices, as well as understandings about literacy teacher education found in the literature and recommendations for practice provided by organizations such as the International Reading Association (IRA), the Common Core State Standards (CCSS) for K–12 settings, and the National Council for Accreditation of Teacher Education (NCATE) Blue Ribbon Panel Report on teacher education. We share a pedagogical philosophy that we bring to this book that includes the following principles:

- *Students must be actively engaged.* Engage preservice/inservice teachers in active and varied learning tasks that foster construction of new knowledge, build on prior knowledge, motivate learning, and overcome misconceptions.

- *Instructors must be actively engaged.* Model, guide, and provide feedback as preservice/inservice teachers engage with and practice instructional, assessment, and reflective tools central to literacy teaching.

- *Learning occurs through social interactions.* Provide opportunities for social interactions with colleagues as members of learning communities. Social interactions are central to learning. In particular, establish habits of collegial and collaborative interactions, and provide opportunities to learn from and engage with others' perspectives.

- *Make explicit connections to classrooms and teacher practice.* Establish close connections between coursework and fieldwork or classroom experiences. These enable the successful transfer of theory into practice, and the opportunity for teachers and candidates to refine their practices.

- *Reflect deeply and sincerely.* Promote and encourage a reflective stance toward teaching and learning with receptivity to growth and change. The diversity of PreK–12 students, the complexity of literacy processes, and the challenges of becoming literate in today's society require that teachers be prepared for the uncertainties and new demands of classroom practice. The willingness and ability of teachers to reflect in and on practice as well as their receptiveness to new ideas are key to teaching in today's classrooms with success and joy.

ORGANIZATION OF THE BOOK

This book is organized around eight areas of pedagogical and content knowledge that a consensus of experts has deemed essential knowledge for the effective literacy teacher (International Reading Association, 2007; Snow, Griffin, & Burns, 2005; National Research Council, 2010). Each chapter begins with an overview of the essential knowledge, understandings, and skills for that chapter's topic, followed by a more thorough explanation of each of the major concepts.

Each chapter also includes exemplary teacher education practices—assignments, activities, or, perhaps, a routine within a course—that a teacher educator or professional developer has found to be particularly powerful in conveying an important understanding, an area of knowledge, or a pedagogical skill. The contributor of each of these activities provides an explanation of the purpose of the activity or assignment, his or her rationale for using it, and the context in which it is used. Many of the activities have online components or can be adapted to online courses. Every college, school district, and group is different; we anticipate that our readers will need to modify the ideas included here to match the particular circumstances of their situations. Our hope is that the contextual information will help professors and professional developers as they make instructional decisions regarding what to use and how to use it. The sheer number of agreed-upon essential understandings prevents us from including an example for each topic. Rather, we provide these activities as models that readers of this book will be able to use to create their own activities for other areas.

Teacher educators may choose to read the entire book to gain a comprehensive view of the entire range of essential knowledge and skills and the many ways to develop them, but each chapter stands alone. Readers should feel free to dip in and out as they look for activities or assignments that support particular objectives for a class or professional development session.

Chapter 1 begins with the foundational knowledge necessary for informed literacy instruction. It encompasses the relationship between oral language and literacy; the affective, social, and cognitive processes related to literacy development; theories of reading and writing processes; literacy development; and an introduction to new literacies. The focus of Chapter 2 is word-level processes and associated instructional strategies. We include the structure of the English spelling–sound system, development of alphabet knowledge, and development of phonological and phonemic awareness, phonics, and word recognition strategies in this chapter. Chapter 3 covers text-level processes, including reading fluency, vocabulary knowledge, reading comprehension strategies, content-area literacy, discussion, and critical literacy. Development of writer identity, along with writing processes, instruction, and assessments, are examined in Chapter 4. The focus in Chapter 5 is learning environments, instructional approaches, and materials. This includes the establishment of structures and routines for literacy learning and the use of a variety of materials. In Chapter 6 we look at the new literacies and multimodal communication. Chapter 7 focuses specifically on student diversity—understanding and addressing the needs of readers and writers from different cultures and language backgrounds, as well as readers and writers who struggle or excel. Chapter 8 encompasses principles of assessment with a focus on the development and use of classroom-based assessments. In the Conclusion, we reflect on the challenges we found in writing this book and our hopes for the power of strong teacher education to assist teachers with the many challenges they will face in practice.

A WORD ABOUT TERMINOLOGY

We hope that this book will be useful to teacher educators who work with individuals already working as teachers, as well as those who teach individuals planning to become teachers. Because we found it awkward to repeatedly use phrases such as "preservice and inservice teachers" or "prospective and current teachers," for the remainder of the book we refer to all of these individuals as *teachers*. Similarly, we decided to use the term *teacher educators* for everyone who provides professional education or training for teachers—professors and professional staff developers, as well as school- and district-based personnel. We reserve the word *students* for the children and adolescents with whom our adult teacher education students work.

Acknowledgments

We wish to thank the Teacher Education Research Group of the Literacy Research Association for inspiring and supporting the conference sessions on Promising Practices in Literacy Teacher Education that led Debby to Susan and Nancy, and ultimately to this book.

We wish to acknowledge each other as well. From start to finish, this was a truly collaborative enterprise. Our many lengthy phone conversations were always a joy; it is rare to find others who share your passions, push your thinking to new places, and whose judgment you can rely on completely.

INDIVIDUAL ACKNOWLEDGMENTS

Debby: Thank you to my husband, Bob, for his support of this project.

Susan: Transitioning to teacher education from elementary classroom teaching was not easy for me. Sheila Valencia, Elizabeth Dutro, Janice Fournier, and Pam Grossman at the University of Washington and Marsh Riddle Buly at Western Washington University were wonderful models and mentors early in my career. I have also been fortunate to work with incredible teacher educators at Boise State University, who keep me on track for lifelong learning. Finally, thank you to my husband, Will, who patiently (or otherwise) abided the long hours of writing, conference calls, and a weeklong "writing retreat."

Nancy: I have had wonderful mentors as a teacher of both adults and children. In particular, Betty Jones and Louise Derman-Sparks at Pacific Oaks College; Pat Carini at the Prospect Institute; and Sheila Valencia, Pam Grossman, and Cathy Taylor at the University of Washington have strongly influenced me as a teacher. Thank you also to my husband, Tom, for his love and support throughout this project.

Contents

Purchasers can download copies of the reproducible tools
from *www.guilford.com/litt-forms.*

CHAPTER 1

Foundational Knowledge about Literacy

Foundational knowledge forms the underpinnings of teachers' instructional practices in literacy. Knowledge of literacy development—and the cognitive, social, and affective processes required to support literacy development—is key to thoughtful instruction. A teacher who is knowledgeable about literacy theory, and connects this knowledge with practice, can critically evaluate texts, flexibly adapt curricula, and intentionally design instruction to meet the needs of students in a range of situations.

This chapter provides a brief introduction to key ideas regarding the relationship between language and literacy, various perspectives on literacy and literacy learning, theories of reading processes, theories of writing processes, developmental progression of literacy, and issues of digital literacy.

THE RELATIONSHIP BETWEEN LANGUAGE AND LITERACY

What Is It?

Oral and written language are intertwined. Written language is the symbolic representation of oral or signed language. Learning the written code in any language rests upon oral or signed language.

What Do Teachers Need to Know?

Oral language proficiency underlies development of reading and writing. Although oral and written languages have much in common in terms of vocabulary, syntax, and use, there are important differences as well. Teachers who understand these commonalities and differences are better equipped to help children use their oral language to become skilled readers and writers.

Grammar and Register

The purpose of all language, whether written, gestured, or spoken, is to enable people to share meanings with one another. Every language follows rules (grammar or syntax) that govern the structure of the language. The vocabulary of the written and oral versions of a language is the same, although certain words are more likely to be used in the written version and others more likely to be used in the oral version. Within any language there are multiple registers—the way teenagers speak among their friends is different from the way they speak to their parents or how they speak to teachers or employers. Written language, too, exists in multiple registers, some more formal than others—a thank-you note, a fairytale, and an article in a scientific journal all vary in levels of formality. Particularly significant for beginning readers is that texts are typically more formal than everyday speech. A challenge for beginners is that written language doesn't always match their speech.

Ordinarily, young writers write the way they speak until taught otherwise, which accounts for the endless run-ons of so many 7-year-olds, and the informal oral register found in inexperienced writers. It is worth remembering, too, that young writers encouraged to use invented spelling, *spell* the way they speak—complete with immature pronunciations. Gaining control in writing of standard English presents a major challenge for many children, particularly those whose spoken language varies considerably from standard English. Because language is tightly connected to cultural identity, teachers need to be sensitive to these children and teach the standard English register while also recognizing the appropriate use of the children's home registers.

Oral Language Is Contextual

Tone, gestures, and facial expressions, as well as proximity and shared context, enable speakers and listeners to more easily understand each other. Without the rich contextual supports available in oral and signed contexts, readers must work harder to construct meaning. However, until very recently in human history, oral (and signed) language was transitory, whereas the permanence of written language enabled written language to bridge across time and space. This was an advantage written language held over spoken language. However, the newly developed ease of recording and disseminating speech and gesture may change this long-standing distinction.

Oral Language Is Natural; Written Language Is a Cultural Invention

Except for rare cases of extreme social deprivation or severe physiological deficits, all children develop oral or signed language. In fact, many linguists believe humans are born with a language capacity hardwired in their brains (Pinker, 1994). Thus, children are said to "acquire" spoken (or signed) language—oral language acquisition is considered natural. On the other hand, written language is a more recently developed cultural invention (approximately 3200 B.C.E.) that requires intentional instruction.

Familiarity with Stories and Books Supports Literacy Acquisition

Children who have familiarity with Western story structure, and the sentence structure and vocabulary found in books can anticipate words and events in stories more easily than those with less familiarity. This familiarity is a valuable support for learning to read and write. Children who are unfamiliar with book language—and whose oral language is at great variance with book language— may not anticipate the words in the sentences they encounter in written texts, or may not recognize when a word does not fit the sentence structure.

Comprehension of Written Text Is Related to Comprehension of Oral (Spoken) Language

The richness of a child's oral language is highly correlated with a child's reading proficiency. Younger children cannot be expected to comprehend written text that they would not understand if it was read to them. However, beyond the beginning phase of reading, reading experience becomes a prime vocabulary and syntax builder. Most avid readers can recall mispronouncing words that have entered their vocabulary via reading. Advanced readers are able to use a host of strategies to understand written text that is *more* difficult than they would be able to understand by listening.

The richness of a young child's oral language—the breadth and depth of the child's vocabulary, and the child's familiarity with a wide range of sentence structures, including those only found in written forms of language—depends on the quantity and quality of the child's interactions with caregivers during the early years. In the United States, vast differences in oral language proficiency exist before school entry between children from rich language environments and children from average or poor language environments. According to Hart and Risley, children raised in typical professional families hear 30 million more words by the age of 3 than children raised in families receiving welfare (Hart & Risley, 1995, 2003). Vocabulary size at age 3 correlates strongly with reading comprehension in third grade and beyond (Sénéchal, Ouellette, & Rodney, 2006). Intensive work to enrich vocabulary once children can read will narrow this gap. We feel that in recent years far too little attention has been paid to the development of oral language.

ACTIVITY 1.1
Using a Venn Diagram to Compare Oral and Written Language
SUSAN D. MARTIN

Activity Type: In-class activity.

Materials: Venn diagram graphic for students and instructor.

Duration: 30–45 minutes.

Professional Learning Focus:
- Recognize the role of language in written language development.
- Recognize foundational commonalities of written and oral language.

Standards Links

IRA Professional Standards:
1.1 Understand major theories and empirical research that describe the cognitive, linguistic, motivational, and sociocultural foundations of reading and writing development, processes, and components.

Common Core State Standards: N/A.

- Recognize differences in oral language development, processes, registers, and conventions.
- Recognize implications for literacy instruction.

K–8 Student Learning Focus:
Purposes for aspects of written language.

Rationale

As proficient users of all aspects of English language—speaking, listening, reading, and writing—we don't always consciously think about or recognize the specific ways in which oral and written language are similar and dissimilar. We shift easily between multiple written and spoken speech genres (Bakhtin, 1986), with seemingly automatic adjustments to the conventions and natures of the genres. Foundational similarities of oral and written language support development of reading and writing. For instance, sentence organization does not alter as we shift from oral to written language. On the other hand, differences between oral and written language registers, genres, and conventions can interfere with efficient reading and writing. While sentences frequently begin with *because* in spoken English, students are admonished to not begin written sentences this way. Conscious recognition of the similarities and differences between oral and written language can assist teachers in understanding some difficulties in students' reading and writing development, while providing them rationales for written language conventions to share with their students.

Description

1. Teachers are given individual copies of the Venn graphic (Figure 1.1). In small groups, they first brainstorm ways that oral and written language are similar for 5–10 minutes. They record their answers in the overlapping section of the graphic.

2. Using a projected e-copy, I solicit responses from students and create a group product. Teachers are encouraged to add to their individual copies as we do this. I make sure that critical points are included. These include communicative purposes, meaning making, syntax, semantics/vocabulary, phonological foundations, as so on. We then discuss implications for literacy learning and the foundational nature of oral language.

3. I then give them another 5–10 minutes to discuss and record differences in their small groups.

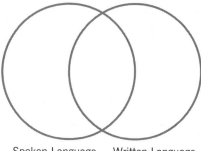

Spoken Language   Written Language

FIGURE 1.1. Venn diagram.

4. We again debrief and I record on our shared product as shown in Figure 1.2. Critical points include the move from a phonological to a graphophonic foundation; oral language as hardwired into the brain, while written language is a cultural invention; great dependence on nonverbal elements in constructing meaning in spoken language; development of meaning in situated, personal contexts versus abstract contexts separated by time and space; joint meaning making in conversation as opposed to the lone reader constructing meaning; and differences in conventions of syntax and vocabulary in oral and written language—including more formalized aspects of written language such as spelling, capital letters, and punctuation. We discuss implications for literacy learning.

5. Teachers turn to a partner and describe one thing they learned during this lesson and implications for their practices.

Discussion

While serving as a teacher/teacher educator in the Peace Corps in the Philippines in 1995, I grappled with issues of working with English language learners for the first time, as well as with notions of psycholinguistics (Goodman, 1986). Trying to make sense of what I was experiencing and reading—and putting it together with knowledge gained from 18 years of classroom teaching—I created a graphic organizer in which I compared and contrasted the four aspects of language—speaking, listening, reading, and writing. This was the first time I had ever paid conscious attention to issues of oral and written language. What an enlightening process this was!

This experience laid the foundation for the Venn activity I now do in both the preservice and inservice courses. As I make sure that critical points are included in the group graphic, I typically draw on deeper understandings about language and literacy that I have developed since 1995. Although simple, this activity appears to generate ahas! for other teachers as well. I have found that comparing just oral and written aspects of language serves appropriate purposes in most of my courses, and is much less confusing—especially for preservice teachers— than comparing speaking, listening, reading, and writing. I do engage experienced teachers in comparing across the four aspects of language.

A good deal of discussion is generated around this activity, particularly in the areas of signed language, English language learning, and technologies that record and preserve oral language. I make sure to discuss how the insights noted on the Venn diagram can be shared with K–8 students to create purposes for aspects of written language. For example, rigid conventions to do with spelling and punctuation can be ascribed to the need to communicate effectively across time and distances. Reasons, rather than rote rule, can be emphasized in the literacy classroom.

Figure 1.2 is a model of a completed chart, with a record of important information.

References

Bakhtin, M. M. (1986). *Speech genres and other late essays* (C. Emerson & M. Holmquist, Eds.; V. W. McGee, Trans.). Austin: University of Texas Press.
Goodman, K. S. (1986). *What's whole in whole language?* Portsmouth, NH: Heinemann.

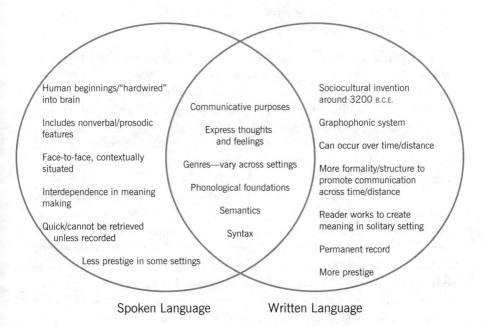

Human beginnings/"hardwired" into brain

Includes nonverbal/prosodic features

Face-to-face, contextually situated

Interdependence in meaning making

Quick/cannot be retrieved unless recorded

Less prestige in some settings

Communicative purposes

Express thoughts and feelings

Genres—vary across settings

Phonological foundations

Semantics

Syntax

Sociocultural invention around 3200 B.C.E.

Graphophonic system

Can occur over time/distance

More formality/structure to promote communication across time/distance

Reader works to create meaning in solitary setting

Permanent record

More prestige

Spoken Language   Written Language

FIGURE 1.2. Completed Venn diagram.

AFFECTIVE, SOCIAL, AND COGNITIVE PROCESSES RELATED TO LITERACY DEVELOPMENT

What Is It?

Our understandings of reading and writing processes as well as literacy learning and development have been enriched by research from many theoretical perspectives. From cognitive psychology and neuropsychology come discoveries about how the brain perceives, processes, stores, and retrieves information, and how children's cognitive functioning changes as they mature. From social psychology, sociology, and other fields come insights regarding the influences of culture, belief systems, emotional development, and social interaction on learning. Teachers need to understand the key insights into literacy learning and development that come from these disciplines to create the most powerful instructional environments. Although we tend to think of literacy learning as primarily a cognitive process, successful new learning also depends on affective factors and social interaction.

What Do Teachers Need to Know?

Affective Processes: Dispositions and Motivation for Engagement in Literacy Learning

What motivates a child's engagement in reading and writing? Curiosity about a topic? The desire to get lost in a good story or share a funny story with a relative who lives far away? The desire to please a teacher or get a good grade? A willingness to persevere on a difficult task and the strong sense of accomplishment that can follow? The answers to these questions have an enormous impact on the learning trajectory of children—with profound implications for classroom practices and teacher decision making.

Children come to school with wide variations in interests, goals, and in dispositions toward literacy learning. They vary in confidence, persistence, and ability to self-regulate in complex tasks, as well as in their understanding of what the value or rewards of reading and writing might be. A growing body of evidence demonstrates that differences in dispositions toward learning affect long-term performance in school and life more than whatever is measured by intelligence tests (Tough, 2012). Similarly, children who view reading and writing as meaningful activities that have value in their lives show more persistence over time and develop greater proficiency than children who view literacy tasks as something required for school or work with little personal value. Attention to the affective aspects of literacy learning is sometimes overlooked, but is an essential component of effective literacy instruction.

Children's and teachers' beliefs about the relationship between intelligence and literacy learning play a major role in student engagement and persistence. Children who believe that intelligence is a fixed trait, and that the ability to learn school tasks such as reading or writing is mostly fixed (a fixed performance frame; Johnston, 2012) give up more quickly when the task becomes difficult than do children who believe that it is mostly the effort put forth that will determine their success in a school task (a dynamic learning frame; Johnston, 2012). Fortunately, teachers have tremendous power to influence how children view themselves as learners. Teachers can assist children in framing positive learning narratives through the language they use (Johnston, 2004, 2012). Avoiding judgmental terms such as *good* or *bad* when referring to readers or writers, and insisting on a growth perspective, teachers can change a child's fixed-trait views. When a child looks to a teacher for confirmation in his or her oral reading, the teacher can turn it back to the child by saying, "Were you right?" demonstrating confidence in the child's own powers while teaching the valuable skill of self-regulation. Limiting praise to very specific actions (Johnston, 2012) and providing accurate and timely feedback builds children's confidence in their abilities to take on new challenges, and, ultimately, their literacy competency (Locke & Latham, 1990).

Deep and serious learning requires risk taking, as we go beyond what we already can do. The social settings in which learning occurs can either hinder or enhance willingness to take risks. A supportive classroom—where the climate invites experimentation, errors are viewed as a natural consequence of learning and trying new things, and children feel protected from ridicule—is of paramount importance for children to develop as readers and writers to their fullest extent. Thus, teachers must create the safe learning environments children need to read aloud, discuss their ideas, or share their writing.

In reading and writing, as with all complex endeavors, there is a direct relationship between practice and proficiency (Anderson, Wilson, & Fielding, 1988; Pressley, Mohan, Raphael, & Fingeret, 2007.) But children will not read or write extensively if they do not enjoy it or view it as a meaningful activity! The widespread use of extrinsic rewards, such as stickers, suggests teachers recognize the critical role that students' motivation for learning plays in classroom settings. But extrinsic incentives to motivate reading have been found to have minimal effects at best—unless tightly linked to the reading task, such as using books for rewards (Gambrell, 2011). More often, extrinsic rewards have negative effects: they undermine children's long-term habitual motivation to read (Schiefele, Schaffner, Moller, & Wigfield, 2012).

However, teachers can encourage the development of a "habitual motivation" to read, as well the development of "current motivation" (motivation to complete a specific literacy task; Schiefele et al., 2012) by selecting engaging literacy activities based on the interests and abilities of their students. This includes expressive reading aloud, helping children find texts that interest them, and helping them choose topics and writing genres of personal relevance. Leveraging students' desire for social interaction by using instructional arrangements such as book clubs, brainstorming with a buddy, or sharing writing with classmates and family is another effective tool for motivating literacy practice. Providing the correct degree of challenge in a text or task also motivates students. However, determining an appropriate degree of challenge is a difficult task for teachers since there is so much variation among students in interest, background knowledge, word identification skill, and persistence at difficulty.

The inherent complexity of reading and writing processes can stymie even proficient readers and writers. Teachers need to help students develop strategies and other tools to tackle and "manage the challenges and difficulties of writing" (Boscolo & Gelati, 2007, p. 219) and reading. Motivating students to tackle complex literacy tasks may require teachers to intentionally shape student understandings of reading and writing as challenging but meaningful activities. In sum, the role of the teacher in fostering positive student dispositions and motivation for literacy learning goes far beyond offering stickers or pizza parties.

Social and Cultural Processes

Learning to read and write is a social and cultural process as well as a cognitive task. In addition to motivating children, the power of social interaction as an aid for taking on new learning can be seen in many of the structures and routines found in the most productive literacy classrooms: turn and talk, literature circles, author's chair, and reciprocal teaching, among others. The role of social processes in learning is highlighted in Vygotsky's (1896–1934) highly influential work on cognitive development, in which interaction with a more knowledgeable other is viewed as key to new learning (Vygotsky, 1978). Vygotsky's theory of the zone of proximal development (ZPD) influences many current practices in literacy pedagogy. The "sweet spot" for new learning, the ZPD is that place just beyond what the learner can accomplish independently, but where the skillful assistance from a more knowledgeable person enables the child to accomplish the task. Success in the new task then pushes the ZPD to another level. This principle can be seen in the practices of shared reading and guided reading, the practice of providing some information about the ideas and words in a text about to be read before the children embark on reading, interactive writing, and in all manner of instructional conversations. In these examples, social interactions with a more knowledgeable other are critical to learning.

An important insight derived from a sociocultural perspective is that children gain understandings of the uses and purposes of reading and writing from how they see literacy used and valued in their families and communities, and that these understandings affect their comfort in and progress at school. Some children grow up immersed in routines of storybook reading and writing very similar to those they will encounter in school, and slide effortlessly into the school culture. Other children have had minimal exposure to written registers before school entry, but may know stories, songs, and poems that were told to them orally. Understanding different home literacy experiences will help teachers capitalize on what children already know, and avoid misunderstandings and mismatches between the culture of the school and the culture of the child that can interfere with learning (Heath, 1983/1996). For example, teachers who use songs and stories from students' communities as literacy texts help students build on their existing knowledge, while also fostering connections between home and school.

Cognitive Processes

The constructivist theory of learning first proposed by developmental psychologist Jean Piaget (1896–1980) continues to inform both literacy learning and literacy pedagogies. In a constructivist orientation individuals are seen to play an active role in their own learning. They interact with, and modify, new information by thinking about it in terms of their existing "schemas," thought structures that are representations of the world based on previous experiences. As learners engage with new information they develop "approximate" understandings that are refined over time as the individual assimilates additional experiences into his or her existing schemas (Piaget & Inhelder, 1971). Children's partial understandings can serve as valuable windows into the ways that learners are thinking about literacy. For example, when a child spells *went* YT, we can surmise he or she is using the rule he or she has constructed that the letter's name includes its sound, as it does for nearly all letters, and has not yet learned all of the exceptions to the rule.

Vygotsky's theory of cognitive development also falls within the constructivist umbrella. As mentioned above, the principle of the ZPD contributes enormously to literacy pedagogy today. The impact of constructivism on literacy instruction can be seen in the use of a careful gradation of difficulty for beginning readers (leveled texts), the recognition that reading involves an interaction between reader and text (Rosenblatt, 1938/1983), the recognition of the importance of stimulating related background knowledge before reading (Anderson & Pearson, 1984), and in efforts to use instructional techniques that foster active participation by the learner—"hands-on" techniques.

More recent work in neuropsychology has contributed new and detailed understandings of literacy processes. Many separate interacting perceptual and cognitive processes, such as visual perception, working memory, and pattern detection, work together to enable reading or writing to occur. Individual differences in all of these factors can contribute to the relative ease or difficulty an individual may experience in learning to read and write.

A key insight for literacy educators from the information processing approach in cognitive psychology is the concept of two aspects of memory: "working memory" (short-term transitory memory) and "long-term memory" (memory available for another time; Sternberg, 2001). Since only a few ideas can be held in working memory (five to nine for adults, fewer than five for children), the development of automaticity in letter and word identification (automatic or instantaneous recognition that does not require conscious effort) is critical. The bigger the chunks (letters, words, or even phrases) a reader can identify or a writer can produce automatically, the more space exists in working memory to focus on comprehension or composition.

Another important idea from neuroscience is "neural connectivity"—the notion that neural connections between parts of the brain can be strengthened through repeated use. The more frequently that connections among the various parts of the brain related to reading—print, letter sound, meaning, and context—are made, the more rapid this connection will become, resulting in more fluent reading and better comprehension.

READING PROCESSES

What Is It?

How is it that we can gaze at some black marks on a piece of paper and develop a vivid picture in our mind's eye of acres of burnt-out forests seen from a moving train, and feel the despair of the man who has lost his young wife and child to that fire (Johnson, 2011)? Models and theories of reading explain how the mind turns the letters on the page into meaningful language. Early modelers of the reading process relied primarily on reasoning and experiments; more recently, computer modeling and brain imaging techniques have enabled researchers to refine our understanding of how the complex cognitive activity we call reading occurs.

What Do Teachers Need to Know?

Reading—constructing meaning from print—is a complex, multifaceted process dependent on attentional, perceptual, emotional, language, and memory systems working rapidly and in concert. Understanding different facets of the process helps teachers understand what they need to do to help children.

Simple View of Reading Processes

One way to understand reading processes is the "simple view of reading" (Hoover & Gough, 1990). The simple view proposes that reading can be described as the interaction of word recognition and oral language comprehension. Severe decoding weaknesses can prevent adequate reading comprehension even when oral language comprehension is normal or advanced. Similarly, a child with excellent decoding skills can have poor reading comprehension if the child's oral language is underdeveloped (*www.balancedreading.com/simple.html*). Once children learn to read, reading experience strengthens both language proficiency and decoding proficiency. Word identification is but one component of this complex, interlocking system.

Multiple Cueing Systems Involved in Word Recognition

Emergent and early readers rely on the redundancies of language to determine the pronunciation of words whose print form is unfamiliar to them. For example, what would you place in the blank of the following sentence: "My _____ wouldn't start this morning?" Most people would say *car* or *truck*, perhaps a few might select *motorcycle*. But if provided with just the initial letter *t*, the list of likely candidates is significantly narrowed. Beginners (and struggling readers) take advantage of that redundancy to combine context (meaning), including any illustrations with syntax (the sentence structure or grammar), and partial letter information to determine unfamiliar words, as in the example above. Meaning (semantics), structure (syntax), and graphophonics (the letter–sound system) are often referred to as the three cueing systems used by readers to assist in word identification.

Eye-movement studies confirm that skilled readers rather unconsciously process all the letters in the words they read, with the exception of some high-frequency function words (Samuels, Rasinski, & Hiebert, 2011). However, context and sentence structure facilitates word recognition for experienced readers, as well as novices, by activating networks of knowledge and expected words. In fact, meaning and syntax *must* be used to determine the pronunciation of words like *read* and *row*.

Interactionist Perspective

Reading does *not* occur through a letter-by-letter, word-by-word assembly process. In an early model of reading, Gough proposed that the reader perceives individual letters in sequence, translates the letters into sounds, turns the sounds into words, the words into sentences, and the sentences into meaning—a strictly linear "bottom-up" theory (Gough, 1972, as cited in Gough, 2004, p. 1180). However, literacy researchers have since realized that word identification is facilitated by the reader's prior knowledge as he or she predicts words and constructs meaning. Nearly all theorists, including Gough (2004), now accept an interactionist view in which the meaning of larger units depends on the recognition of individual words, but at the same time word recognition is facilitated by the overall meaning being constructed by the reader. This is referred to as a "top-down" effect. Brain-imaging studies have found rapid, near simultaneous activation from areas of stored knowledge to the area used for word recognition, which confirms the interactionist view. Nevertheless, our experience with beginning teachers leads us to believe that most teachers unconsciously hold a model very similar to Gough's (1972, as cited in Gough, 2004, p. 1180) original model. As teacher educators and professional developers, we need to help teachers develop a more complex and nuanced understanding of reading processes.

Comprehension Depends on Background Knowledge and Vocabulary

Background knowledge is organized into schemas, networks of related information. The more an individual already knows about a topic—the more developed the schema—the more easily that individual will comprehend written (or oral) information about the topic (Anderson, 2004). Constructing meaning from text on an unfamiliar topic requires creating a new concept from scratch, and is far more difficult. The schemas possessed by the reader, including the reader's knowledge of language patterns and text structures, helps a reader anticipate upcoming ideas and words and, thus, facilitates word recognition as well as comprehension. Jokes and puns often depend on this facilitation effect for their punch; we anticipate a word and then revel in an unexpected turn. Vocabulary is a particularly critical component of background knowledge. When a reader encounters a high density of unknown or only weakly understood words, he or she will experience great difficulty understanding the text even at a literal level. Sometimes even one or two unknown words will prevent a reader from grasping the meaning of a selection, if the word is key to the meaning of the text.

Because each reader has unique life experiences, each reader will apply a different set of schema to a text, coloring his or her interpretation of it. When a reader already has a well-developed schema for a topic he or she is reading about, he or she will generate mental pictures, and often sounds, smells, and even kinesthetic responses. The reader's memory of the text will include the images and other sensory details evoked from the print. This memory, or encoding, in multiple senses is referred to as dual coding (Sadoski & Pavio, 2004). Readers retain their sensory responses to a text long after the details fade, remembering the loss triggered by Charlotte's death (White, 2004) or the inward terror evoked by a thriller.

Reader Response Theory

Reader response theory (Rosenblatt, 1938/1983) provides another useful lens with which to view the comprehension process. Rosenblatt asserts that the meaning of a text does not lie solely in the words on the page, but is constructed from *transactions* between the reader and what the author has written. Thus, each reader will have a unique response to a work of literature because each reader brings his or her own experiences and worldview to the work. Rosenblatt developed the useful construct of two types of reading: *aesthetic* for when we read primarily for the emotional and/or aesthetic value of the experience and *efferent* for when we read for gathering information.

ACTIVITY 1.2
Role of Schema in Text Comprehension
DEBORAH G. LITT

Activity Type: In-class activity.

Materials: Copies or projection of one of the experimental passages from Anderson's (1994) paper "The Role of Reader's Schema in Comprehension, Learning, and Memory" or a passage with similar ambiguities.

Duration: 15–20 minutes.

Professional Learning Focus:
Insight into the role of background knowledge in reader interpretation and comprehension of text.

K–8 Student Learning Focus: Need to integrate background knowledge with text information.

Standards Links

IRA Professional Standards:
1.1 Recognize major theories of reading and writing processes and development, including first and second language acquisition and the role of native language in learning to read and write in a second language.

Common Core State Standards: N/A.

Rationale

Teachers' recognition of the enormous role a reader's background knowledge plays in comprehension is one of the foundational understandings I believe is most important for teachers to deeply comprehend. I believe that when teachers understand this idea they are more likely to make the effort to (1) develop children's background knowledge to enable them to understand what they are about to read and (2) understand why a child misunderstands a text. I developed this simple activity to ensure that teachers understand and remember the critical role schema plays in comprehension.

Description

I distribute or project the "Tony" passage from Anderson's 1994 article and ask the teachers to read it and jot down what they think it is about. When everyone has finished reading I ask what they thought the passage was about. They are usually surprised to discover that not everyone thought it was about the same topic. Some think it is about a prisoner, others think it is about a wrestler, and a few have suggested that Tony is a dog or another animal in captivity. I probe further to ask why they came to the conclusions they did. No matter which interpretation they take, they inevitably point to the same pieces of information in the text—desire to escape, a mat, and early roughness—as leading to their interpretation of the topic of the passage. I then guide the teachers in understanding that each individual's background knowledge and schemas influence their interpretation. Participants or fans of wrestling might be more likely to think of wrestling when they see the words *hold* and *mat*, whereas fans of police procedurals would be more likely to think of prison.

Discussion

I find that having teachers experience for themselves how mature, educated readers can have differing interpretations of a short text makes the principle memorable for them. When used in a semester course, the activity provides a touchstone I can refer to throughout the remainder of the semester. Sometimes teachers ask me what the "real" answer is and I explain that the passage was created to be intentionally ambiguous for an experiment. In the study Anderson (1994) describes in the article, college students who wrestled or followed the sport thought the passage was about wrestling, while others assumed Tony was a prisoner.

Reference

Anderson, R. C. (1994). Role of reader's schema in comprehension, learning, and memory. In R. Ruddell & M. Ruddell (Eds.), *Theoretical models and processes of reading* (pp. 469–482). Newark, DE: International Reading Association.

ACTIVITY 1.3
Informational Illustration Charts
MARY ANN CAHILL and ANNE GREGORY

Activity Type: In-class activity.

Materials: Premade charts; pens.

Duration: 20–30 minutes.

Professional Learning Focus: Provide information multimodally (visually and verbally) to enhance learning.

K–8 Student Learning Focus: Use information gained from illustrations (e.g., maps, photographs) and words to demonstrate understanding of the text (e.g., where, when, why, and how key events occur).

Standards Links

IRA Professional Standards:
1.2 Explain language and reading development across elementary years using supporting evidence from theory and research.

Common Core State Standards: Reading Anchor Standards
7. Integrate and evaluate content presented in diverse media and formats, including visually and quantitatively, as well as in words.

Rationale

Informational illustration charts are powerful, multimodal presentation tools that make complex vocabulary and concepts related to literacy comprehensible to teachers, especially to novices who have little or no understanding. The multimodal presentation occurs both verbally and visually. We draw charts in front of our students as we talk. We find that informational illustration charts are a useful tool to help them visualize concepts while simultaneously providing them with information, therefore making concepts more easily encoded into memory (Troje & Giurfa, 2001). Using informational illustrations in our literacy courses enables us to activate prior knowledge, build background (i.e., both conceptual and specific for the lecture selection), introduce content specific vocabulary, and provide a visual representation of the concept for students.

Furthermore, strategies such as the informational illustration provide a means for teacher educators to model the instruction they wish to see occurring in classrooms; in this way, such strategy use serves as a bridge between theory and instruction (Kucer, 2005). We have successfully used informational illustration charts in our work over the last 4 years with teachers and students in several elementary and middle schools.

Description

Creating and presenting an informational illustration chart is a two-step process for teachers: designing and presenting the illustrations.

Planning

We typically begin by identifying the key vocabulary that will be used (such as *phonological awareness, analytic phonics*, and *synthetic phonics*, as noted in our examples below), and then follow through with identifying background knowledge, prior knowledge, and examples. These steps are outlined below.

1. *Vocabulary.* We critically examine the ideas and concepts to be presented and write down all the words related to these that might need clarification. While doing this, we try to think like an education student in our classes . . . whatever will be confusing and needs clarification and should be written down.

2. *Background knowledge.* We carefully consider the background knowledge that students must have to understand this concept. We often assume that our students have this background, but in actuality, they may not. It will be necessary to bring this knowledge to students if the concept is to be understood.

3. *Activating background knowledge.* While thinking about the concept, we consider what questions will help to activate students' prior knowledge to make connections and retrieve background knowledge they may already possess.

4. *Examples.* We determine the concept and list several key examples that specifically pertain to it. For example, *alliteration, syllables, onsets, rime*, and *phonemes* for the concept of phonemic awareness.

5. *Sketch out informational illustration.* Using the above information, we create a sketch that illustrates the idea/concept being presented. To do this, we use light pencil on a piece of chart/butcher paper surrounded by information, words, and ideas that we wish students to understand. This, in essence, becomes the outline for the presentation. This chart will be a dynamic part of the classroom; additional information will be added to it in subsequent classroom sessions.

Presenting Illustration to Students

1. *Reveal.* Using a large piece of chart/butcher paper, we begin to draw out the sketch that was previously prepared using a dark marking pen. Some storytelling generally goes along with this. This should be considered to be a lively and engaging discussion about the concept/idea, in which students are asked to interact with the information. Additionally, we are sure to include discussion of pertinent information and important vocabulary as it is written on the visual representation. This is the opportunity to impart a great amount of knowledge to them. Sometimes they don't even realize they are learning!

2. *Retelling.* On subsequent days, we encourage students in small groups to "retell the illustration." We distribute vocabulary words and/or pictures to the students. As we retell the illustration, students are encouraged to come to the visual representation and affix the vocabulary/picture card to the proper part of the chart as it is occurs in the retelling. While this may seem somewhat basic, we have found that this constant repetition of conceptual information helps students remember this information.

Discussion

This strategy has literally changed the way lectures occur in our classrooms. Students are engaged and motivated as the picture takes shape before their eyes. We have found that many students either draw the illustration along with us, or take a picture of the illustration with their cell phones. They also request that we post all the pictures on our websites because "it helps us study." We have used this strategy to teach many concepts in literacy, such as the phonological umbrella, the differences between analytic and synthetic phonics, and the bell-shaped curve. Students looked forward to the informational illustration and exhibited excitement when they came into the class and poster paper was draped across the white board. Students in our classes consistently mentioned informational illustrations in their exit slips and evaluations as one of the favorite methods for presenting information. One student stated, "I love the story boards and creative approach to the lessons . . . helps me understand and remember."

The most challenging part of this strategy is figuring out how to represent the concept visually, as not all topics lend themselves easily to this idea. When this occurs, it is often necessary to embed the concept/idea in a picture book or other experience that is shared with students. For example, to represent an analytic approach to teaching reading, we drew Mrs. Wishy-Washy from Joy Cowley's book, as we had previously used *Mrs. Wishy-Washy* to illustrate this type of approach for teaching phonics. In this way, a picture from the story or of the experience can serve as the illustration of the concept/idea, helping students to connect their experiences with the concepts being studied and modeled. In addition, if drawing is not your forte, simply find a picture from the Internet that illustrates your concept and project this image onto a smartboard or projection screen. Then, drape a large piece of chart/butcher paper over the image, and lightly trace in pencil. In our experience, this alternative to PowerPoint has been an equal or better way to present foundational concepts to students. The overwhelming belief by students is that these visual lectures help them to retain the information better.

Supporting Materials

Our examples in Figure 1.3 are finished products taken directly from our teaching in a comprehensive literacy course for preservice teachers.

References

Kucer, S. B. (2005). *Dimensions of literacy: A conceptual base for the teaching of reading and writing* (2nd ed.). Mahwah, NJ: Erlbaum.

Troje, N. F., & Giurfa, M. (2001). Visual representations for memory and recognition. In N. Elsner & G. W. Kreutzberg (Eds.), *Proceedings of the 28th Göttingen Neurobiology Conference* (Vol. I, pp. 608–613). Stuttgart, Germany: Georg Thieme Verlag.

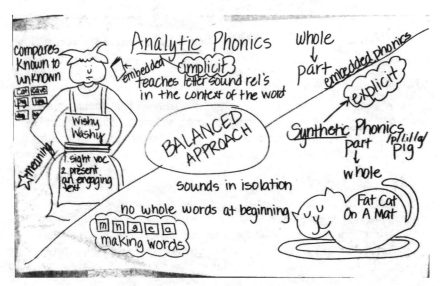

FIGURE 1.3. Examples of informational illustration charts.

ACTIVITY 1.4
Connecting Theory to Practice:
Taking Stock of Who Sits on Your Shoulder
KATHY GANSKE

Activity Type: In-class activity.

Materials: N/A.

Duration: N/A.

Professional Learning Focus: Solidify understanding of research and theory through application to classroom practices; realize the dominant philosophical stance that is influencing instructional decisions; determine one or more ways to use the knowledge acquired about research to practice connections to impact future teaching.

K–8 Student Learning Focus: N/A.

Standards Links

IRA Professional Standards:
1.1 Recognize major theories of reading and writing processes and development, including first and second literacy acquisition and the role of native language in learning to read and write in a second language.

Explain the research and theory about effective learning environments that support individual motivation to read and write (e.g., choice, challenge, interests, and access to traditional print, digital, and online resources).

2.2 Select and implement instructional approaches based on evidence-based rationale, student needs, and purposes for instruction.

Common Core State Standards: N/A.

Rationale

Teachers should know which research and scholarly writings ground their practice, as this is part of what it means to be an informed decision maker and a professional. The knowledge can also serve as a powerful tool when someone challenges a choice of approach, text, or strategy that is being used. This learning activity provides opportunities for teachers to apply their understandings of theory to their practices. The title of the activity alone demystifies what for some can be intimidating—learning about theorists and models and delving deeply into scholarly writings. In my experience, teachers have often read about theories as "over-there matter," not something that touches their daily teaching lives in significant ways. Teachers with whom I've used this activity have viewed the experience as eye-opening and have acquired a heightened identity of who they are as teachers through their completion of the activity. They've come away considering ways to incorporate more of the practices they value into their daily teaching, even in the use they are expected to make of mandated materials and practices.

Description

For this activity teachers take stock of their teaching, materials they use, students' learning (assessments), and the classroom environment to increase their awareness of the everyday influences of scholars whose work they've read and learned about. The activity assumes that (1) teachers have a working knowledge of several different reading/learning theories, and (2) there has already been modeling of the process and a small-group work through. Although I use the activity with graduate students who are teaching in challenging urban middle schools, the activity could easily be used with elementary or secondary students at the graduate or undergraduate level. For students in initial licensure programs, the activity might be used as part of a practicum experience.

1. *Identifying aspects of teaching/learning to explore.* Ask teachers to brainstorm a list of some of their practices (strategies or approaches, such as thinkaloud or Book Club), materials (such as leveled texts or word sorts), assessments, and aspects of their classroom environment (such as a reading corner). Provide time for them to share their lists with a partner or small group. This sometimes generates additional overlooked possibilities. Next, ask them to choose seven of the practices to explore. Among those selected, there must be at least one materials item, one assessment, one selection related to the classroom environment, and at least two strategies or approaches. Distribution of the other two selections is a personal choice. For each practice, material, assessment, or context chosen, teachers are expected to:

- Identify the item or practice and describe it so that a reader can clearly understand what is being talked about; incorporate into the discussion at least one photo or photocopy of what was chosen.
- Explain which theory, model, and/or research the selection exemplifies. The explanation should include a detailed rationale that clearly expresses the teacher's thinking and makes explicit connections to relevant characteristics of the research.
- Provide evidence for a dominating influence but should also show that teaching and learning are influenced by multiple scholars.

2. *Philosophical stance: Who does sit on your shoulder?* After describing and providing a rationale for each of the selections, teachers synthesize what they've learned/discovered about their teaching and their teaching environment. The synthesis should:

- Reveal what is at the core of the teacher's philosophy of teaching. What matters, and why? (In teaching situations where mandated practices are pervasive and represent different groundings than those of the teacher, teachers may have to think deeply about how the scholars who sit on their shoulders nonetheless influence their practice).

- Demonstrate how knowledge gained through the activity will be used to impact future teaching and learning.
- Include references to relevant texts and theorists read.

3. *Follow-up.* Designate a class session to sharing and discussing teachers' discoveries and questions.

Discussion

I think part of the strength of this activity for forging research/practice connections lies in its authenticity—from the modeling to teachers' own taking stock of what goes on in their classrooms. Teachers experience the same sort of excitement and sense of "Eureka!" as I did when they find that the "over-there matter" is really right there in their classrooms and teaching. In her project, Aubrey Kuppler, a teacher in the course, highlighted an activity she asks students to complete as a means for raising their consciousness about the role that literacy plays in their lives and futures—they write and illustrate why they need reading for the career they want as an adult. In her explanation she wrote:

> Although I didn't know it at the time, I was engaging the students in the critical literacy theory practices of Freire linking the ability to read to success in a career as an adult. Before this semester, I have always discussed with my students the need to be able to read and write to be successful in life. This activity is one example of the students in fifth grade completing an activity that was developmentally appropriate for them to think and internalize the link between literacy, power, success, and financial success as an adult.

In her synthesis the same teacher said:

> "I have to admit that I learned something about myself through this assignment. While I have been teaching for four years, I have never looked at my teaching through the lenses of theorists. . . . It is just jumping out at me that I am a teacher that uses the social learning perspectives to plan and facilitate my classroom. My hope is to continue to release the learning to my students by implementing more and more social learning theory practices in my classroom."

Such testimonials are common among the projects and speak to the fact that, although it may be challenging to build theory to practice connections, there are ways to bring it about and ways that are not only effective but also engaging and meaningful to teachers.

WRITING PROCESSES

What Is It?

Writing is the means by which one's thoughts and feelings become visible through written language. Writing is thus intimately personal—a means for self-expression and reflection, a tool that can be used to organize one's thoughts and extend memory. On the other hand, it is ultimately social—a communicative act with the capacity to enlighten and entertain others, with the power to topple governments and transform our worlds. Writing, then, serves multiple purposes. As Graham, MacArthur, and Fitzgerald (2007) remarked, "Writing is a powerful tool for getting things done" (p. 2).

What Do Teachers Need to Know?

Writing processes are multifaceted, involving physical, cognitive, affective, and social processes. Teachers who understand the complexities of writing processes will better understand how to meet the learning needs of their students.

Complex Cognitive Processes

Beginning in the 1970s, writing researchers attempted to understand writing processes by asking adults to think aloud as they wrote (Graham, 2006). One outcome of this early research, the Flower and Hayes (1980) cognitive processing model, hypothesized numerous mental operations that occurred during composition, such as retrieving knowledge of topic and audience from long-term memory, generating ideas, rereading text already produced, and monitoring one's progress. An important aspect of this theory is that these subcomponents can influence one another in ways that can inhibit or enhance writing.

Building on his own and others' research, Hayes (1996, 2006) revised the model adding motivation/affect, work with collaborators, social contexts, and writing tools. Current understandings, further building on these early cognitive models, suggest that strategies (such as brainstorming ideas) consciously selected by writers work in conjunction with foundational skills—those abilities that are typically automatic in proficient writers, such as handwriting and spelling.

Social Processes

Although writing demands complex cognitive processes, it is actually the social and communicative contexts that drive an individual's writing. Social contexts and/or discourse communities (Gee, 1999) determine the purposes and forms for most of our writing. For example, almost all of us could identity a recipe at one glance and describe its purposes. Written products are social artifacts for which there are inherent purposes and audiences. Sociocultural theorists argue that writing is collaborative even when a writer appears to be writing on his or her own as the lone writer is utilizing an "array of sociohistoric resources . . . that extend beyond the moment of transcription and that cross modes and media" (Prior, 2006, p. 58). Writing is fundamental to ways of being and doing in our society.

Challenges to Developing Writing Proficiency

Scardamalia and Bereiter (1991) have argued that developing writing proficiency is one of the most difficult academic expectations. Foundational skills such as handwriting, spelling, and written conventions take years of instruction and practice to master. For most children, composition strategies must be explicitly taught (Graham, 2006; Graham et al., 2007). Furthermore, foundational skills and composition strategies interact. For example, troubles with handwriting (use of writing tools) were found to affect students' perseverance in writing (Berninger & Swanson, 1994).

Given the complexities of writing, Scardamalia and Bereiter (1986) theorized that writing can occur at two levels: (1) *knowledge telling*— essentially connecting one thought with another as they sequentially come to mind and writing them down; and (2) *knowledge transformation*— a problem-solving process as one engages in composition of particular texts. As a problem-solving activity, writing is viewed as an open-ended task that can be continually improved rather than mastered. Writers must self-regulate and persevere in the face of the challenges in writing. Highly complex and interrelated composition processes, coupled with the demands of writing for particular purposes and audiences, require sophisticated instructional approaches. These may include teacher direction, strategy instruction and practice, and supportive learning environments.

DEVELOPMENTAL PROGRESSIONS OF LITERACY

What Is It?

Literacy—understandings about the functions of print and the ability to write and read—develop in predictable ways beginning in infancy and continuing throughout the lifespan.

What Do Teachers Need to Know?

Practice and Guidance

Just as in any complex endeavor, an individual needs a great deal of practice to become highly proficient in reading and writing. Ongoing practice with literacy processes is central to children's development. Children need to read in order to learn to read; they need to write in order to learn to write.

Literacy development is fostered by active engagement on the part of students, but it also requires active teachers. Ongoing practice needs to be guided and scaffolded to optimize development. Children cannot be left to guess at or intuit complex and invisible mental processes or social purposes on their own. Literacy development needs to be supported by thoughtful instruction (Coker, 2007).

Teachers play critical roles in children's development as they engage students in reading instructional-level texts, foster engagement with purposeful writing activity, and provide explicit instruction and modeling that gives children a window into invisible literacy processes. They assess for, plan, and implement effective literacy instruction differentiated for students' developmental levels.

Development Occurs on Multiple Aspects of Literacy

Literacy development occurs simultaneously on physical, cognitive, social, and affective levels. For instance, children need continued opportunities to practice foundational skills and strategies at the same time they are developing understandings of social purposes and personal appreciation for reading and writing. Learning-to-read instruction does not end in third grade. Both spelling and writing process skills develop over several years.

Development of some aspects of literacy, such as letter–sound knowledge, concepts about print, and fluent letter formation are skills with a limited set of items—usually mastered with a year or two with instruction. Most need to become automatic. Constrained skills (Paris, 2005) are necessary foundational skills for fluent reading and writing, but do not guarantee either comprehension or construction of written text.

In contrast, development of vocabulary, ability to comprehend and interact deeply with text, and effective use of writing processes and strategies are open-ended skills and processes that continue to grow throughout a reader's life. Development of understandings and strategies specific to comprehension and writing processes, as well as understanding the power and purposes of reading and writing, can serve as tools that foster lifelong literacy development, as the scaffolding is released.

Predictable Patterns of Development

Both reading and writing develop in predictable patterns with recognizable features and milestones. From Chall's (1996, cited in McKenna & Stahl, 2009) six-stage model of reading development to Bear's (Bear, Invernizzi, Templeton, & Johnston, 2012) synchronous model of literacy development to Chapman's (1997) continuum for writing development, designating specific patterns of development can be helpful in understanding individual progress. Spear-Swerling (2004) has even developed a highly informative "road-map" diagram that shows how and where readers can get off track to become reading disabled.

Understanding the typical progression of knowledge and skills enables teachers to avoid unreasonable expectations and to plan instruction that will be within the learning reach of a child. However, while stages can provide insight into children's development, there will always be individual variations.

Importantly for teachers, patterns of development are visible as children learn to speak, listen, read, and write. What a child uses, doesn't use, or uses but confuses (Bear et al., 2012) provides a window into that child's developmental level. Knowing what to expect, coupled with close attention—noticing, reading, and listening to children's voices—and appropriate assessments, enables teachers to view children's errors not as mistakes but as insights into their current thinking and to celebrate and acknowledge the partial understandings that children demonstrate as important steps in learning to read and write.

Literacy Beginnings

Literacy development is a lifelong process that begins long before children come to school. In modern societies, children are surrounded by letters and words—on television and T-shirts; on storefronts and street signs; on cereal boxes and toothpaste tubes; and in books, e-readers, and cell phones. Literacy development begins with young children's first efforts at making sense of those ubiquitous symbols, and in their imitations of the literacy practices of their home and community. Creating meaningful representations through drawing are considered precursors to beginning writing (Dyson & Freedman, 1991). Children who see their parents reading or making shopping lists will do the same as they pretend to read to their dolls or scribble make-believe lists.

These early approximations demonstrate young children's understanding of the symbolic nature of print, and their desire to enter what Frank Smith termed "the literacy club" (Smith, 1988). Children who are encouraged in their explorations of print ask many questions about the print they see, and conduct their own explorations with writing. One of us fondly remembers her 5-year-old bringing strings of letters she had written and asking her to read them. When she said, "It doesn't really say anything, but this is what it would sound like," and uttered a string of nonsense sounds, they both had a good laugh. This child-initiated game was helping her child to gain important insights into how print in an alphabetic language works—not every group of letters represents a word, yet the letters provide information about sounds. Through their explorations, young children can develop important insights into how print works. They discover such things as the message is meant to communicate something, the message stays the same time after time, the directional principles of the language, and that longer spoken words require more letters (Clay, 1975).

In this emergent phase, where children are gaining the preliminary understandings that enable conventional reading and writing to develop, reading and writing are interconnected reciprocal processes. Although many of us used to think that children learned to read first and write later, many young children learn to read through writing. Children encouraged to use "invented spelling" gain extensive practice in connecting sounds to the letters that represent the sounds. Early attempts at writing often enable children to learn the conventional spelling of high-frequency words, knowledge that supports them in reading their first little books. Alternatively, some children learn the spelling of high-frequency words such as *the, like,* or *can* when an adult points to the words he or she is reading during shared reading of enlarged print in the classroom or lap reading at home, and bring the conventional spellings into their writing. Understanding the importance of early literacy experiences helps teachers value and build on the literacy knowledge that children bring with them from home.

Concepts of Print

Every written language follows conventions regarding the direction that the printed words are read, and has means of representing phrasing and tone through punctuation marks, print size, and density. Children need to understand these conventions in order to read and write. In English, we read left to right with a return sweep to begin the next line. Understanding and being able to consistently use the left-to-right pattern within words as well as across the page is a critical development for learning to read and write. Teachers may not realize they need to intentionally teach directional principles because it is so instinctive.

Another key early understanding is concept of word (sometimes abbreviated as COW). In oral language words are strung together with no separation. Children must grasp where the individual word breaks are, understand that in print these breaks are indicated with white space, and be able to match a spoken word to the written word, even if they cannot yet perceive all of the letters individually. Fingerpoint reading, where a child can accurately match a memorized text to the groups of letters on the page, is a major milestone in literacy development, and an absolute prerequisite to conventional reading. Sometimes young children confuse syllables with words, and can be observed pointing to two groups of letters when they say a two-syllable word.

Phonological Awareness

Young readers in alphabetic languages need to learn how letters map to the sounds of their language. To be able to map the sound in words to the letters and groups of letters that represent those sounds, a prospective reader/writer must develop the insight that words not only have meaning but that they also are composed of sounds. Typically, children are first able to hear, identify, and manipulate words; then, beginning sounds and rhymes; and finally, individual phonemes. This awareness enables them to understand the alphabetic principle—that each sound is represented by a letter or a combination of letters—and opens the gate to decoding. Phonological awareness is also a milestone because it marks the first instance of language metacognition: the ability to think about language apart from meaning.

Word Recognition and Production

From drawings and preconventional scribbles to phonetic spellings to fluent conventional spelling, children's early word production is striking (Chapman, 1997).

Ehri's widely accepted explanation of how readers at different levels of experience and proficiency identify written words (Ehri, 1998) is very helpful to teachers who work with beginning or struggling readers. The typical developmental path moves from prealphabetic or logographic readers who identify words based strictly on context ("McDonald's") and write a combination of pseudoletter forms and real letters, as in the script for a play written by a kindergarten child in Figure 1.4; to partial

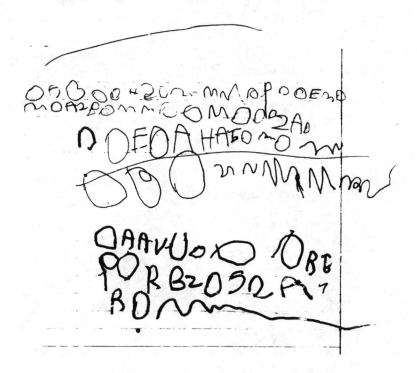

FIGURE 1.4. Script for a play by a kindergarten child.

alphabetic readers who do not use all of the letters to identify and write new words (e.g., *baby* might be spelled as BB), as in the "tree house" story in Figure 1.5; to full alphabetic readers who are able to read and write words by assigning each sound to a letter or letter pattern (e.g., spelling *baby* as BABE), decoding letter by letter as in the "first-grade" story in Figure 1.6; to consolidated readers who can use multiletter chunks and correctly spell most words; to automatic readers who can quickly identify and write most words that they see in text (Ehri, 2005). While a young reader might have a dominant mode for identifying unfamiliar words, readers at all levels read words automatically once the word is sufficiently familiar (Share, 1999). Children experiencing difficulty learning to read are often stuck in the partial alphabetic or full alphabetic mode of reading words; they have trouble developing fluency in word identification that results in a slow, laborious and unfulfilling reading experience.

As Stanovich (1986) pointed out in "Matthew Effects in Reading: Some Consequences of Individual Differences in the Acquisition of Literacy," those individuals who learn to read relatively easily in the early grades find reading a pleasurable activity, and can read with relative fluency. Those children choose to read, and gain further reading proficiency as well as vocabulary and knowledge growth through their reading. Their vocabulary and knowledge then supports them in reading more difficult text. In contrast, the children who struggle to figure out the words on the page find reading laborious and unrewarding. These children often avoid reading, or read so slowly they are not exposed to as many words during a reading session as their more able peers, leaving them further and further behind. Ironically, the individuals who have

FIGURE 1.5. "I am in my tree house," by a kindergarten child.

FIGURE 1.6. "I am in first grade. I am learning how to read."

more difficulty learning to read need *more* practice than their faster progressing peers to attain the same level of proficiency, yet these are precisely the children who typically read less.

Development of Comprehension

Reading development models describe a progression of capacity to understand, describe, analyze, evaluate, discuss, and synthesize increasingly complex text across an array of genres. Readers are expected to become increasingly strategic in the ways they make sense of text, monitor their understanding, read different kinds of text, and see connections across different texts. In fact, central to the Common Core State Standards (CCSS) for reading are expectations for increased text complexity from kindergarten to 12th grade, along with increased expectations to understand and interact with text and across texts.

Long-term support of comprehension development is critical to development of readers' abilities to construct deep understandings of texts and meet the CCSS. Supportive classroom contexts, explicit strategy instruction, teacher modeling, guided practice, independent practice, and high-quality discussion are important components of instruction that support the development of comprehension processes (Duke & Pearson, 2002).

Development of Composition

Children's composition begins in visual representations of thoughts. Coupling of drawing and writing is typical to the language experience approach and in kindergarten writing journals. Drawing and visualization precede the generation of language in these instances.

As they develop understandings of and skills with writing processes and strategies, children move in a "progression of refinement from more unconventional and gross approximations to more conventional and specific ones" (Chapman, 1997, p. 28).

Learning to compose is challenging, as children must develop understandings of communicative purposes for writing, ability to write in various genres, and effective utilization of writing processes and strategies, as well as fluency and automaticity with handwriting and conventions. Even as a first grader writes one simple sentence, he or she will need to retrieve memories or ideas; consider his or her teacher's (audience) expectations; grapple with sentence organization, as well as spelling, letter formation, and spacing; and use conventions of capitalization and punctuation (Coker, 2007). Thus, depictions of developmental patterns in writing, such as that designed by Chapman (1997), typically list several development components along a continuum of stages—such as beginning, emergent, developing, consolidating, and expanding writer—along with typical age levels.

Social contexts are also considerations for writing development. Understanding and utilizing concepts of audience awareness, as well as features, formats, and communicative purposes of written genres, are important to development of effective writers. Furthermore, agency— willingness to take risks, expose one's thoughts and feelings, and develop one's voice in writing—is important to writing development. Children need to develop a sense of themselves as writers in their worlds, using writing to serve important purposes.

NEW LITERACIES

What Is It?

Bound books, the printing press, ballpoint pens, and the typewriter are examples of technological changes that have influenced the ways in which written language is created and consumed in society. The advent of the computer and the World Wide Web—the most recent technological advances in written language—have created changes of historic magnitude. Technology is rapidly changing the intensity and complexity of literate environments (National Council of Teachers of English [NCTE], 2008). Both multimodal and highly social genres (e.g., texting and tweeting) have profoundly influenced how and where we access information, as well as expanding access to audiences. Through the Internet, immediate communication with individuals from other cultures around the world provides rich opportunities for learning about diversity.

What Do Teachers Need to Know?

Attitudes, Knowledge, and Skills

To help students achieve the "literacies of their future" (Leu, 2002, p. 310), instructional practices will need to shift (International Reading Association [IRA], 2002). The NCTE (2008) has set standards for sophisticated digital literacy skills needed by readers and writers. These include:

- Develop proficiency with the tools of technology.
- Build relationships with others to pose and solve problems collaboratively and cross-culturally.
- Design and share information for global communities to meet a variety of purposes.
- Manage, analyze, and synthesize multiple streams of simultaneous information.
- Create, critique, analyze, and evaluate multimedia texts.
- Attend to the ethical responsibilities required by these complex environments.

Preparing children for literacy in the digital age involves embracing and envisioning new ways of reading and writing, as well as knowing strategies for using and managing digital tools and resources. Developing one's own knowledge and skills around digital literacies—in collaboration with students' literacy development—is important to effective literacy instruction.

Changes to Written Products

Digital technologies have opened up a wide array of possibilities for written representations. In fact, regular change is regarded as one aspect of new literacies (Leu, 2002). Text, visual representations, and sound intersect in digital genres in ways that can contribute to rich multimodal products. Information in new genres may be linked rather than linear. Conventions of language have already been altered, such as in texting, to match to new purposes and ways of communicating.

Changes to Literacy Processes

Despite the changes wrought by digital literacies, it is important for teachers to know that "new literacies build on, but do not usually replace previous literacies" (Leu, 2002, p. 315). Reading and writing are even more important in the digital world. On the other hand, important changes have already occurred in digital literacy processes. For instance, rather than turning to the next page while reading for research or information, readers employ various strategies to search through the nonlinear text organization to find relevant information and construct meaning (Coiro & Dobler, 2007). Ability to evaluate trustworthiness of websites and information has become critical, placing new demands on readers' abilities to find, evaluate, and select a seemingly limitless amount of information. As computer tools and emerging genres add visual and auditory layers to the final products, writing in new digital genres will require more complex ways of generating and organizing ideas in multimodal products. With the Internet, issues of audience and authorship take on new meanings.

ACTIVITY 1.5
Literacy Research Position Statement: Deepening Knowledge, Finding Voice
ANTONY SMITH

Activity Type: Assignment with in-class components.

Materials: N/A.

Duration: Semester project; two 30-minutes sessions in class, middle of semester; 60–90 minutes during the final course session.

Professional Learning Focus:
- Read and analyze current literacy research.
- Synthesize research on a literacy topic relevant to practice.
- Develop purpose, audience, and voice in persuasive writing.

Standards Links

IRA Professional Standards:
1.1 Candidates understand major theories and empirical research that describe the cognitive, linguistic, motivational, and sociocultural foundations of reading and writing development, processes, and components.

Common Core State Standards: Writing Anchor Standards

Text Types and Purposes
1. Write arguments to support claims in an analysis of substantive topics or texts, using valid reasoning and relevant and sufficient evidence.

- Develop leadership and perspective as a learning community member.

K–8 Student Learning Focus:

- Understand elements of persuasive writing, with a specific focus on argument and supporting claims with evidence.
- Understand importance of establishing purpose and identifying audience as part of the writing process.

2. Write informative/explanatory texts to examine and convey complex ideas and information clearly and accurately through the effective selection, organization, and analysis of content.

Production and Distribution of Writing
4. Produce clear and coherent writing in which the development, organization, and style are appropriate to task, purpose, and audience.

Research to Build and Present Knowledge
8. Gather relevant information from multiple print and digital sources, assess the credibility and accuracy of each source, and integrate the information while avoiding plagiarism.

Rationale

In a time when the terms *research based* and *evidence based* are used often and found in a variety of curriculum and instructional materials, it is important for teachers to develop a deep knowledge of literacy and become critical consumers of research. This knowledge, developed in tandem with a critical inquiry stance toward research, helps teachers ground instructional practice and fosters a sense of empowerment. Many of my students (who are also classroom teachers) come to class eager to explore issues and questions related to their school contexts, instruction, and students. Through a process of analyzing and synthesizing research on chosen topics, teachers have the opportunity to deepen their literacy knowledge and articulate this knowledge by crafting position statements that are meant to be shared with real audiences.

Description

The position statement assignment is a culminating project for a master's-level research seminar that is part of a reading endorsement program. Below I outline steps to introduce and model this assignment so that teachers are prepared to compose their position statements and then read them aloud on the last day of class.

1. In the first class session I have students read the annual "What's Hot, What's Not" feature of *Reading Today* and other IRA publications (e.g., Cassidy, Valadez, Garrett, & Barrera, 2010) to begin thinking of specific literacy research topics to explore across the semester. This exploration, which includes facilitating research-article discussions and creating an annotated bibliography, culminates with the position statement assignment. Teachers choose their topics early and dig deep.

2. About two-thirds of the way through the semester, once teachers have gained experience reading and analyzing research articles and assembled their annotated bibliographies, I use about 30 minutes of class time to introduce the position statement assignment:

- First, I share the basic criteria of the genre, including a clear position on a topic, an authentic audience, the need to support claims with specific evidence, that the statement be concise (two to three pages), and that the statements will be read aloud.
- Next, I hand out example position statements from IRA and NCTE. Teachers review these statements in class, discussing their observations and reactions in small groups.
- Finally, I share some of my own ideas about position statement topics and audiences and then prompt teachers to brainstorm ideas in small groups.

3. During the following class session, I take another 30-minute period to share and discuss a draft position statement I composed, one that examines oral reading fluency as a measure of formative assessment. Teachers discuss my example, ask questions, and brainstorm in small groups to come up with a list of essential criteria for the position statement assignment. Typical criteria include:

- Clear topic and purpose.
- Statement of a position—choose a side.
- Importance of the issue.
- Background information on the issue.
- Support for the position—three or more references.
- Future of the issue.
- Classroom implications.
- Identified audience.

4. After brainstorming these criteria, I prompt teachers to consider connections between this assignment and the kinds of writing projects they assign their students. We discuss elements of persuasive writing, ways to use details to support claims, and how to back up statements with evidence. I show examples and interactive lessons from the website *readwritethink.org* to facilitate this discussion.

5. On the last day of class, teachers come prepared to share their position statements. One by one, without interruption, each teacher stands at the lectern,

identifies his or her intended audience, and reads the statement to the class. I have found that this process takes approximately 5–8 minutes per teacher. After everyone has shared, I facilitate a discussion exploring themes and ideas that have emerged from the statements. We also debrief the experience of reading a piece of our own writing aloud to an audience. Finally, we outline next steps in sharing our statements with their intended audiences outside of class.

Discussion

While most teachers have opinions about various literacy topics, these opinions are not always supported by research. The position statement allows teachers to ground their ideas in research and to develop an informed position on a topic of importance. This assignment also helps teachers establish connections to school and classroom contexts by identifying a specific audience for their statement and actually sharing it with this audience after completing the course. One outcome I have observed is a strong sense of voice teachers develop as they craft their position statements. Here is one excerpt that illustrates the strong sense of voice that comes through in teachers' statements:

> "The explicit inclusion of instruction centering on expository text is necessary in the elementary grades. Students must have expository skills in order to meet the expectations set forth in content-based classes in later grades. Modeled and guided instruction on text structure in conjunction with exposure to a multitude of texts and an emphasis on its value are pivotal, and should therefore be regularly present in all elementary classrooms." (Chris, elementary school teacher)

Another outcome is a palpable feeling of empowerment among teachers, a feeling that encourages them to become leaders and active members of school or district professional learning communities. One primary grades teacher, for example, chose reading fluency as her topic, writing a position statement for the purpose of communicating assessment concerns to other teachers and the school principal. Another teacher wrote his position paper on adolescent student reading motivation, with the goal of using it to initiate discussion among his middle school peers teaching language arts. During the following semester, these teachers stopped by my office to let me know they had shared their statements with these audiences. They both felt they had the knowledge base and critical inquiry stance to support their position and articulate their ideas. Both were excited to help facilitate meaningful discussion and promote change.

Feedback on course evaluation forms indicates an appreciation for working through challenging research articles, developing deep literacy knowledge, and articulating an understanding of this knowledge through the position statement assignment. After teaching this seminar many times, what I always appreciate most is a rather sudden transformation I have observed of teachers' experience: from nervous anxiety to informed confidence. I can't think of another assignment that fosters such a sense of empowerment through just a few pages of writing!

Supporting Materials

Syllabus Project Description

This paper is a statement you make on one of the literacy research issues considered over the quarter. Using course readings, class discussions, peer-annotated bibliographies, and information you have gathered on current trends in literacy research, you will craft a statement asserting your position on this issue. This position will need to be supported by readings and discussions. The audience for this statement could be the parent community at your school, the school board of your district, a local newspaper editorial page, or a local or state-level elected official. Your finished paper should be two to three pages in length, double-spaced (not including references). You will share this position statement by reading it aloud on the last day of class.

Example Position Statements Used in Class

- NCTE Position Statement on Writing Assessment.
- NCTE Position Statement on Reading.
- IRA/National Middle School Association (NMSA) Position Statement on Young Adolescents' Literacy Learning.

For Teaching the Position Statement Genre to Students

- Persuasion map interactive at *readwritethink.org*: *www.readwritethink.org/files/resources/interactives/persuasion_map*.
- Position Statements outline from *readwritethink.org*.

Position Statement Scoring Criteria

Statement

- Statement of the position is clearly articulated.
- Importance of the issue and the position is justified.
- Supporting points are identified and discussed.

Issue

- Background information on the issue is included.
- Future of the issue is addressed.
- Classroom implications are noted.

Audience, Format, Style

- Specific audience is identified.
- References and reference list (with proper American Psychological Association style) are provided.
- Maximum three pages (not counting references) double-spaced, read with authority and conviction.

References

Cassidy, J., Valadez, C. M., Garrett, S. D., & Barrera, E. S. (2010). Adolescent and adult literacy: What's hot, what's not. *Journal of Adolescent and Adult Literacy, 53*(6), 448–456.

National Council of Teachers of English. (2008). NCTE Framework for 21st century curriculum and assessment. Retrieved from *www.ncte.org/library/NCTEFiles/Resources/Positions/Framework_21stCent_Curr_Assessment.pdf.*

CHAPTER 2

Word-Level Processes

In reading, *word-level processes* refers to the recognition of printed words; in writing, *word-level processes* refers to the production of words. The topics addressed in this chapter include the structure of the English spelling/sound system and the development of word recognition and decoding. Because word recognition and production in alphabetic languages depends on learning letters and their relationship to the sounds of the language, this chapter also includes letter learning, phonics, and phonological awareness (awareness of the sounds in words).

Since the skills and conceptual understandings that support word-level processes are the central focus of literacy instruction in the early school years (and the focus of many high-stakes assessments), it is all too easy for early years teachers to lose sight of the goal of reading or writing—to comprehend or communicate ideas conveyed through print. We think it is critical for teachers who work with emergent and early readers to build the desire to read and write through read-alouds and meaningful opportunities to write, while simultaneously building the foundation for comprehending written text through the intentional development of oral language and background knowledge. Letter knowledge will ultimately be fully mastered by all children, and will be mastered more quickly by 6-year-olds than 5-year-olds, and by 5-year-olds than 4-year-olds. Early years curricula that emphasize the constrained skill of letter recognition (Paris, 2005) at the expense of developing a love for reading and writing along with vocabulary and background knowledge undermine the long-term literacy proficiency of children.

STRUCTURE OF THE ENGLISH
SPELLING/SOUND SYSTEM

What Is It?

The structure of the English spelling/sound system—its orthography—refers to how the alphabetic system maps onto the phonology (sounds) of spoken English.

What Do Teachers Need to Know?

Teachers need a sophisticated understanding of how the complex orthographic system of English works to appropriately guide emergent and developing readers. Teachers ought to be able to accurately parse the sounds in words to help children link speech sounds to letters and letter combinations. An accurate understanding of the meaning of the terminology associated with phonics and word-level instruction enables teachers to understand research, curriculum guides, and professional development associated with instruction for emergent and beginning reading. Figure 2.1 offers an overview of useful terminology for teaching at the word level.

The Complexity of English Orthography

Many people assume that all words can be "sounded out" by which they usually mean worked out letter by letter. While such an approach works in alphabetic languages where single letters map to single sounds such as Spanish and German, a letter-by-letter strategy does not work for all words in English. In fact, many of the most commonly occurring words—the high-frequency words—cannot be figured out using a letter-by-letter sounding approach: *the, one, was, two, said, night*. Thus, teachers need to understand that English has a complex orthographic system. In English:

- A single letter can represent more than one phoneme or sound: *c, g, y, x,* all vowels.
- The same sound is represented by more than one letter or combination of letters—for example, /s/ by *s* and *c*; /k/ by *c, k, ck,* and *q*; /ay/ by *ay, eigh, ai, a_e,* and more; /f/ by *f, ph, gh* (but for *gh* only in the final position of a root word).

Word	Definition	Example
blend	Two or three consonants without a vowel between them; each one is pronounced.	*str* in *string* *cl* in *clap* *st* in *fast*
consonant	All the letters except the vowels.	
digraph	Two letters that represent a single sound.	*sh* *ch* *th* *ea* *oa*
dipthong	A vowel sound that changes from one sound to another as it is uttered.	*oy* in *toy* *ou* in *found*
irregular word	A word with an unexpected pronunciation given its spelling.	*was* (Why doesn't it rhyme with *has?*) *move* *women*
long vowel	The sound a vowel stands for when it "says its own name."	*a* in *cake* *i* in *night*
morpheme	The smallest meaning unit in a word.	*rap* has one morpheme *rapper* has two morphemes
onset	The initial letter or letters in a word up to the vowel.	*r* in *rap* *str* in *strap*
phoneme	The smallest sound in a word that when changed, changes the meaning of the word.	*rap* contains three phonemes; if you change the first, second, or third sounds, you will have a different word *rap–cap*; *rap–rip*; *rap–rat* *chap* also contains three phonemes
prefix	A part added to the beginning of a base or root to change its meaning.	*un* *re* *anti*
rime	The part of a word from the vowel to the end that rhymes with other words.	*at* in *cat* *ind* in *grind*

(continued)

FIGURE 2.1. Useful terminology for teaching at the word level.

Word	Definition	Example
short vowel	One of the two most common sounds represented by a vowel.	*a* in *cat* *e* in *jet* *i* in *fish* *o* in *stop* *u* in *run*
suffix	A part added to the end of a word.	*ed* *ing* *ous* *tion* *ly*
syllable	The number of beats or claps in a word.	*rap* has one syllable; *rapper* has two syllables
vowel	The letters *a*, *e*, *i*, *o*, *u*, and *y* when it sounds like an *i* or *e* as in *my* or *happy*. The sounds represented by vowels are made with an open mouth and free air flow. The most common sounds these letters stand for are called "long" and "short," explained above. There are many additional sounds that fall into neither category.	Vowel sounds that are neither "long" nor "short": *a* in *father* *i* in *bird*

FIGURE 2.1. *(continued)*

- The same combination of letters can represent more than one sound—for example, *ea* in *great, head, seat, beauty, meander,* and more.
- Certain phonemes are represented *only* by letter combinations: /sh/ by *sh*, /th/ by *th*.

English spelling is more regular when viewed at the pattern or *rime* (the written part of a word from the vowel to the end that rhymes) level than the individual letter–sound level, particularly because long vowel sounds are represented by multiple vowel combinations. Words that share the same rime unit, such as *pail, sail,* and *jail,* will be spelled with the same letter sequence; the novice's task is to learn which pattern a word belongs to (*tale, male, sale* or *tail, mail, sail*). The spelling of words in English is also related to meaning, where a consistent spelling provides insight into meaning even when pronunciation changes. For example, *sign*, *signal*, and *significance* all share the same meaning (morphological) root.

ACTIVITY 2.1

Word Sorts for Teachers: Helping Teachers Recognize Decodable and Nondecodable Words for Students at Different Reading Stages

DEBORAH G. LITT

Activity Type: In-class activity

Materials: Handouts of word lists; scissors.

Duration: 10–25 minutes.

Professional Learning Focus:
- Identifying regular and irregular words.
- Recognizing which words children at different levels of decoding ability can figure out independently.

K–8 Student Learning Focus:
Decoding.

Standards Links

IRA Professional Standards:
2.2 Use appropriate and varied instructional approaches, including those that develop word recognition, language comprehension, strategic knowledge, and reading–writing connections.

Implement and evaluate instruction in each of the following areas: concepts of print, phonemic awareness, phonics, vocabulary, comprehension, fluency, critical thinking, motivation, and writing.

Common Core State Standards: Reading Standards: Foundational Skills
3. Know and apply grade-level phonics and word analysis skills in decoding words.

Rationale

When beginning reader Albert pauses at a word he does not know in print, should the adult *tell* him the word, make a suggestion (give him a prompt) that will enable the child to figure the unfamiliar word out on his own, or wait to see if Albert can figure it out himself? If Albert asks for help, then what should the teacher do?

Knowing how to respond in this common situation is a key skill for teachers who work with beginning readers. And teachers at any level may find themselves with beginners in their classrooms. To respond in a manner most advantageous to the student's progress, the teacher must be able to quickly determine whether or not the student has the capacity to figure out the word independently.

Adults who have never worked with emergent and beginning readers typically overestimate what these early readers are capable of figuring out. This faulty understanding leads teachers to ask children to sound out words using a letter-by-letter sounding procedure when the pronunciations of the letters do not follow expected patterns (*one, was, said, through*) or when the children do not yet have the letter–sound knowledge to figure out the word, for example, as when a teacher directs a child who has not learned about the silent *e* to sound out *cake.*

Children who struggle without success to figure out many words in a relatively short text may become discouraged readers, often becoming quite clever at avoiding the task. Even if they do not become discouraged, they can become habituated to slow, choppy reading. On the other hand, telling children words that they are fully capable of decoding on their own can make them passive, and unwilling to take on the challenge and responsibility of figuring out words on their own.

Teachers need to know which words their students have the capacity to decode. Therefore, it is critical for teachers to learn to distinguish the words they can reasonably expect their students to figure out on their own from those the teacher needs to provide. What makes this a particularly challenging skill is that teachers must make their decisions on the spot with little time to think. On top of that, teachers face a constantly moving target. As the children gain experience, they become capable of figuring out more of the words independently.

I use word sorting to help teachers discover that words they may have thought of as easy because they are very common or short may not necessarily be easy for a beginning reader. I also use word sorts to provide teachers with opportunities to practice deciding which words students with a different sets of knowledge about words and letter–sound relationships could be expected to figure out. Experiencing the power (and pleasure) of sorting with material that is at the teachers' level makes it more likely they will use sorting as an instructional technique in their own classrooms.

Description

As with word-sort activities used with children for spelling and word study, I give teachers a list of words to cut apart and sort into columns according to criteria I specify. I ask them to sort the words for different characteristics (easy vs. hard, regular vs. irregular, a spelling–pronunciation combination with only one example such as found in the words *one* or *was* vs. a spelling–pronunciation combination with multiple examples such as *dove, shove, love.* I also give them student descriptors and ask them to determine which words a child or group of children would be capable of decoding (see Figure 2.3). They work with one to three other teachers and discuss their choices and reasoning as they place the words into columns. I circulate around the room commenting and posing questions as the teachers are working. I ask the teachers to reflect on what they learned from the activity.

A sampling of the questions I use for reflection on the word sorts are:

"What surprised you?"

"What did you learn about reading English words that you didn't realize before?"

"Will you respond differently from now on when listening to a child read? If so, how?"

"What do you need to know more about? What do you need more practice with?"

"What questions do you have?"

After sufficient time has passed for most groups to finish or nearly finish I ask each group share a point or two with the whole class from their reflective discussion.

Figures 2.2 and 2.3 show some examples of word sorts I have used to help adults learn to distinguish decodable from nondecodable words matched to different sets of decoding knowledge.

Discussion

The teachers with whom I have used this activity uniformly report that it is very helpful. During discussion after the sorts they voice their new understandings regarding what makes a word easy or hard for a student to figure out. Some have asked for more opportunities to practice, but rather than create more word sorts for them, I point out that they can practice on their own. They can and should determine what phonics understandings each child has mastered and which words each child knows. They can then examine the words in the texts available for instruction to determine which words each child already recognizes, which ones each child should be able to decode, and which words each child will need to be told. If there are too many in that last category, that tells them that the text is too difficult for those children at the moment.

After several practice sessions with the word sorts, I see improvement in teachers' ability to appropriately determine when to encourage children to work out a difficult word independently This can be seen through the practice exercises themselves, items on quizzes, and, most importantly, in the audiotaped recordings of their interactions with beginning readers.

to	the	can	up
was	thought	two	one
said	laugh	women	want
come	move	home	went
eight	day	understand	lunch
car	will	morning	green
red	love	who	they
blue	hat	what	could
know	black	again	guess
two	have	there	bird

1. Which of these words can be figured out with a letter-by-letter sounding approach? Sort into three columns: Yes, No, Not Sure.

2. Which words follow the rules? Which words are probably exceptions? Sort into three columns: Follows the Most Common Rules, Does Not Follow, Not Sure.

3. Discuss with your group your "ahas" and surprises. What did this activity make you aware of that you were not aware of before?

FIGURE 2.2. Word sort sample 1.

PHONOLOGY, PHONOLOGICAL AWARENESS, AND PHONEMIC AWARENESS

What Is It?

Phonology refers to the study of the sounds of a language and how they are organized. Phonological awareness encompasses recognition of the sounds within words as well as the ability to manipulate subword sound units (syllables, onsets, rimes, phonemes). *Phonemic* awareness refers to the ability to perceive and manipulate the smallest sound units within words, the phoneme. *Phonemic* awareness is a subset of *phonological* awareness. *Phonics* is the application of the sound value of letters or groups of letters to unfamiliar words.

hit	player	fish	power
pot	hop	hope	but
shut	mad	made	fist
said	tall	boy	now
thick	sick	litter	slower
filling	much	stage	drive
laugh	the	filled	which

Directions: Sort these words into three columns: Decodable, Nondecodable, Not Sure (?) depending on the phonics knowledge described.

Sort 1: Susie, Sam, and Sita
- Know all consonant sounds.
- Know all short vowel sounds, but no digraphs (*sh*, *ch*, *gh*, etc.).

Sort 2: Kareem, Kate, and Karl
- Know all consonant sounds and all short vowel sounds.
- They also know the CVCe rule.

Sort 3: Amalia, Andre, Antoine, and Ama
- Know all consonant sounds and all short vowel sounds.
- They also know the CVCe rule and these digraphs: *sh*, *ch*, *wh*, *th*.

Sort 4: Jake, Jenna, Juan, and Josie
- Know all consonant sounds and all short vowel sounds.
- They also know the CVCe rule and these digraphs: *sh*, *ch*, *wh*, *th*.
- They also know as units (phonograms or rimes) *ay*, *all*, and how to use these chunks to figure out unknown words.

Sort 5: Mia, Megan, Mark, and Manuel
- Know all consonant sounds and all short vowel sounds.
- They also know the CVCe rule and these digraphs: *sh*, *ch*, *wh*, *th*.
- They also know as units (phonograms or rimes) *ay*, *all*, *ow*, *er*, and how to use these chunks to figure out unknown words.

FIGURE 2.3. Word sort sample 2.

What Do Teachers Need to Know?

Phonics and Phonological Awareness Are Not the Same

Though they are often confused, *phonological awareness* is *not* the same as *phonics*. Whereas phonics refers to the reading strategy of using the sound value of letters and groups of letters to figure out unfamiliar printed words, phonological awareness tasks are related entirely to sound. They can be performed entirely orally, without looking at print. Common phonological awareness assessment tasks include rhyme detection, syllable counting, alliteration detection, initial consonant substitution, and sound deletion (say *sunshine* without saying *sun* or say *track* without saying /t/). Even though they refer to separate skills, phonological awareness is more easily developed when teachers provide letters as references during phonological awareness instruction.

Relationship between Phonological Awareness and Early Reading Skill

A minimal level of phonological awareness is necessary for access to printed words, specifically the ability to recognize the same phoneme in different words, known as *phoneme identity*. Children find it easier to develop phoneme identity when instruction includes the letter associated with the sound than when the instruction is solely oral (Bus & van IJzendoorn, 1999; Stahl & Murray, 1998). In fact, Stahl and Murray found that letter knowledge typically *preceded* the development of phonological awareness (1998). Learning letter names and reading alphabet books appears to help children develop phoneme identity.

Reading proficiency and phonological awareness have a reciprocal relationship. Reading in an alphabetic language cannot begin until the child develops the beginnings of phoneme identity and can recognize when words begin with the same sound. Many children can already recognize rhyme and syllables before they can read, but others develop these phonological awareness skills as they learn to read. The more advanced phonological awareness skills such as taking a word apart into all of its separate phonemes, recognizing a word from its separate phonemes (blending), and deleting a consonant within a consonant cluster (if you take /l/ from *split* you get _____) develop as a consequence of learning to read and write in an alphabetic language (Adams, 2011). Children who enter kindergarten with well-developed phonological awareness rarely go on to experience difficulty learning to read (Scarborough, 1998). These children also enter school with large vocabularies, some letter knowledge, and have heard many stories read to them—all factors contributing to success in initial reading acquisition (Stahl & Murray, 1998). Contrary to a widely held belief, less developed phonological awareness in a kindergarten child does not necessarily mean the child will experience difficulty learning to read. Only *some* of those children experience difficulty learning to read (Scarborough, 1998).

Fostering Phonological and Phonemic Awareness

Teachers can foster the development of phonological awareness through singing songs, reciting rhymes and chants, and through the reading of alphabet books. Sorting objects or pictures by sound is particularly effective in fostering phonological awareness, and can be used to target a specific area such as initial sounds, rhyme, or vowel sounds. Phonological awareness instruction is more powerful when children are shown letters to represent sounds (Bus & van IJzendoorn, 1999). In some school districts so much time is allotted to phonological awareness development that other activities that support long-term literacy development have been neglected. Early years teachers need to provide a balance of activities.

Children develop *phonemic* awareness—the awareness of each individual sound in words—when they write, especially when encouraged to create temporary or invented spellings for words they do not yet know how to spell conventionally. Phonemic awareness also develops through blending letter sounds when reading unfamiliar words. Elkonin boxes (see Activity 2.2) are a very powerful technique for developing phonemic awareness.

Assessment of Phonological and Phonemic Awareness

Each aspect of phonological awareness is a different skill, demanding a different item type to assess it. Even within one aspect of phonological awareness, there are different levels of difficulty and different ways of assessing it. To assess rhyme awareness, for example, a child may be asked to decide whether a pair of words rhymes or which word in a set of three is the "odd one out" because it doesn't rhyme or to produce a word that rhymes with one provided by the teacher. The three tasks are not equivalent. Rhyme recognition is easier than rhyme production, and some children may perform poorly on an "odd one out" task because of working memory limitations, despite adequate rhyme recognition.

Many phonological awareness skills can be assessed through careful observation during class activities. Is a child accurate when clapping the syllables of classmates' names? Does a child provide a rhyming word when the class makes up new verses to songs? Invented spelling provides a particularly rich data source for analyzing children's perception of speech sounds. There are also commercially developed and open source assessments for these skills.

ACTIVITY 2.2
Elkonin Boxes
DEBORAH G. LITT

Activity Type: In-class activity.

Materials:

For teachers:
- Pencil.
- Paper.

For instructor:
- Whiteboard, overhead projector, or similar device (camera projector).
- Material used for demonstration depends on group size.
- Optional: Video clips (*www.pioneervalleybooks.com/news/maddies-story-writing-lessons*).

Standards Links

IRA Professional Standards:
2.2 Use appropriate and varied instructional approaches, including those that develop word recognition, language comprehension, strategic knowledge, and reading–writing connections.

Select and implement instructional approaches based on evidence-based rationales, student needs, and purposes for instruction.

Implement and evaluate instruction in each of the following areas: concepts of print, phonemic awareness, phonics, vocabulary, comprehension, fluency, critical thinking, motivation, and writing.

Note. Elkonin boxes were invented by a Soviet psychologist, Daniel Elkonin. The technique first came to the attention of Western educators in 1973, when a description of the technique was published in English (Elkonin, 1973). Based on this description, Marie Clay developed a version of the technique for the Reading Recovery early intervention program.

Duration: 10–20 minutes.

Professional Learning Focus:
- Know when and how to use the Elkonin box procedure.
- Be able to teach and support children with the Elkonin boxes.
- Determine the number of phonemes in words.

K–8 Student Learning Focus:
- Development of phonemic awareness.
- Development of sound to letter mappings.

Common Core State Standards: Reading Standards: Foundational Skills

Phonological Awareness
2. Demonstrate understanding of spoken words, syllables, and sounds (phonemes).

Rationale

Elkonin boxes (also called sound boxes) are an exceptionally powerful technique for fostering both phonemic awareness and an understanding of the complex relationship between letters and sounds in English orthography. When I was a Reading Recovery teacher, I often saw children's faces light up with sudden understanding as soon as I introduced the boxes. One little girl even said to me, "Now, I get it!" Because it is such a powerful technique I think all literacy teachers ought to have it in their instructional toolboxes, and I take the time in my classes to teach the procedure to ensure teachers do it correctly. Performed incorrectly, the technique would confuse, not enlighten children. I have found it important to provide teachers with practice and corrective feedback to ensure they will demonstrate the technique correctly. (I provide an explanation of the common confusions in the Discussion section below.)

Description

1. I begin with a brief history of the technique and an explanation of its purpose—that Elkonin boxes help beginning readers (and older struggling readers or spellers) understand in a concrete way how letter sequences in written words are related to the sound sequences of spoken words. I explain to the teachers that I will be leading them through the same steps they should take when introducing Elkonin boxes to children and then proceed to do just that, starting with two-phoneme words and working up to words with four phonemes.

2. I draw or project an Elkonin box diagram for a two-phoneme word and ask everyone to draw a rectangle and divide it into two like the one I am showing.

3. I point to my knee and ask, "What am I pointing to?" I ask them to repeat the word *knee* and stretch it out slowly as I articulate it slowly along with them. (I use *knee* because the initial sound can be stretched out without adding a vowel sound to it.)

4. I demonstrate pushing my index finger into one box at a time as I say *knee*, coordinating the articulation with the movement. I do not separate the sounds. With this technique, the sounds are simply stretched out, not isolated.

5. Then I ask everyone to use the index finger of their dominant hand and to push and say *knee* just as I have demonstrated. I walk around the room to check that each person is coordinating the articulation and the pushing correctly, that no one is separating the sounds, and that each person is using only one finger. If correction is needed, I provide it to the teacher who needs the assistance.

6. I hold up a small picture of a sun and ask the teachers to pronounce the word. I ask them to say it slowly, stretching it out, and we practice doing that together a few times. I ask them to draw three boxes. I draw or project three Elkonin boxes and then demonstrate how to slide my index finger into each of the three boxes as I articulate *sun* slowly.

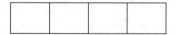

7. I ask the teachers to practice pushing their fingers into the boxes for the word *sun* and again walk around the room checking the coordination of pushing the index finger with the articulation.

8. I repeat the procedure with *mask* and *fist*, words that require four boxes.

9. With a volunteer teacher, I demonstrate how to scaffold and support children who have difficulty properly coordinating the speaking with pushing their finger. I show how I can say the word slowly while the volunteer pushes his or her finger into the boxes, making sure to match my voice to his or her movements; how we can exchange roles and I match my movements to his or her articulation; and, finally, how I can say the word together with my partner while gently sliding his or her finger for him or her. Alternatively, the volunteer can put his or her finger on top of mine. I have used all of these techniques to help young children master the coordination.

10. I write and pronounce an assortment of words containing three, four, and five phonemes, using an assortment of letter-to-sound mappings more complex than the single letter-to-sound mapping of the demonstration words, for example, *meat*, *dish*, *plan*, *pull*, *lunch*, *straw*, and *stripe*. I ask the teachers to determine how many boxes they need to draw. (Figure 2.4 shows how the letters are placed in the boxes for these words.) This provides me with an opportunity to show how to handle the silent *e* at the end of words and to emphasize that these are boxes for the number of sounds, not letters. If only one sound is heard, as in /sh/ or the *ea* in *meat*, then both letters are placed in the single box. However, even though the sounds occur very close together, each sound of a cluster or blend can be heard and felt in the mouth.

I explain that when children have difficulty noticing some of the sounds, such as the /l/ in *play* or the *n* in *find*, it is often helpful to provide a small mirror and direct the child to watch his or her mouth and tongue as he or she pronounces the word. Another technique for drawing children's attention to a sound they are not perceiving, is to touch the child gently on the jaw just as he or she is producing the sound and say, "Right there. That's what I mean. Can you feel it?"

11. Finally, I show a video clip of a child using the boxes as she writes a short message. While I use clips of my own Reading Recovery lessons, a clear illustration can be found at *www.pioneervalleybooks.com/news/maddies-story-writing-lessons*.

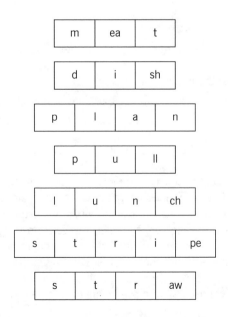

FIGURE 2.4. Elkonin box examples.

Discussion

I have found it important to provide teachers with practice and corrective feedback in determining the number of boxes to draw to represent the phonemes. Some teachers consider consonant blends or clusters to be one sound. Thus, they would draw only three boxes for the word *strap*. To help them understand that each letter within a cluster represents a separate, audible sound, show related words such as *rap*, *trap*, and *strap* or *low* and *slow*. Occasionally, teachers will think that the letters in consonant or vowel digraphs need to be in separate boxes. The other common error we have seen is teachers who try to push into all of the boxes simultaneously, rather than one at a time synchronized to the phoneme they are pronouncing. It is important that the teachers' confusions and misunderstandings are corrected before they introduce the procedure to children.

Reference

Elkonin, D. B. (1973). U.S.S.R. In J. Downing (Ed.), *Comparative reading: Cross-national studies of behavior and processes in reading and writing* (pp. 551–579). New York: Macmillan.

LETTER KNOWLEDGE

What Is It?

Letter knowledge involves recognition of the distinctive shape of each letter of the alphabet in both upper- and lowercase, associating the correct letter name with each shape, and associating the correct speech sound or sounds with each letter.

What Do Teachers Need to Know?

Teachers can expect a wide range in the letter knowledge of incoming kindergartners and first graders. Some kindergarten children recognize no letters at all; others recognize nearly all of them. Children may know the names of letters, but not know the associated sounds. A surprising number of children don't realize that the uppercase letter stands for the same sound as the lowercase letter of the same name. Certain letters are particularly confusing or difficult to learn such as *b/d* and *p/q*. Unlike children's previous experience with objects, the spatial orientation of a letter is key to its identity. For most letters in English, the name of the letter provides a strong clue as to the sound it represents, but when the letter name is not related to its sound some children take a long time remembering the sound it stands for. Fast, automatic recognition of letters that triggers the associated sound is an essential underlying skill that supports fluent reading.

How to Foster Letter Knowledge

Letter learning involves two major tasks—learning to distinguish the shapes associated with each letter, and learning the sound or sounds associated with the shape. Letter sorting helps children learn the distinctive features of each letter. Magnetic letters can be sorted by feature—circles, lines, diagonals, humps, tall, short, descenders, and line first or circle first. Children can also sort letters by case or letter (i.e., put together all forms of *a* or find the *s*'s among a group of letters). Another activity to develop letter recognition is to have children highlight particular letters in discarded newspapers or magazines. Repetition of these activities helps children gain speed in recognizing the distinct forms of each letter. For learning to associate a letter form with a sound, children can match pictures or small objects with letters and work toward speed in the task.

Frequent reading of alphabet books is sometimes all children need to learn the letters. In addition to reading the book through from A to Z, the teacher should open to random pages out of sequence to help children gain automaticity of recognition. An alphabet chart can be read out of sequence—down columns, diagonally, or across rows but skipping every other letter—again to assist in developing automatic recognition.

When introducing letters and their sounds, begin with high-contrast letters with continuant sounds such as *m* and *s*, which can be emphasized without distortion. Teach the name of the letter, how to write it correctly (children can write in the air and trace with their fingers on the floor or table), and the sound that it represents. Letters should not be taught in alphabetical order as this can create a dependency on reciting the entire alphabet to recognize a target letter. Teachers should move quickly through all the letters and review. There is no need to spend a week per letter as is common in many kindergarten programs because what is important is teaching children how to notice the distinguishing features of letters. When children realize what they need to pay attention to, their letter learning accelerates. Finally, assessing students on their alphabet knowledge and teaching letter knowledge in small groups enables teachers to instruct according to need. For those children experiencing the most difficulty in letter learning, a highly effective technique is for the child to read a simple alphabet book (only one illustration per letter) and to trace the letters with the soft pad of their pointer fingers while saying the letter name. The child then points to the picture and says its name: "A, *a*, *apple*" (Richardson, 2009).

CONCEPTS OF PRINT

What Is It?

Concepts of print refer to a set of understandings regarding how print works such as the direction of reading (left to right across words and lines followed by a return sweep to begin the next line at the left); the idea that printed words consist of a group of letters surrounded by white space; and, critically, it is the black marks, not the illustrations, that are what a reader reads. Understanding the use of punctuation marks is also a component of print concepts.

What Do Teachers Need to Know?

The development of a concept of word in print—the understanding of word boundaries—enables an emergent reader to "finger-point read" or match spoken words to written ones, a critical foundational skill for reading. However, children need to understand where the word boundaries are in speech to master finger-point reading, also known as one-to-one matching. Adults often assume children arrive at school knowing where word breaks occur, but many children are not aware of word boundaries in speech prior to school entry. This is entirely understandable because spoken language does not contain pauses between words; in fact, words slur together. Adults experience this same difficulty in recognizing individual words when listening to people speak in an unfamiliar language.

The directional rules for reading print are so ingrained in adults that adults often aren't aware there *are* any rules and take for granted that children implicitly know them. While many children understand the directional rules for reading by the time they enter kindergarten, others do not. In addition, some children move left to right across the *lines* of print, but may not look consistently left to right across every word and letter, leading to confusions between words that share letters such as *was* and *saw* or *form* and *from* or similarly formed letters such as *b/d* and *p/q*. The fact that the order of letters within a word is significant and invariant is another unspoken "rule" controlling print that may need to be brought to a conscious level. Two of us have encountered several children—all readers who struggled—who expressed surprise when told that the sequence of letters matters.

Fostering Understanding of Print Concepts

Children develop initial concepts of print when being read to while simultaneously viewing the print. Children can see print in a lap-reading setting at home or through enlarged print in the classroom. Big Books, paper charts, and digital text projected onto screens or interactive white boards enable children to see print in classroom situations. Teachers foster concepts of word and directionality by crisply pointing to the words they are reading in enlarged print that all the children can see. By consciously using the words *picture, letters,* and *words* in context while pointing teachers help children grasp the distinction between those concepts. In addition, children can be asked to use their fingers to frame specific *letters* or *words,* or to show the *first* letter in a word, or to frame punctuation marks. Counting words in spoken contexts as well as in print helps children develop an understanding of the concept of word.

The instructional technique of *interactive writing,* where the teacher and a group of children co-construct a short piece of writing is another highly effective means of conveying concepts about print (McCarrier, Fountas, & Pinnell, 1999). In this technique, the teacher and children talk together to develop a few sentences to write. Initially, the teacher models by writing aloud. He or she talks through the entire process of writing—where on the page to start, using a capital letter for the first word, leaving a space between words, rereading after he or she has written a few words to remember what to write next, and so forth. But, very quickly the teacher invites children to take over writing individual letters, words, or groups of words, while prompting for spaces, punctuation, and capital letters as needed.

Assessment of Print Concepts

Teachers can assess children's understanding of print concepts through observation of their reading and writing. Teachers can learn about directionality and reverse sweep when children are still in the pretend writing stage. The original Clay Concepts About Print assessment (Clay, 2006) or one of the many commercial or open-source variants can also be used.

WORD RECOGNITION AND PRODUCTION

What Is It?

Word recognition is simply the recognition of the print version of words. Similarly, word production is simply the writing or spelling of a word, producing a written version of a word.

What Do Teachers Need to Know?

Words Are Identified Multiple Ways

Fluent reading depends on fast, accurate word recognition, a skill that develops over time. Words can be identified in multiple ways. Readers may (1) make a guess based on the context, perhaps guided by illustrations; (2) use partial letter information (often the initial letter) and context; (3) assemble the word sound by sound using individual letters (sounding out); (4) assemble the word using groups of letters (syllables or other larger units within the word); (5) analogize the new word to a familiar word (knowing *night* enables the reader to figure out *bright*); or (6) recognize the entire word automatically known as sight-word identification (Ehri, 1997). Beginners may use any of these approaches. Proficient readers recognize nearly all words by sight, though they will occasionally need to assemble parts of a long, unfamiliar word such as a foreign name.

Many of the most frequently occurring words in English are *irregular* or *exception* words, that is, their pronunciations do not conform to expectations based on the most typical sound–letter associations. For example, in most one-syllable words containing a single vowel surrounded by consonants, the vowel represents the "short" sound as in *sit* or *stuck*, but in the word *was*, the *a* does not match the "short" sound of *a* in *apple*. Therefore, beginners cannot be expected to figure out these words using decoding techniques. They must be told what these irregular words are, and then they need to learn to recognize them automatically. Four techniques used in rapid succession are very effective: (1) "mix and fix" (scrambling and assembling the word with magnetic letters), (2) "What's missing?" (asking students to identify the missing letter in the word formed with magnetic letters), (3) "table writing" (writing the word with the fleshy part of the dominant finger), and (4) writing the word on a whiteboard (Richardson, 2009). A video demonstrating these techniques in a guided reading session can be found in the clip titled "New Sight Word—4 Steps" at *www.janrichardsonguidedreading.com/video-clips*.

Teaching children how to create a letter-by-letter mental image of a word is another powerful technique, and one often needed by children performing significantly below age or grade expectations in reading or spelling.

When selecting words to teach directly, make sure the words meet these three criteria: (1) the child does not already know the word, (2) the word will be encountered often (high-frequency words), and (3) the word is in a text the child is going to be reading immediately so that it can be practiced in context.

Word recognition can be roughly assessed by asking a child to read a list of words. Lists of high-frequency words and grade-level word lists can be easily found on the Internet and in informal reading inventories. Grade-level word lists enable a teacher to determine if a student recognizes a sample of words that are typically found in texts at that grade level. Word lists require children to read words in isolation, without the support of surrounding context. Children must either recognize the words automatically or be able to decode them phonetically. The ability to read a grade-level word list does not guarantee that students can comprehend text at that grade level. Some children who are not able to recognize words in isolation can identify them within the context of connected text.

Phonics and Decoding

Decoding is simply the term used for determining what word a string of letters represents when the word is not automatically recognized as a whole. Phonics refers to the decoding procedure of applying the sound value of individual letters or groups of letters to figure out a word.

There are several important aspects to decoding. First, blending—putting back together the smaller parts of an unfamiliar word—is an important skill for independent reading. There are two methods of letter-by-letter blending—isolated blending and cumulative or "blend-as-you-go" blending. Today's commercial phonics programs typically use the isolated approach. The reader pronounces the sound of each letter in the word—/f/-/a/-/s/-/t/—and then tries to blend the sounds together. An alternative method is for the reader to accumulate the sounds as he or she works through the word—/f/-/fa/-/fas/-/fast/. Isolated blending often so distorts the target word (What is /fuh/-/a/-/suh/-/tuh/?) that the reader cannot determine the target word. Readers can also use the meaning of the text to help decode a word, as long as that word is in their speaking vocabulary.

A second important aspect of decoding is the understanding that multisyllable words are composed of smaller, regular words or word parts. Once a reader knows the most common prefixes and suffixes, longer words can be figured out by peeling off the prefixes and suffixes and then working out the rest of the word in parts. If taught to look for "parts that they know," children are able to break longer words into "chunks" and then blend these larger chunks together: *ad-ven-ture, im-poss-ible, pre-his-tor-ic.* (Gunning, 2013, p. 258, calls this the "pronounceable word part strategy.")

When they need to work out an unfamiliar word, proficient readers use the largest units available to them, that is, they analogize to a familiar spelling pattern or use a part-by-part approach. Rarely do proficient readers use a letter-by-letter approach. For this reason, and because letter-by-letter blending is slow and often unsuccessful, students should be taught to decode using larger units as soon as possible. In fact, current research demonstrates that instruction in morphology—knowledge of word roots, prefixes, suffixes, and how they work together—contributes to gains in spelling, word recognition, vocabulary development, and reading comprehension (Carlisle, 2011).

Role of Oral Vocabulary

When a reader encounters an unfamiliar word that is not in his or her oral vocabulary, the reader will have no way of knowing if an attempt is correct. Even if pronounced correctly, the reader will not know what the word means. Strong decoders with low receptive vocabularies, including English language learners, sometimes deceive teachers into thinking they understand a text better than they actually do with accurate pronunciations of words whose meanings they do not know.

Cross-Checking and Multiple Information Systems

Because of the complexities of English orthography, an initial attempt to determine an unfamiliar word often produces only an approximation of the actual word. The reader needs to check the "word" produced with what fits with the syntax of the sentence and the meaning of the text to confirm the actual word.

Meaning, structure or syntax, and graphophonic or visual (the letters) comprise the three major information systems readers rely on to determine unfamiliar words. Some authorities believe the information systems are equal in importance; others argue that the graphophonic system—the letters and sounds—is preeminent. It is our view that readers in different stages of development rely differentially on each information system. For example, an emergent reader may use only the initial letter in combination with the pictures and sentence structure to predict an unfamiliar word and then check his or her prediction by looking at the rest of the letters in the word. A more advanced reader may blend an unfamiliar word letter by letter and then check the result against what makes sense and sounds right in the sentence.

Fostering Cross-Checking

At the beginning stages of reading, many children over-rely on one system. Some beginners are so focused on analyzing the letters to figure out unfamiliar words that they pay no notice to their nonsensical miscues. Others, relying on illustrations and their expectations for what the text will say, ignore letters and produce readings that make sense but are inaccurate. Such children need teacher guidance to learn to coordinate all the information systems. Teachers foster this coordination when listening to beginners read by allowing children time to notice their own errors before intervening, and by using prompts that foster this coordination such as "Did that look right and make sense?" or "That made sense, but did it look right?"

Assessment of Decoding and Cross-Checking

Children's skill in decoding as they read continuous (connected) text can be assessed informally through running records (records of oral reading) and miscue analysis (analysis of reading errors). Teachers analyze the errors to see what letter–sound information children are using and what they are ignoring. A common misunderstanding is that when a child fails to pronounce final letters he or she does not know his or her ending *sounds*. Since the letters represent the same sound no matter their position within a word, the more likely explanation is a failure to *look* all the way to the end of the word. Children who speak strong varieties of African American Vernacular English (AAVE) may drop final sounds because they are matching the recognized word to their own speech pattern. In the latter case, the miscue should be interpreted as an alternate pronunciation and as evidence of comprehension. Cross-checking can also be assessed by using running records and miscue analysis. These assessments help teachers use students' errors and self-corrections as windows into the strategies that they are using to recognize unknown words.

Numerous commercial and open-source assessments of decoding in isolation are also available. Pseudowords or nonwords are often used to assess decoding because accuracy can't be confounded by use of words known by sight. Children who read for meaning are confused by pseudowords and may try to turn nonwords into real ones, thus nonwords may underestimate their true proficiency in decoding. The use of pseudowords results in confusion on the part of children around the idea that reading should make sense. An additional disadvantage to the use of pseudoword assessments is the use of instructional time for practicing the reading of nonsense words. There is no evidence that such practice improves the ability to apply decoding strategies when reading continuous text, which is what is important for reading development.

For assessing skill in handling multisyllabic words, teachers can use readily available lists of multisyllabic words that contain high-frequency word parts within them such as the Names Test (Cunningham, 1990; Duffelmeyer, Kruse, Merkley, & Fyfe, 1994) and the Nifty-Fifty-Thrifty (Cunningham, 2013).

ACTIVITY 2.3
What to Say When Coaching Beginning Readers: Guiding Teachers to Prompt for Self-Regulation
DEBORAH G. LITT

Activity Type: In-class activity.

Materials:
- Move–effect thinking guide.
- Key to what to say when.
- Optional: Copies of the text of a little book and an altered version of that text if the activity is preceded by a simulation of a beginning reader and teacher interaction.

Duration: 30–45 minutes

Standards Links

IRA Professional Standards:
2.2 Select and implement instructional approaches based on evidence-based rationales, student needs, and purposes for instruction.
Implement and evaluate instruction in each of the following areas: concepts of print, phonemic awareness, phonics, vocabulary, comprehension, fluency, critical thinking, motivation, and writing.

Professional Learning Focus:
- Purpose of prompting for self-regulation and independence.
- Recognition of the effective and ineffective teacher actions for promoting self-regulation and independence.

K–8 Student Learning Focus: Self-regulation for comprehension and accuracy in reading.

Common Core State Standards:
Reading Standards: Foundational Skills

1. Demonstrate understanding of the organization and basic features of print.

3. Know and apply grade-level phonics and word analysis skills in decoding words.

4. Read with sufficient accuracy and fluency to support comprehension.

Rationale

I have observed that most adults have only two responses to children's oral reading miscues and hesitations. They either correct the miscue immediately, or say, "Sound it out." Another common adult behavior is to provide confirmatory responses or praise after each correctly read sentence and after a beginner has correctly worked out an unfamiliar word. I view the development of self-regulation (an internal reading conscience) on the part of the developing reader to be the critical component for becoming an independent reader. Overcorrection and monitoring *for* the child on the part of a teacher can undermine a child's developing self-regulation system. Correcting miscues before readers have a chance to read on and notice that what they're reading no longer makes sense, interferes with learning to detect and correct their own errors. Providing verbal and nonverbal confirmatory responses as the child is reading also interferes with the development of internal monitoring on the part of the child. In addition, because of the limitations of working memory, *any* talk directed at the beginning reader has the potential to interfere with the student's reading and thinking. For all of these reasons, I try to convey to the teachers and prospective teachers I work with the value of teaching for self-regulation rather than just helping a child get through a text, and I teach them other ways of responding. This activity is designed to challenge and change the manner in which most adults "assist" beginning readers.

Description

Coaching Simulation

Before discussing the "move–effect" questions, I usually have the teachers simulate coaching a beginner. In groups of three, one teacher takes the role of the child, one the role of the teacher, and one observes taking notes on the "teacher's" moves (e.g., prompts, praises, nonword vocalizations). I provide the "child" with an altered version of the text that includes errors and stage directions regarding when to appeal for help. The "teacher" listens and responds the way he or she would typically respond when working with a beginner. After each group finishes the simulation and the observer reports to the small group the prompts and other moves observed, the groups share out loud the teacher moves observed and I compile a list of all reported prompts and moves. I add any additional commonly heard phrases or common teacher actions if they aren't observed in any of the simulations.

Establish the Goal of Independence and Self-Regulation

I set the stage by explaining that the true, long-term goal of any teacher should be to foster self-regulation and independence in his or her students. I use the phrase I first heard from Shelley Harwayne in class: "The real job of a parent (or teacher) is to put yourself out of a job." While that may sound obvious, teachers and even experienced teachers are often more focused on being helpful and needed in the short term; they do not always think through whether the short-term assistance they are providing is fostering independence in the long term. Alternatively, they may assume that assisting a child in producing an accurate reading is sufficient to develop long-term independence. Analogies to how parents and teachers approach self-care tasks such as dressing and brushing their teeth can be useful in establishing the importance of thinking long term.

Guided Thinking and Discussion

I give teachers 10–20 minutes to work with a partner or a small group to consider whether each described teacher action or words on the thinking guide (see Figure 2.5) actually promotes self-regulation or independence. Typically, during the small-group discussions, teachers come to the realization that many of the most common moves (frequent confirmatory noises or immediate correction) do not foster self-regulation. To ensure that everyone in the group understands which moves truly promote self-regulation and which ones are likely to foster continued dependency, after most of the groups have finished I lead a discussion with the entire group.

I explain how some of the moves they might think are helpful are not, and challenge the common belief that abundant praise is helpful. I help them to see that whereas some moves are never helpful—correcting a beginner immediately after the error and before the child has had a chance to read further to notice the other—other moves are helpful in some circumstances but not in others. If a child has no way of figuring out a word on his or her own, it *is* appropriate to tell him or her the word, but not when the child could do it him- or herself. An important principle is that adults should use prompts that children will be able to use for

Type of Action	Language Heard	Does This Action Promote Self-Regulation and Independence?*
Global praise	Good. Great. Good job. Super.	
Correction	[Teacher corrects a miscue immediately after student makes it.]	
Check-in move	Um-hmm. Yes, yes, good. [Providing frequent approving feedback.]	
Hint	[Example:] It's what birds do [the word was *fly*].	
Prompt (a call to action)	Sound it out.	
	What's that word?	
	What letter is that?	
	What sound does that letter make?	
	Does that make sense?	
	Were you right?	
	Read that again.	
	Check the picture.	
	Did it match?	
	Get your mouth ready and think about the story.	
	What can you do to help yourself?	
	Does that sound right?	
	Does that look right?	
	Do you see a part that you know?	

*Will being on the receiving end of this action enable the student to do it for him- or herself the next time?

FIGURE 2.5. Reading with beginners: Move–effect thinking guide.

themselves when the adult is not there. A child can always ask him- or herself, "Did that make sense?" or "Is there a part in that word I know?" but cannot provide him- or herself a hint that depends on already having read the word!

When the discussion is over, I provide a "key" to the prompts—a chart that indicates what prompts and actions to use, what circumstances are appropriate for particular prompts, and what prompts and actions they should avoid. This becomes the teacher's guide for his or her tutoring project. (The chart "Key for What to Say When" is provided in Figure 2.6.) Lists of prompts that encourage student self-regulation can be found in many textbooks, as well as in Fountas and Pinnell (1996) and Richardson (2009).

Extension

Teachers can assess their own progress in fostering self-regulation and cross-checking by recording and transcribing samples of their interactions when listening to children read aloud. They compare what they said and did with the prompting key I have provided. In their tutoring project, a major assignment for my reading course, teachers transcribe and analyze their interactions five times over the course of a semester.

Discussion

Most individuals who choose teaching as a profession do so because they want to be helpful. Teachers are often quite surprised to discover that their instinctive responses, particularly their praising and cheerleading, might not be helpful. I often take great pains to acknowledge their good intentions, but then go on to explain how they will be helping in a deeper and longer-lasting way if they maintain a more neutral pose and learn to turn responsibility for monitoring back to the reader. This guided thinking activity successfully draws teachers' attention to some of their unexamined assumptions and ways of acting; it has long-term effects on their responses to beginning readers.

References

Fountas, I. C., & Pinnell, G. S. (1996). *Guided reading: Good first teaching for all children.* Portsmouth, NH: Heinemann.

Richardson, J. (2009). *The next step in guided reading: Focused assessments and targeted lessons for helping every student become a better reader.* New York: Scholastic.

What You Might Do or Say	When to Use	How Often to Use
Good job. Great. Good for you. [Etc.]	Do not use. Avoid these "check-in" moves that are monitoring *for* the reader.	Almost never. If you feel the need for positive reinforcement, ask "Were you right?" when a child is correct. When a child answers "Yes," say, "Yes, you were right. It made sense, looked right, and sounded right. That's how you know you were right."
Good.	Do not use. Avoid these "check-in" moves that are monitoring *for* the reader.	Almost never.
Mm-mm; unh-hunh.	Do not use. Avoid these "check-in" moves that are monitoring *for* the reader.	Avoid.
I liked the way you . . . [specific action praised].	When the child does something new that you want repeated.	Every opportunity, *but* don't interrupt reading often. Wait for a natural pause or sneak it in quickly during a page turn.
What letter is that?	Only when a child uses an incorrect letter sound, and it is an appropriate opportunity to work on more careful visual analysis.	Rarely, but if at all, *after* a child has finished the section of text. *Never* immediately after the error.
What word is that?	When going back into the text *after* the first reading. *Never* immediately after the error.	Rarely.
Sound it out.	Avoid if possible. What this *should* signal is "Figure it out," but it can signal an inefficient means of getting to an unfamiliar word.	Avoid if possible. Other options: "Get your mouth ready." "What can you do to help yourself?" "Do you see any parts you know?" "Get your mouth ready and think about the story."

(continued)

Note. Children should always be given the chance to notice their own errors to enable them to self-correct. Wait for a child to finish a page, sentence, or an entire (little) book before intervening.

FIGURE 2.6. Key for what to say when: Teacher coaching moves and prompts for beginning readers.

From *Literacy Teacher Education: Principles and Effective Practices* by Deborah G. Litt, Susan D. Martin, and Nancy A. Place. Copyright 2015 by The Guilford Press. Permission to photocopy this figure is granted to purchasers of this book for personal use only (see copyright page for details). Purchasers can download and print a larger version of this figure from *www.guilford.com/litt-forms*.

What You Might Do or Say	When to Use	How Often to Use
[Tell or correct a word without an appeal immediately following a miscue.]	*Never.*	*Never.*
[Ask a question or give a hint to help a child come up with the word.]	*Never, never, never.*	*Never.*
Check the picture.	When the picture could help a child figure out a word.	Early levels until a child learns to do this for him- or herself.
What sound does that letter make?	When a child uses an incorrect letter sound, and it is an appropriate opportunity to work on more careful visual analysis, or when a child needs help getting started using a visual-to-sound analysis.	Not often. *After* a child has finished the section of text, although sometimes this will help a child get going with solving a word.
[Repeat the word for the child.]	When a child seems tentative; provide support and affirmation.	Not often; try to get beyond that.
Did it match? Did you have enough/ too many words?	Early levels when a child's words don't match the number of words in the text.	When you see a child off (i.e., when the number of the child's spoken words do not match the number of words on the page) and he or she didn't notice; *often*. Get one-to-one matching under control as quickly as possible.
Did/does that make sense?	Whenever a child says something that doesn't make sense.	*Often.*
Did/does that look right?	When the word said by the child does not correspond to the sounds represented by the letters on the page. For example, the child says "fish," but the word is actually "tadpole." The printed word "fish" doesn't look like the printed word "tadpole."	*Often.*
Did/does that sound right? Can we talk like that?	When the miscue is obviously grammatically wrong—for example, "I *lucky* ice cream" (for *like*). Do *not* use just because there is a miscue.	When a child is reading and does not notice such an error. *Note* that when a child reproduces his or her own speech pattern—for example, "He *fixeded*"—this prompt will not help.

(continued)

FIGURE 2.6. *(continued)*

What You Might Do or Say	When to Use	How Often to Use
Are/were you right?	*Often; both when right and wrong.*	*As often as possible.*
Get your mouth ready.	When a child comes to an unknown word and pauses, knows how to do this, and hasn't tried this. When getting started with the word will likely lead a child to figuring out the word.	Often at the early stages when a child is just learning to use letter–sound information and doesn't automatically make the initial sound. It is important to balance "Get your mouth ready" with other prompts.
Do you see a part in that word that you know?	When a child pauses or exhibits difficulty with a word and there is a "chunk" that he or she recognizes.	Often when this technique will help a child figure out the word.
What can you do to help yourself?	When a child has paused and doesn't seem to be doing anything, but already knows ways of solving words.	*Often* once a child knows multiple problem-solving techniques.
Go back and read it again.	After a child has had to do a lot of work and may have lost the thread of the story. When you feel a child will benefit from putting the sentence(s) together before going on. *Not* to be used just because a child made an error.	Not too often. If needed often, then the texts may be too difficult. More likely to be needed at Levels A–E.
[Tell a word after an appeal.]	When a child is truly stuck. After three attempts.	Occasionally. Telling a word may be the only move available in the earliest stages because the child does not have the tools to figure the words out independently. However, if more than three are required in a book with 75 words or less, either the book was too hard or the book introduction failed to provide sufficient support.
[Make a comment about the text.]	At natural pauses and placed within a story. After reading.	*Always* comment about the text in a natural fashion when a child has completed the text. Intersperse brief remarks sparingly during the reading, perhaps during a page turn. These comments focus on the meaning and serve to build comprehension, motivation, and engagement.

FIGURE 2.6. *(continued)*

CHAPTER 3

Text-Level Processes

In this chapter we explore a variety of instructional techniques for teaching novice teachers to help young readers comprehend *connected* text. The strategies and abilities highlighted in this chapter focus on the foundational skills of fluency and vocabulary knowledge, as well as those specific to meaning making: comprehension strategies, content reading strategies, discussion, and critical literacy.

To a proficient adult reader reading a comfortable text—perhaps the daily newspaper with breakfast or a novel at bedtime—comprehension feels effortless. But when readers are challenged with texts outside their comfort zones, such as legal contracts or recent research in particle physics, in which both the concepts and the vocabulary are unfamiliar, it becomes becomes painfully obvious that full comprehension does not automatically accompany the ability to pronounce the words on the page. One of the truly great contributions of cognitive and education research of the last 30 years is that strong comprehenders apply strategies to understand text (August, Flavell, & Clift, 1984; Garner & Krauss, 1981; Paris & Myers, 1981) and that weak comprehenders can be taught to use the same techniques to improve their comprehension (Almasi, Palmer, Madden, & Hart, 2011; Dewitz, Carr, & Patberg, 1987; National Reading Panel, 2000; Palincsar & Brown, 1984; Pearson & Dole, 1987; Pressley, 2000).

As classroom teachers, each of us has worked with children who could pronounce words, but who didn't understand what they were reading. We have also met many students who could comprehend at the literal or surface level, but could not comprehend at a deep or critical level. Furthermore, some students understand narrative, but experience great difficulty understanding or learning from expository text. Many people come to teaching, however, with an implicit belief that comprehension follows automatically from word recognition. This naïve belief often leads to instruction with a heavy emphasis on word recognition, and insufficient attention to comprehension. We feel strongly that this unconscious belief must be disrupted, and that teachers must embrace the research on comprehension development and develop the skills that foster—not just assess—comprehension.

READING FLUENCY

What Is It?

Reading fluency refers to the rate, accuracy, and prosody of reading (Kuhn, Schwanenflugel, & Meisinger, 2010; Wolf & Katzir-Cohen, 2001). In fluent oral reading, the skilled reader conveys the author's meaning through the rise and fall of his or her voice, and through pauses in appropriate locations. The reading is smooth, without hesitations or pauses in inappropriate locations. In silent reading, the reader groups words in appropriate phrases internally.

What Do Teachers Need to Know?

Fluent reading facilitates or enables comprehension. When reading is slow and labored, attention and limited working memory capacity are devoted to figuring out individual words, limiting the reader's ability to construct meaning. However, we have seen slow readers who comprehend well, and readers who sound fluent, but don't comprehend. Fluency does not always accurately predict comprehension. Students often equate fast reading with good reading; such students may believe fast word recognition is the goal of reading and may not attempt to understand what they are reading. Teachers, too, can be misled into thinking that fluent reading is merely fast reading because so many of the commonly used measures of fluency consider rate and accuracy, but exclude phrasing and prosody.

To read fluently, readers must have a large number of words they can recognize automatically, that is, by sight. A reader can be fluent when reading one text and halting when reading another depending upon the percentage of unfamiliar words, the reader's familiarity with the subject matter, and the complexity of syntax. It is important that readers understand that they should vary their rate to match the difficulty of the text— fast reading is not always beneficial to meaning making.

Teachers can foster fluency development in many ways. Two critically important practices to support fluency development are (1) providing ample time for children to read meaningful text at an appropriate level of complexity and (2) modeling fluent reading through engaging read-alouds. Students who do not phrase appropriately or ignore punctuation need direct instruction and supported practice.

ACTIVITY 3.1
Self-Adjusting Fluency Rates for Meaning Making
SUSAN D. MARTIN

Activity Type: In-class activity.

Materials: Stopwatch; two sets of reading materials—one text that is easy for teachers to read and one text that is difficult.

Duration: 30 minutes.

Professional Learning Focus:
- Adjusting reading rate for meaning making.
- Awareness of differences in oral and silent reading rates.

K–8 Student Learning Focus:
- Reading fluency.
- Adjusting reading rate for meaning making.

Standards Links

IRA Professional Standards: Curriculum and Instruction
2.2 Candidates use appropriate and varied instructional approaches including those that develop word recognition, language comprehension, strategic knowledge, and reading–writing connections.

Common Core State Standards: Reading Standards: Foundational Skills
4. Read with sufficient accuracy and fluency to support comprehension.

Rationale

When I first started reading journal articles in my doctoral program, I remarked to one professor that it had taken me 2 hours to read one article. He replied that it took him that long to read some articles as well. Most likely, neither of us would pass any fluency assessments at these rates, even at the first-grade level! My focus was not on how fluently I could read. Instead, I had a vested interest in making sense of dense content and connecting to prior understandings of the topic. However, I can speed through many novels without sacrificing comprehension or my ability to think about ideas encountered in the novel while reading it. Like all proficient readers, I automatically alter my reading rate to adjust for meaning making.

I believe that the current emphasis on rate in oral reading fluency has promoted both teacher and student misconceptions of fluency. Some of my students, especially preservice teachers, equate fluent oral reading with comprehension ability. They also fail to realize that production of oral text is not necessarily a reflection of how we "read" in our minds.

For some teachers and students, oral reading fluency has become an end in itself, rather than a foundational skill for proficient meaning making across a range of written genres. This is a recommendation from the CCSS. I worry that we have K–8 students who believe that good "reading" is reading quickly. One teacher described how her students take a deep breath and then "read, read, read, read, read," as fast as they can. With this activity, I want to disrupt misconceptions and deepen teachers' understandings of the complexities of fluency and its contributions to meaning making.

Description

1. I come to class with a stopwatch and two sets of reading materials for the class. From our departmental book/materials closet I gather narratives written at a third- to fifth-grade level. Additionally, I find a written passage in another content area, such as physics, that is conceptually dense and contains unfamiliar vocabulary. I copy one page of text for each teacher.

2. In class, teachers are asked to read to gain meaning from the text. Then I give two 1-minute timings of the easy text. I have teachers first read a passage silently and then another orally—quietly to themselves. Teachers count and record how many words they read in each passage. I ask for data that lets us get at some issues. For example, how many people read more quickly in the silent mode? Oral mode? What was the range of difference between your scores? I record this data on the board, as trends across individuals are important to note.

3. We then engage in a conversation in which we discuss the differences in their rates and any other issue that teachers wish to raise. Very few teachers read faster orally. This is a point to have teachers delve into, and have individuals describe why they read faster orally.

4. Then we do the same processes with the difficult text.

5. At this point, there are typically some lightbulbs going on, so that teachers lead the discussion. But some prompting questions that might be helpful include "So what do you think is going on when everyone's rate is so much lower in the difficult text?" "What does this mean for your students?" and "How would these timings have been different, if I had not prompted you to read for meaning?"

6. I bring closure to this activity by linking it directly back to practice. Teachers discuss what their students need to know and be able to do in the area of fluency, and what they need to do instructionally to make this so.

Discussion

No matter which course, I can predict that lessons on fluency will engender a great deal of conversation—more so than other topics. I sometimes suspect it's because the current emphasis on rate goes against what teachers intuitively know about reading. Experiential activities such as this one, that engage teachers with their own reading, can bring to the forefront greater understandings of fluency processes. I certainly notice the ahas! being expressed during class debriefings of the activity.

Unfortunately, teachers will continue to be constrained by policies that focus on one-size-fits-all notions of fluency rates. However, I believe that activities such as this will help teachers understand that elementary fluency instruction needs to include development of awareness that proficient reading is not about rate, but about adjusting rates while making sense of text.

VOCABULARY KNOWLEDGE

What Is It?

Vocabulary refers to those words an individual understands while listening or reading—receptive vocabulary—and those words an individual uses either in speech or writing—expressive vocabulary. Vocabulary knowledge, understanding what words mean is a crucial factor in reading comprehension. If a reader does not understand a sufficient number of words in a text, he or she will not comprehend the text.

What Do Teachers Need to Know?

Most word learning occurs incidentally through exposure to oral and written language. Due to differences in family communication patterns, children arrive at school with vocabularies of vastly different sizes

(Biemiller & Slonim, 2001; Hart & Risley, 1995). Attention to vocabulary development in school can help children accelerate their vocabulary growth—many studies show growth in vocabulary and comprehension when effective practices are used in the classroom (Boulware-Gooden, Carreker, Thornhill, & Joshi, 2007). Unfortunately, the most familiar vocabulary practice—looking up words in a dictionary, copying the definition, and writing a sentence using the word—is *not* an effective approach (Boulware-Gooden et al., 2007).

Extensive reading is one means of expanding vocabulary; the amount of time that students spend reading books is among the best predictors of vocabulary size (Nagy, Anderson, & Herman, 1987), and some researchers (Anderson & Nagy, 1992) believe reading to be the *most* important contributor to vocabulary growth. However, explicit instruction in how to extract meaning from context can increase the power of reading (and listening); teachers need to learn how to do this.

Word learning tasks differ. Learning a new word for an existing concept, for example, *scarlet* for *red* is easier than learning a new concept along with its label, as in *metamorphosis* or *habitat*. Learning concrete words—words that can be illustrated, for example, *curlicue*—is easier than understanding words for abstract ideas, for example, *democracy*. Other word learning tasks include learning a new meaning for a known word (a *hole* in an argument or *hand* as a unit of measurement), learning more specific words that expand and refine meanings of known words (e.g., *damp, soggy, clammy*), and learning to recognize the printed version of a word in the reader's receptive vocabulary.

Vocabulary instruction needs to encompass (1) direct instruction on the meanings of selected words, (2) instruction that fosters student independence in learning words, and (3) activities and routines that generate a desire and interest in learning new words—what Graves and Watts-Taffe (2008) call *word consciousness*. Since it is not possible to directly teach all the words students will need to understand, it is important for teachers to think about which words to select for vocabulary study. A new interest in teaching *morphology*—the study of word roots and the network of derived words using that root—is a promising approach that combines independence in learning the meaning of words with direct instruction in selected word meanings (Bowers, 2010; Carlisle, 2011).

ACTIVITY 3.2
Choosing "Tier Two" Words
NANCY A. PLACE

Activity Type: In-class and homework.

Materials: "Filling Station," a poem by Elizabeth Bishop (available on the Internet in many locations, including *www.poemhunter.com/poem/filling-station*), or another poem of your choosing; teachers bring a text that they will be using with their students.

Duration: 1 hour.

Professional Learning Focus: Selection and teaching of appropriate vocabulary words.

K–8 Student Learning Focus: Vocabulary development.

Standards Links

IRA Professional Standards: Curriculum and Instruction
2.2 Candidates use appropriate and varied instructional approaches including those that develop word recognition, language comprehension, strategic knowledge, and reading–writing connections.

Common Core State Standards: Reading Anchor Standards (Vocabulary Acquisition and Use)
5. Demonstrate understandings of word relationships and nuances in word meanings.

Rationale

Vocabulary knowledge is an important predictor of reading comprehension (Anderson & Freebody, 1983). With the great variation in the amount of vocabulary knowledge that students bring to school, it is crucial that teachers pay attention to the vocabulary development of their students. Wide reading and learning how to learn words in context are key to vocabulary development, but it is also important for teachers to specifically instruct children in words that will help them understand a specific text or become more proficient writers. This kind of instruction is particularly significant for those students who are disaffected or struggling readers, those who may not be reading text in much quantity or with much complexity. However, teachers cannot teach all the words that students need to learn. It's important for teachers to thoughtfully select the vocabulary words that they want children to know.

In *Bringing Words to Life: Robust Vocabulary Instruction* (2002), Isabel Beck, Margaret McKeown, and Linda Kucan shine a light on the kinds of decisions that teachers might make when they choose words for instruction. One of their most important ideas is the description of a three-tier system for approaching vocabulary instruction. This organizational system helps teachers determine which words might be most valuable to teach in a given situation. Tier One consists of basic and familiar words, such as *house, happy*, and *yes*, with which most native English speakers and conversational-level English language learners are familiar. Tier Two words include words more commonly used, such as *skittered, slouched*, and *reputation*. These words are useful for crafting and understanding precise language in a variety of domains. Tier Three words are those that are limited to specific disciplines (academic language) and not in frequent general use, such as *photosynthesis* and *plate tectonics*. Aside from teaching the academic language required for participation in an academic discipline, Tier Two words are the most useful words for instruction because they may be unknown or only partially known to most students, they help students to more clearly understand a piece of text and to develop precision in writing and speaking, and they have the most opportunity for use.

Description

Before class the teachers are asked to bring a text that they will be using with their students.

1. I give a general introduction to vocabulary development and instruction followed by an overview of the three tiers of vocabulary words based on the work of Beck and her colleagues (2002).

2. I do a shared reading of the poem "Filling Station' by Elizabeth Bishop. I picked this poem because I love it and because it offers good possibilities for talking about words on a variety of levels with adults. Before reading the poem I ask the teachers to think about what the poem might be about, and following the reading we discuss this. I read the poem a second time and this time I ask them to pay attention to the language. After the second reading students identify any words that are unfamiliar.

3. I model a selection of Tier Two words from the poem. I share the criteria developed by Beck et al. (2002) for the selection of these words: importance and utility, instructional potential, and conceptual understanding. I ask the students to consider the following questions:

- How useful is the word? Will it help students describe their own experiences with more precision?
- How does it relate to other words or ideas the students have been learning?
- What does the word bring to the text or the learning situation? (Beck et al., 2002, p. 29)

In the case of this poem, I selected the words *translucent, extraneous*, and *hirsute*. The teachers are often surprised by my selection of *hirsute* and this gives me an opportunity to show that a teacher might want to pick a word that is not necessarily Tier Two but is chosen because of its importance to the text, in this case, to the meaning and structure of the poem. After I model my selection of words with rationale, I ask the teachers to each pick two additional words that they might teach as Tier Two words. We discuss these words as well as those words we consider Tier Three.

4. I model how I might teach the three words I have chosen using strategies from *Bringing Words to Life*. I begin with "student-friendly explanations" (Beck et al., 2002, p. 35) by explaining the meaning in "child" language and giving examples of how it is commonly used. This is more difficult than it sounds! For example, with the word *translucency* I say, "In the poem we read about a 'black translucency.' *Translucency* means that light can pass through something. You can see that there is light on the other side, but you can't clearly see through to the other side. Say the word with me: *translucency*."

I continue by adding common examples: "I have a shell from the Philippines that has a white translucency. We had baked chicken last night with a jell that had a brown translucency. What do you know that has translucency?"

Teachers then follow the same procedure with one or two Tier Two words that they have selected in the poem and share out loud.

5. Finally we discuss how to further instruct toward developing a deeper understanding of these words and the importance of understanding words in relationship to one another. I model some vocabulary instruction activities that relate words to one another, such as linear arrays, semantic mapping, semantic feature analysis grid, and Venn diagrams (Nagy, 1988). Teachers also share the ways that vocabulary is taught in their classrooms. Finally, teachers then begin to choose Tier Two words in the texts they have brought to class, developing student-friendly explanations and vocabulary activities. This activity is completed as homework.

Discussion

This activity provides an opportunity for teachers to consider the importance of word learning and their role in promoting it. For some young teachers the word *filling station* is unfamiliar, as is the setting of the poem and some of the vocabulary words (*taboret, marguerite, daisy stitch, monkey suit*). This allows us to discuss which words teachers might explain quickly "on the fly," to talk about why the poet made certain word choices (*taboret*), and how teachers might link an unfamiliar setting to children's lives. Many of the teachers use materials in their own classrooms that include recommended vocabulary words so they have not previously had to consider the utility of the words they are teaching. An understanding of Tier Three words has generally caused teachers to develop their own "word consciousness" (Graves & Watts-Taffe, 2008) about the ways that their students use language, become more intentional in their instruction, and more selective about the ways that they utilize suggested vocabulary lists.

References

Anderson, R. C., & Freebody, P. (1983). Effects on text comprehension of differing pro-
portions and locations of difficult vocabulary. *Journal of Literacy Research, 15*(3),
19–39.

Beck, I., McKeown, M., & Kucan, L (2002). *Bringing words to life: Robust vocabulary
instruction.* New York: Guilford Press.

Graves, M. F., & Watts-Taffe, S. (2008). For the love of words: Fostering word consciousness in young readers. *The Reading Teacher, 62*(3), 185–193.

Nagy, W. E. (1988). *Teaching vocabulary to improve reading comprehension.* Newark, DE:
International Reading Association/ National Council of Teachers of English.

ACTIVITY 3.3
Online Dictionary Scavenger Hunt
LEE ANN TYSSELING

Activity Type: In-class, homework, or online course activity.

Materials: Teachers bring a short story or other type of reading material appropriate for students in third through eighth grade.

Duration: 30–60 minutes.

Professional Learning Focus:
- Exploration of available online dictionary/references.
- Critical analysis of strengths/ weaknesses of various online reference resources for word study.
- Increased comfort with using digital resources in the K–8 classroom.

K–8 Student Learning Focus:
- Dictionary and reference resources.
- Vocabulary development.

Standards Links

IRA Professional Standards: Curriculum and Instruction
2.2 Candidates use appropriate and varied instructional approaches including those that develop word recognition, language comprehension, strategic knowledge, and reading–writing connections.

Common Core State Standards: Reading Anchor Standards
4. Interpret words and phrases as they are used in a text, including determining technical, connotative, and figurative meanings, and analyze how specific word choices shape meaning or tone.

Rationale

This activity is designed to expose teachers to a few of the online dictionaries available and encourage them to consider their individual strengths and weaknesses.

Learning to use dictionaries and other reference resources is an essential literacy skill, yet often given perfunctory attention in the classroom. Some core reading series include an activity or two about using guide words in paper dictionaries, using diacritical markings to pronounce words, or reading dictionary definitions, but these are infrequent and do not transfer well to actual use. Even in the most recent versions of popular spelling or word study programs little attention is given to the technical aspects of using dictionaries and even less attention to online resources available to help define and refine word meanings. Yet, vocabulary continues to be cited as an essential literacy skill in various topics such as making the transition to "reading to learn," the fourth-grade slump, content-area (disciplinary) literacy, word choice in writing, and text complexity.

A common assignment is to have students copy definitions from a dictionary. This assignment has several flaws: students may select a definition that does not match the context the teacher intended, students may not think carefully about the definitions as they copy them, and it is a relatively low-level task. I've seen my children copy definitions while they watch television or between turns on video games. Consequently, copying definitions often becomes handwriting practice rather than an opportunity to learn new word meanings. The time devoted to vocabulary study is better spent in activities that encourage deeper thinking about word meanings than the copying of definitions.

Vocabulary study can be exciting and engaging. The many online dictionaries and reference resources provide a delicious smorgasbord of definitions, examples, and illustrations. Readers of all ages now can have instant access to online dictionaries and word study reference resources through computers, cell- or smartphones, and tablet devices. Many of these online resources are superior to *dictionary.com* (which has lots of advertising and spyware) and are designed with a younger audience in mind. Exposing teachers to the choices available and providing an opportunity to critically evaluate the various resources can change forever their approaches to dictionaries, online references resources, and vocabulary exploration.

Description

1. In preparation for the vocabulary scavenger hunt it is important that the teachers have a short story, unit from a textbook, or other short piece of reading typically required for third- to eighth-grade students. I encourage the use of "challenging" text, text that is at upper ranges of text complexity for the grade range. In situations that do not allow teachers to select materials in advance I will supply a short reading that has some interesting vocabulary for exploration.

2. I begin the class or workshop with a freewrite, brainstorming, or think–pair–share activity in which I ask them to describe the vocabulary activities that they remember from their K–8 school days. We share our experiences and reflect on them as both learners and teachers. Most remember copying definitions for lists of words and taking a test at the end of the week or unit. When asked to reflect on this practice they have a range of responses. Some teachers have fond memories of this activity; others found it an onerous task. Very few are able to endorse this activity as being particularly effective. Typically they describe memorizing the definitions for the test and immediately forgetting them.

3. We discuss their current practices for learning new words or exploring intriguing vocabulary terms. Most rely on *dictionary.com*. Typically a few of the group will share their personal passion for learning new words. Others will admit to rarely looking up unfamiliar words, instead skipping over them hoping to pick up enough clues through the surrounding text to understand the author's meaning.

4. I introduce the scavenger hunt (see Figure 3.1). There are exciting online resources available to explore word meanings. I demonstrate two that are not widely known, but very interesting to learners of all ages: *www.wordnik.com* and *www.visualthesaurus.com*. If I know that if I have a high number of teachers who are primarily interested in primary grades or second-language learners, I may substitute *www.visual.merriam-webster.com* for Wordnik. There are many other interesting online dictionaries or reference resources available. These include specialized dictionaries such as *www.artlex.com* (an art dictionary), dictionaries of medical and scientific terms, or even dictionaries of text speak. Many of these are listed in my *Delicious.com* social bookmarks in the vocabulary stack. (My Delicious account is open to the world; feel free to visit *www.delicious.com/BSU-Lee*.)

5. Teachers are asked to select one important/interesting word for the material they have brought to class or that I have provided. The word they explore is up to them, but the choice is important. I suggest that they select a "just-right" word—one that would be "new" or be used in a new way by third- to eighth-grade students but not so exotic that the students would not see it again for years. The word should be one that they would hope that their students would understand in deep and nuanced ways at the end of a unit. Teachers then search from at least three different online resources and explore the definitions and examples that are available for that word. They copy and paste these resources into an activity template or print a copy to submit. After exploring the resources they write a reflection about the various resources available, the strengths and weaknesses of each, and their thinking about possible student responses. This generally takes about 20 minutes.

6. After everyone has completed their reflection (often at the next meeting) they share in small groups. These discussions are very interesting. Some teachers

have strong positive or negative reactions to specific online resources. Often others in the group will have the opposite reaction. The value of this discussion is that the responses of our third- to eighth-grade students to these resources will be as varied as ours. Choice is important but so is exposure. Too often we rely on a familiar resource rather than opening ourselves to something that is unfamiliar, but perhaps ultimately of more utility.

Directions: Create a document with your last name and "vocabulary" as the file name (e.g., Smithvocabulary). There will be three sections. Use the following subheads to identify the required elements:

1. Topic and Word:
2. Definitions from Three Online Dictionaries:
3. Reflection:

Selecting a Word: Pick an important word from the reading passage. This should be a word that is essential to understanding the main idea of the reading or is a "high-utility" general vocabulary word. Record the word and a brief explanation of why you selected it. (Remember, the amount of time you will have in your classroom to thoroughly teach words is limited. To make every minute count you need to select important [concept critical] or high-utility [interesting, descriptive, but not exotic] words for study.)

The Hunt: Explore the meaning of this word in at least three of the online resources listed in my vocabulary stack at *www.delicious.com/BSULee*. For each of the three resources you explore, copy and paste into your saved document a substantive portion of the map, definition, discussion, or illustration. (You may also print it and submit a paper copy in class.) Take a few minutes to read the definitions and explore each resource. You will be asked to compare them in your reflection. Try to think about how a student in a third- to eighth-grade classroom would experience the resource.

Thinking about Online Dictionaries: After you have explored (and copied) the definitions of your word from at least three resources reflect on your explorations. You might respond to the following questions: Which resource is most helpful? Why do you prefer one resource over the other? How do you think third- to eighth-grade students will respond to these various resources? Which would be most helpful to learners without much background knowledge? Which would be most helpful to English language learners?

Be prepared to discuss your reflections on the three different resources with a small group.

FIGURE 3.1. Assignment for vocabulary/dictionary scavenger hunt.

Discussion

Teachers are amazed at the variety of resources available for vocabulary study. The highly interactive and visually appealing resources are a revelation to many. For the last 2 years I have been working closely with two teachers who have been using online resources for vocabulary development in their classrooms. Overall the responses of their students are extremely positive. The teachers report improved scores on vocabulary tests (or vocabulary questions in unit tests). Recently I was able to show our new African immigrants how they could add French words to the word map in Visual Thesaurus. Their eyes lit up! I showed Hispanic students how they could add Spanish words to the maps as well and they were equally excited. Several other students who were trying to learn Spanish or German were thrilled to know they could look up words in those languages as well as add the Spanish or German words to an English word map. The one disappointment came from one of our Russian immigrants—he was very disappointed that Visual Thesaurus did not offer the option of adding Russian words to the map.

This activity is really a first step in changing approaches to vocabulary study in the classroom. Once teachers have been exposed to some alternative online resources, the next step is to change the vocabulary activities they plan for K–8 students. It is a good idea to emphasize that this particular activity is probably not good for most elementary classrooms. Once teachers are familiar with a wide range of online dictionaries and resources they can begin to introduce them to their students and demonstrate how to use them. Vocabulary activities in the classroom can be modified to take advantage of the rich visual and language resources these digital resources offer.

READING COMPREHENSION STRATEGIES

What Is It?

Reading comprehension strategies are those processes in which readers make "deliberate, goal-directed attempts to control and modify the reader's efforts to decode text, understand words, and construct meanings of text" (Afflerbach, Pearson, & Paris, 2008, p. 368). Comprehension strategies are those that focus on making sense of and interacting with text. Self-initiated strategic interventions arise in good readers when meaning making does not go smoothly. For example, a reader may choose to preview a text, construct mental images, and/or question the text during reading when confronted by dense text in an unfamiliar content area. Comprehension strategies thus involve self-monitoring, and deliberate, flexible problem-solving processes. With continued practice, some comprehension strategies will develop into comprehension skills—automatic actions used in meaning making (Afflerbach et al., 2008). Comprehending strategically goes hand in hand with effortless and fluent meaning making.

What Do Teachers Need to Know?

As comprehension involves invisible mental processes, understanding how to engage deeply with text can be a mystery for children. We cannot take for granted that children will learn on their own to create mental images when they read. Fortunately, text comprehension can be improved through explicit instruction (Almasi et al., 2011; Dewitz et al., 1987; National Reading Panel, 2000; Palincsar & Brown, 1984; Pearson & Dole, 1987; Pressley, 2000). Use of semantic organizers, answering/generating questions, and summarization are among the researched strategies that can aid students in developing and strengthening comprehension skills. Effective comprehension strategy use is complex, as intentional strategies require that students self-regulate and take responsibility for their own learning (Afflerbach et al., 2008). Comprehension strategy instruction includes these elements: (1) description of the strategy—what it is, why use it, and when to use it; (2) teacher modeling of the strategy, including *think-aloud* procedures to reveal invisible processes and self-monitoring; (3) guided practice—students engage in using the strategy with teacher guidance; and (4) independent practice or application—students practice with the strategy until they can use and choose it fluently. Students need to be taught how to use strategies flexibly and in combination to understand text (Pearson, Rohler, Dole, & Duffy, 1992).

ACTIVITY 3.4
Think-Aloud Comprehension Strategy Lesson
DEBORAH G. LITT

Activity Type: Assignment with in-class presentation or video.

Materials: Planning guide, as well as instructor-made materials as appropriate—sample lesson plan, rationale statement, text or texts selected for demonstration, and rubric (see model below).

Standards Links

IRA Professional Standards: Curriculum and Instruction
2.2 Candidates use appropriate and varied instructional approaches including those that develop word recognition, language comprehension, strategic knowledge, and reading–writing connections.

Duration: Approximately 3 hours of class time, depending on number of students; several weeks for preparation.

Professional Learning Focus:
- Comprehension strategy instruction.
- Think-aloud technique.
- Matching instruction to student needs.

K–8 Student Learning Focus:
Comprehension strategies.

Common Core State Standards: Reading Anchor Standards
Depending on the particular strategy modeled, this activity could address any one of the nine reading standards for Literature and Informational Text. The Common Core Standards below are those most often selected for modeling.

Key Ideas and Details
1. Read closely to determine what the text says explicitly and to make logical inferences from it; cite specific conclusions drawn from the text.

2. Determine central ideas or themes of a text and analyze their development; summarize the key supporting details and ideas.

Craft and Structure
4. Interpret words and phrases as they are used in a text, including determining technical, connotative, and figurative meanings and analyze how specific word choices shape meaning or tone.

Rationale

I believe that a well-conducted think-aloud is an especially powerful instructional tool, one that all teachers should know how to use. Through the structure of the assignment, I hope to ensure a basic level of competence in delivering think-alouds appropriate for particular children and learning contexts. Although many of the teacher candidates with whom I work will be delivering premade lessons as classroom teachers, I believe they will be better equipped to evaluate and adapt lessons produced by others if they understand the principles behind lesson development and learn to create their own lessons geared to particular students. Some schools and school districts use rigid curriculum guides that require teachers to provide lessons in a predetermined sequence whether or not their students are ready or need the skill, so I feel it is especially critical for teachers to have practice matching instruction to the needs of the learners.

Description

Teachers develop and present a think-aloud lesson demonstrating a comprehension strategy. For this assignment I limit the lesson to a think-aloud that models one of the major comprehension strategies documented in the literature, such as monitoring, questioning, summarizing, visualizing, inferring, determining importance, clarifying, or connecting. The teachers submit a written lesson 1 or 2 weeks before they present their lesson in class or teach it in a classroom. The lesson format includes a rationale statement explaining why the teacher thinks this group of students needs the lesson and how the teacher knows the students are ready for it; a verbatim script for the opening, closing, and think-aloud portions of the lesson; and the activities they will use for guided practice, independent practice, and assessment. I don't want the teachers to read their script when they present the lesson, but scripting forces them to think carefully about the words they will use, and also enables me to review the lesson ahead of time. I give them feedback such as "Think about the words you're using. Do you think your second graders will understand them?" or "You are modeling here. How might you say this so that it is not a question/answer routine?"

The teachers "present" the opening, the think-aloud portion, and the closing to the class as if the other teachers were their students or use a video taken of the lesson with students. The assignment is graded with a rubric (see Figures 3.2 and 3.3). The rubric is quite specific, providing clear guidance to the teachers.

Discussion

Over the years, I have experimented with different versions of the assignment. Some years I have required a video recording of a lesson taught in front of children, other years the lesson must be taught in the university classroom, and some years I give the teachers a choice. The advantage of the video is that it is an authentic experience, and for preservice teachers it is another opportunity to try their wings in front of real students. However, obtaining permission for video recording can be extremely difficult. Also, if the teacher makes a major error such as using the IRE pattern (the common interaction pattern in which a teacher asks a question, one student responds, and the teacher evaluates the response) instead of a true think-aloud, there is often less opportunity to redo the assignment.

Before my teachers tackle this assignment I prepare them with extensive explanation and modeling. I explain the purpose and value of think-alouds, and model a few for them. Because so many of my students have difficulty moving away from the IRE pattern, I emphasize the need to use first-person language—for example: "So, *I'm* wondering, why . . .? Then *I* remembered *I've* heard of something like that on TV so *I* think it must be . . ." I provide them with a planning guide and several samples of the plan for the lesson, including one that I teach to them just as if they were a group of fourth graders.

Reading strategy to be modeled: _____

Title of text: _____

Page(s): _____

Cue you will use to show when you are thinking aloud:

Opening sentences in which you succinctly explain what you will be demonstrating, why you are bothering to show this, and what the students stand to gain when they can to do it themselves:

Places where you will stop and think aloud (indicate paragraph, word, etc., or mark in your own copy of text):

FIGURE 3.2. Planning sheet for a think-aloud assignment.

	Approaches 6.5　7.0　7.5	Meets 8.0　8.5　9.0	Exceeds 9.5　10.0
Strategy Selection **Counts double**	Too advanced or already mastered and unnecessary or no evidence presented of need.	Strategy selected worthwhile and appropriate for target audience.	
Written Rationale	Missing or illogical or no evidence of need presented.	Clear explanation; logical support based on student needs for selected strategy.	
Rationale to Students	Missing, confusing, or inaccurate.	Reasonably succinct statement in student-friendly language. Students understand why they are learning the strategy—how it will help them.	Crystal-clear statement in student-friendly language; fosters student desire to master the strategy.
Example(s)	Weak selection; difficult-to-understand strategy.	Good selection; clear example of strategy.	Excellent selection; very easy-to-understand strategy from the example.
Language Choices and Modeling **Counts double**	Language used was too complex much of the time or candidate talked "down" to target audience or too vague. Or candidate used a question–answer or IRE pattern. Incorrect use or pronunciation of words and/or multiple errors of standard usage. Delivery moribund or tentative; would not motivate students.	Language used was mostly appropriate for intended age group and words accurately conveyed principle intended. Could contain an occasional lapse in word use, pronunciation, or standard usage. Candidate stayed in first person, *modeling* his or her own thought process. Clear when teacher is "thinking" versus talking or reading. Delivery audible and clear throughout; sufficiently animated to hold students' attention.	Language was crystal clear and appropriate for target audience throughout. Precise word use. Correct pronunciation and standard usage throughout. Exceptionally enthusiastic and positive delivery that would be motivating to students.
Overall Demonstration	Somewhat to very confusing.	Overall, the demonstration would help students understand what they ought to be doing in their minds when interacting with text.	In addition to "Meets," exciting and inviting.

FIGURE 3.3. Think-aloud strategy lesson presentation or video rubric.

From *Literacy Teacher Education: Principles and Effective Practices* by Deborah G. Litt, Susan D. Martin, and Nancy A. Place. Copyright 2015 by The Guilford Press. Permission to photocopy this figure is granted to purchasers of this book for personal use only (see copyright page for details). Purchasers can download and print a larger version of this figure from *www.guilford.com/litt-forms.*

I discuss each component to share the thinking behind my choices. I talk them through how I would analyze student needs to decide on a comprehension strategy to model, and show how this leads to a rationale statement. Since I have found that many students have difficulty with the rationale statement—and I think this is critical because it forces the teacher to think about what the learners need—I now provide a demonstration and partner practice in class on writing rationale statements. I review the written lessons and provide feedback before they teach the lesson.

The in-class presentation portion of the assignment provides me with an opportunity to observe teachers' delivery. Is their speech audible, clear, and appropriately animated, or do they mumble or speak in a monotone? Do they use language that would be comprehensible to the children they are directing the lesson toward, or are they talking way above or below them? The words teachers use can determine whether or not students will grasp the concept they are trying to convey, and the tone that they use can determine whether or not the students tune in. I want them to become conscious of the language they use with their students, as well as the tone and energy they convey. All of these factors contribute to the effectiveness of their lessons.

I find that despite my modeling, and the examples available in the textbook or online, about 1 in 10 students uses a question–answer or IRE discourse pattern. To me, the failure to take on true modeling language is proof of how deeply ingrained these discourse patterns are, and how closely tied they are to our cultural notions of instruction. But, it could also be true that talking one's thoughts aloud just feels awkward to some individuals, or because it appears easy when I model, the teachers don't realize how much effort and practice the lesson demands. Despite modeling and practice, adequate rationale statements continue to pose difficulty for a small portion of my students.

The teachers benefit not just from developing their own think-aloud lesson but from seeing their classmates' lessons. They appreciate being exposed to children's books they were previously unfamiliar with, seeing demonstrations of different comprehension strategies, and observing different ways of approaching the same strategy. And whether or not they appreciate it at the time, I think they benefit tremendously from the opportunity to receive a thorough, close critique of a single lesson.

ACTIVITY 3.5
Practicing Reading Comprehension Strategies with Adult Text

JOANNE DURHAM

Activity Type: In-class activity, may also be adapted for online course activity.

Materials: Reading passage that is challenging for adults.

Duration: 45 minutes.

Professional Learning Focus:
- Comprehension strategy instruction.
- Metacognition.
- Engagement and motivation.
- Reader response theory.

K–8 Student Learning Focus: N/A.

Standards Links

IRA Professional Standards:

2.2 Select and implement instructional approaches based on evidence-based rationale, student needs, and purposes for instruction.

Implement and evaluate instruction in each of the following areas: concepts of print, phonemic awareness, phonics, vocabulary, comprehension, fluency, critical thinking, motivation, and writing.

Common Core State Standards: N/A.

Rationale

Unlocking the door to comprehension is one of a reading teacher's most important roles and research shows that teaching children to use strategies while they read is one of the most useful keys. As proficient readers, adults use strategies automatically; we don't even realize we are visualizing, searching our background knowledge to help us when we are confused, filing in gaps with our inferences, or letting our own questions propel us forward through text. It's when we are confronted with text that is complex or difficult for us—as adults—that it becomes easier to recognize what our minds are really doing when we read. Therefore I have found that introducing reading strategies by having teachers or teacher candidates read and think through text that is written for and presents challenges to adults is an effective means for helping them get inside the process. When teachers have this experience, instruction in reading strategies begins to change from a list of objectives into an authentic tool for supporting readers.

Description

I present a short piece of text—sometimes a poem, a nonfiction article, or a book excerpt—that is challenging for most adults to read. One of my favorites is an excerpt from Yale medical doctor and researcher Sally Shaywitz's book *Overcoming Dyslexia*, which is definitely not an easy read. The process is as follows:

1. I ask participants to read a difficult text, using sticky notes to mark where they are confused and what strategies they use to deal with the confusion. If participants are unsure how to begin, I model my own confusions and strategies on the first paragraph.

2. I circulate and prompt as needed, and I help those who are stuck notice what they are thinking. I might ask, "What are you thinking in this part?" or "Is anything confusing to you?" Then I repeat back to them their thoughts and encourage them to jot them down on their sticky notes.

3. Participants turn and talk to a colleague and share what they were thinking as they read. Again I circulate and listen. Sometimes I need to redirect those who begin to talk about the implications for teaching children or the challenges of the task rather than unpacking their thinking about the passage.

4. We share our thinking in the whole group, examining any thoughts that I modeled as well as those from the participants. We then categorize them as specific reading strategies, such as questions, connections, inferences, or visualizations. I always include something that is simply a reaction, to emphasize that every thought doesn't necessarily fit into a predetermined list of strategies. Then I share the research on comprehension strategies and how good readers use them.

5. We conclude by reflecting on what participants learned from this exercise.

I have also adapted this activity for use in an online course on reading comprehension. I post the text in a Word document, with my confusions and coding of the first paragraph of the text shown in the comments section of Word under "Review." I ask the participants to code the remaining text on their own using the same comments function. After posting, they respond to at least two colleagues' posts, noting similarities and differences and what they learned by coding the text.

Discussion

This activity provides a very clear assessment of what teachers already know about reading comprehension strategies, and whether they are able to articulate their own thinking process. I have often noticed that the teachers are hesitant at first, feeling somewhat intimidated by the passage and not sure they will give the "right" answers. Teachers are used to instructors asking questions of students, not deconstructing their own process of thinking about text. If I have done initial modeling, I may categorize my thoughts before teachers continue trying to capture their own thinking to provide extra support. I usually prefer to wait to categorize until teachers have coded their text, however, to promote genuine responses from the participants, and allow them to inductively recognize strategies such as inferring and visualizing through their own use of them. Some groups that are completely new to strategies benefit from naming the strategies first.

This exercise helps teachers to directly experience what reader response theory (Rosenblatt, 1994) and schema theory (Anderson, 2004) have shown: that reading is an interaction between the reader and the text, and that we are constantly making use of our background knowledge, expanding or readjusting it as we read. For example, on reading "Reading is a code, and no matter who we are, each of us must somehow represent print as a neural code that the brain can decipher," one teacher talked about watching her 2-year-old just beginning to realize that squiggles on the page transmit meaning. Another used that experience as a springboard to imagining what it would be like for someone for whom the squiggles never do turn into meaningful sequences. These connections helped the participants translate scientific jargon into everyday realities. Teachers inevitably say, "I never thought about it that way before." Turning and talking about one another's thinking adds richness because other people's background knowledge becomes incorporated into our own as we share.

Following this type of reflection, I asked one group if they would have gotten as much from the article if I had used a typical Initiate-Response-Evaluate (IRE) mode of instruction with them, such as asking, "What does Shaywitz mean by 'the neural code'?" They all laughed; it was so obvious that letting them enter the text through their own thinking, and sharing with one another to struggle with ideas, was so much more powerful. The activity helped them understand why it is so important to guide children to develop their own thinking, not just require them to respond to teacher-made questions.

Supporting Materials

Any engaging and complex short passage of text works well with this activity. In addition to expository nonfiction, poetry is very effective, as it always brings forward a variety of interpretations that deepen understanding and appreciation of the text. "The Voice You Hear When You Read Silently," a poem by Thomas Lux that I used for the online course, is intriguing because its topic is the inner conversation one has while reading.

References

Anderson, R. C. (2004). Role of reader's schema in comprehension, learning, and memory. In R. B. Ruddell & N. J. Unrau (Eds.), *Theoretical processes and models of reading* (5th ed., pp. 594–606). Newark, DE: International Reading Association.

Rosenblatt, L. M. (1994). The transactional theory of reading and writing. In R. B. Ruddell, M. R. Ruddell, & H. Singer (Eds.), *Theoretical models and processes of reading* (4th ed., pp. 1057–1092). Newark, DE: International Reading Association.

CONTENT-AREA LITERACY

What Is It?

Content-area literacy refers to the special skills and strategies readers must employ to *comprehend* and *learn* from texts found in different content areas. Learning from text (whether traditional print-based text or nonprint "text" such as film) requires intentional effort. Helping students understand the organization of expository text, which most students find more difficult to understand than the (usually) more familiar narrative form, is another major component of content-area literacy.

What Do Teachers Need to Know?

To master the content of a particular subject area, students must learn to think like experts in that area—mathematicians, historians, biologists, or sociologists, for example. A major component of a discipline's manner of thinking is how experts read and write in their fields. Teachers need to be skillful in their use of think-alouds, as described in the section on comprehension strategies, to induct students into the type of thinking done by experts in the subject.

A student's background knowledge on the topic and the genre has a profound influence on whether a student will understand and be able to learn from a particular text. Techniques for activating background knowledge, building background knowledge prior to reading, understanding features of the subject-area genres, and connecting new information in a text to a reader's existing background knowledge are part of content-area literacy.

Preservice teachers often assume that a good reader can understand all types of texts equally well, but being able to comprehend text in one genre—perhaps mysteries or sports articles—is no guarantee that a reader will be able to understand a poem, learn from a chapter in a science textbook, or grasp the significance of a primary source document in history. Most students benefit from some explicit instruction and guided practice in the strategies proficient readers use to understand these texts. Explicit instruction of expository text awareness has a positive effect on reading comprehension (Duke & Pearson, 2002). Such instruction involves learning to identify different organizational patterns, learning to use the text features peculiar to expository texts (headers, picture captions, glossaries, indexes, etc.), drawing attention to signal words and phrases and their meanings, and using graphic organizers specific to the text type.

Teachers also need to know how to teach students a variety of strategies they can use to understand and remember content material including methods of helping students organize and process the information they are learning, various forms of note taking, and other writing-to-learn techniques.

DISCUSSION AS AN INSTRUCTIONAL APPROACH TO MAKING MEANING OF TEXT

What Is It?

Discussion-based lessons, whether teacher- or student led, are typically complex and rich learning opportunities designed to promote students' conceptual and linguistic development around text (Goldenberg, 1993). Discussion can provide opportunities for students to hear multiple perspectives, support their own ideas with evidence from the text, and provide sites for comprehension strategy practice (Berne & Clark, 2008). Reciprocal teaching (Palincsar & Brown, 1984), in which teachers and students took turns leading small-group dialogue focused on summarizing, question generating, clarifying, and predicting processes, was the first instructional approach that emphasized a group effort in making meaning of text. Book Club, as an elementary literacy instructional approach, has been researched and used in classrooms for more than 15 years. Student-led discussion groups, as well as writing about reading, teacher instruction, and community sharing, are basic to this instructional approach (Raphael & McMahon, 1994; Peterson & Eeds, 1990).

What Do Teachers Need to Know?

Although research clearly indicates the benefits of teacher- and peer-led discussion around text, this is not an easy instructional approach to implement. Both reciprocal teaching and the Book Club model are multifaceted: student-led discussion is only one facet of these approaches.

Some research has suggested that student-led discussions can yield deeper interactions with text (Almasi, 1995) than those that are teacher led. On the other hand, other studies indicate that power differentials developed in peer groups left on their own (Evans, 2002), or that students were unable to manage to stay focused on the task at hand when they were on their own (Martin, 2004). Clearly, discussion-based instruction requires teacher modeling and clear expectations for desirable/

undesirable behaviors in discussion (Berne & Clark, 2008). Daniels (2002) has developed particular roles, such as summarizer, illustrator, or word wizard, to help students engage in what he terms *literature circles*.

ACTIVITY 3.6
Book Clubs in a Methods Course
SUSAN D. MARTIN

Activity Type: Multifaceted assignment that involves reading, in-class discussion, question generation, reflection, and presentation.

Materials: Books selected by participants for Book Club.

Duration: 6 weeks, with 20–30 minutes per week spent in class.

Professional Learning Focus:
- Develop knowledge base in writing processes and/or instruction.
- Develop knowledge of group discussion as a model for social learning that helps to deepen each participant's understandings and connections to the book.
- Learn to generate thought-provoking and higher-level questions around text.
- Identify key points of a text.
- Understand the value of keeping a reading log/journal.
- Use reflective habits.
- Experience motivational factors involved in self-selection of text to gain understanding of the power of self-selection of text.
- Collaborate with colleagues to produce an informative presentation.

Standards Links

IRA Professional Standards:
2.2 Candidates use appropriate and varied instructional approaches including those that develop word recognition, language comprehension, strategic knowledge, and reading–writing connections.

5.4 Candidates use a variety of classroom configurations (i.e., whole class, small group, and individual) to differentiate instruction.

Common Core State Standards: Speaking and Listening Anchor Standards

Comprehension and Collaboration
1. Prepare for and participate effectively in a range of conversations and collaborations with diverse partners, building on others' ideas and expressing their own clearly and persuasively.

Presentation of Knowledge and Ideas
4. Present information, findings, and supporting evidence such that listeners can follow the line of reasoning and the organization, development, and style are appropriate to task, purpose, and audience.

K–8 Student Learning Focus:
- Learn to engage in discussion.
- Learn to deepen understandings and connections to text.
- Learn to support ideas with evidence from text.
- Learn to evaluate the ideas and perspectives of others and reconsider first thoughts.

Rationale

Book Club, as a literacy instructional approach, has been studied and used in classrooms for more than 15 years. Basic to this classroom approach are student selections of texts, written responses to reading, student-led small-group discussions, teacher instruction, and community sharing (Raphael & McMahon, 1994). I have used this assignment at both preservice and inservice levels as an opportunity for teachers to experience firsthand the benefits of small-group discussions of text. I have used Book Club discussions in writing methods courses where the content of the selected texts focuses on writing processes and writing instruction. Since the processes are reading/discussion centered, I am able to expeditiously cover many aspects of literacy practices.

Description

1. At the beginning of the semester, I discuss the assignment (see Figure 3.4). I give brief book talks on the books that teachers can select for their Book Club book. Teachers sign up for their first three choices. I try to give them their first choice, but there have to be at least two and no more than six in each group. However, more than one group can read the same book. This provides opportunity to discuss classroom organization for book clubs—students in multiple books or everyone in the same book. I have used *Bird by Bird* by Anne Lamott and *On Writing: A Memoir of the Craft* by Stephen King. Each of these is a fast, fun read. Narrative writing is the focus of each book, but the authors delve into issues of writing processes. Other books I have used include *Reading, Writing and Rising Up: Teaching about Social Justice and the Power of the Written Word* by Linda Christensen and *Mentor Texts: Teaching Writing through Children's Literature, K–6* by Lynn Dorfman and Rose Cappelli.

2. About 3 weeks later, to allow teachers time to obtain the books, we begin the weekly Book Club meetings. The first week, each group decides on a reading plan that will enable them to complete the book within a 4- to 5-week period. As part of the plan, they assign discussion leader(s) for each of the 4 weeks. Discussion leaders must prepare three to five questions and/or discussion points, and

To promote development of your knowledge base in an area that you deem important, you will select a book on writing/writing instruction to read. You will be involved in small-group discussion of this book as a model for social learning that helps to deepen each participant's understandings and connections to the book. You may find these in the bookstore or order them online. **Please order your book the first week of the semester.**

Book choices:
- *Bird by Bird*, Anne Lamott, 1994.
- *On Writing: A Memoir of the Craft,* Stephen King, 2000.
- *Reading, Writing and Rising Up: Teaching about Social Justice and the Power of the Written Word,* Linda Christensen, 2000.
- *In the Middle, Second Edition*, Nancy Atwell, 1998.

1. Your group will decide on a reading plan together so that you have each finished reading your Book Club book over a 5-week period, **February 8–March 10**. You will keep a **reading log** that denotes pages read and any questions/comments that occur to you as you read.

2. Each group member will take a turn as a **discussion leader** for a particular chapter or part of the book. As discussion leader you will prepare questions/discussion points and facilitate the discussion to include all group members. Post three to five questions/points on your group's BlackBoard site by the **Sunday night before class**. Once everyone has been discussion leader, decide for yourselves how you want to facilitate the conversation.

3. You will actively participate in your group discussions each week.

4. You will complete a final one-page reflection on this assignment. It should include:
   - Main points of what you learned about writing in the book.
   - How will you apply these points in your own classroom?
   - Thoughts, feeling, and ideas about the reading logs/Book Club process.
   - Could/would you use this instructional approach in your own classroom?

5. The final product for this activity will be completed in class. You are expected to share with your classmates.

Evaluation:
20 points based on:
   - Thorough and complete reading log.
   - Quality of your questions/discussion points as group leader.
   - Participation in group discussions.
   - Individual reflection.
   - Product to share with classmates.

FIGURE 3.4. Book Club activity assignment.

facilitate the discussion to include all group members. Discussion leaders post their questions on our class website by Sunday evening. I also provide guidelines for a reading log/journal, and during their first Book Club meeting, teachers discuss how they will keep a reading log that denotes pages read and any questions/comments that occur while reading.

3. Groups meet for about 20 minutes in class for the next 4–5 weeks.

4. The last day of Book Club takes about 45–60 minutes. I ask teachers to come to class with a list of what they think the key ideas of the book might be. I allow about 15 minutes for the groups to discuss key ideas, identify connections to teacher practices and classroom learning, and give the book a recommendation (or not). Then I allow them another 15 minutes to create a presentation about their book for the other groups using supplies that I have brought to class, such as paper of various sizes, markers, yarn, and scissors. At the end of the 15 minutes we watch the 1- to 2-minute presentations and debrief any commonalities across books.

5. The following week their "product" for Book Club is turned in: log, group leader questions/comments, and a one-page reflection on the assignment that must include responses to these prompts:

- Main points that you learned about writing while reading the book.
- How you will apply these points in your own classroom.
- Thoughts, feelings, and ideas about the reading logs/Book Club/presentation processes.
- Would you use this instructional approach in your own classroom?

6. Assessment: I use a checklist assessment for this assignment as I want to model one of the assessments we learn about in the course. A checklist assessment works well as the tasks in this assignment are so completely different from one another. Each of the five criteria is worth the same amount (4 points out of 20 total). There is no rubric, but I use comments to explain my assessment scores:

- Thorough and complete reading log.
- Questions and discussion points developed as a group leader.
- Participation in group discussion.
- Individual reflection.
- Product to share with classmates.

Discussion

When I first taught this class, I had teachers select a book to read independently and then give a poster presentation at the end of the course. I love the switch to book clubs and the briefer in-class presentation format. These briefer presentations have freed up course time for other important assignments. This activity promotes a high-leverage reading instructional approach (Ball & Forzani, 2011) while simultaneously helping teachers deepen their understandings about writing and writing instruction.

I must confess, when I started using a Book Club approach I felt a loss of control over the conversation. But, over time, I learned to trust that teachers will interact deeply with one another around text. In fact, now I do very little "cruising" of the room. I am well aware of the change in group dynamics when I listen to or join in a conversation: instead of looking at one another, they all turn their eyes on me. My trust in this method has grown as I have consistently observed the high quality of the discussion leaders' questions, the teachers' reflective writing, and their discussions about text. I learned from my teachers that group members put high effort into these discussions because they feel so obligated to one another. Over time, my beliefs that student-directed conversations promote deeper understandings and the ability to see multiple perspectives have been well supported through documentation in my research. Book Club activities provide rich opportunities for development of content knowledge and instructional practices.

References

Ball, D. L., & Forzani, F. M. (2011). Building a common core for learning to teach: And connecting professional learning to practice. *American Educator, 35,* 17–21, 38–39.

Raphael, T. E., & McMahon, S. I. (1994). Book club: An alternative framework for reading instruction. *The Reading Teacher, 48,* 102–116.

ACTIVITY 3.7
Rotating Envelopes:
Developing Higher-Level Responses to Reading
JOANNE DURHAM

Activity Type: In-class activity.

Materials: Envelopes; prepared discussion questions, each one heading a sheet of paper.

Duration: 1 hour.

Professional Learning Focus:
- Read professional literature closely and analytically.

Standards Links

IRA Professional Standards:
2.2 Select and implement instructional approaches based on evidence-based rationale, student needs, and purposes for instruction.

6.2 Display positive reading and writing behaviors and serve as a model for students.

- Deepen analysis through discussion.

K–8 Student Learning Focus:
Reading text closely and analytically.
Collaborative discussion.

Common Core State Standards:
Reading Anchor Standards

Key Ideas and Details
1. Read closely to determine what the text says explicitly and to make logical inferences from it; cite specific textual evidence when writing or speaking to support conclusions drawn from the text.

2. Determine central ideas or themes of a text and analyze their development; summarize the key supporting details and ideas.

3. Analyze how and why individuals, events, and ideas develop and interact over the course of a text.

Rationale

Whether in a K–12 setting, or in classes in higher education, participants need to read and analyze articles, book chapters, videos, or other sources of relevant information. We want a class discussion of these texts to fully explore the author's viewpoint for deep understanding as well as critical analysis. We also want every participant to be actively involved in the discussion. Since we espouse moving away from an IRE format (teacher initiates a question, student responds, teacher evaluates) with students, the discussions we lead with teachers should model ways to effectively leave IRE behind as well.

I have found that the cooperative learning structure of "rotating envelopes" is useful in demonstrating the power of small-group collaboration as well as leading to higher-level interpretations of the text under consideration.

Description

1. I place participants in groups of two to five members. They are assigned or volunteer for tasks of reader, scribe, and messenger/timekeeper (and optionally facilitator and reporter).

2. I provide an envelope to each group that contains a different question written on the top of a sheet of paper. The question is relevant to a piece of text that the participants have been assigned to read and study. It is usually an open-ended, thought-provoking question for which several appropriate responses can be derived from a careful reading of the text. Often I simply provide a significant

quotation from the text and ask for an interpretation of the passage and its implications for instruction.

3. The reader is signaled to open the envelope, and reads the question to the group. The facilitator keeps the group on point, encourages participation from everyone, and helps sum up what they decide to write. The scribe records their response on the paper. The messenger/timekeeper keeps track of the allotted time to complete the response. When the time is up, the messenger places the paper with its response back in the envelope, and takes the envelope to the next group.

4. The process is repeated as many times as there are questions, optimally about four times. When each group receives its second, third, and fourth question, the reader reads both the question and the responses from all of the previous groups. The group then must create a new response, not repeating any already written.

5. After each group has responded to all the questions, the messenger returns the envelopes to the original groups, that then read all the entries and discuss the various ideas. After, the reporter for each group synthesizes key points with the whole class, focusing on how the group's thinking was expanded by the responses that came after their own.

Discussion

Each time a group receives a new question, they have to think harder to answer it, because the more obvious responses are already written by other groups. Thus this activity spurs deeper and more creative thinking based on the text. It requires the group members to revisit the text and study it more carefully to craft a new response. The game-like quality of the activity, as well as the collaboration among the group members, spurs motivation and engagement in exploring the text, and usually keeps participants focused on their interpretations of the reading. When the group's initial question returns to them, they are quite interested in what the other groups' interpretations were. They also notice how multiple perspectives on the same question are not only possible but deepen understanding.

Like other cooperative learning structures, rotating envelopes increases the likelihood that all participants actually participate. The opportunities for discussing their ideas, supporting one another in analyzing the text, and listening to others enrich the quality of each person's interaction with the text. Instead of a whole-class discussion almost inevitably dominated by a few vocal members, everyone's ideas are much more likely to be heard, explored, and to contribute to more insightful comprehension.

I have found this activity works well with discussions of visual media as well, such as viewing a video of a lesson. For example, after viewing a reading conference and being provided with a written transcript, I have asked participants to note one type of conferring move that the teacher made and explain its purpose and effects. As the most obvious examples were written down, the subsequent groups had to reread the conference very carefully and analytically to provide meaningful responses.

A further benefit of this activity is that teachers not only gain insight into the reading for their course but they also experience an activity that is equally beneficial to implement in their own classrooms. The skills to dig deeply into a variety of types of texts and make meaning from them are critical ones for the teachers to teach to their students as well. Rotating envelopes is an effective and motivating way for students to discuss themes, character traits, or important ideas in books they are reading.

This activity can be modified by using large chart paper posted in various parts of the room instead of paper inside an envelope. At the signal, each group rotates to the next chart and follows the same process of reading the question and previous responses, and adding its own. This brings movement to the activity for everyone, not just the messenger, and makes the final discussion more visual since everyone can easily see the responses from all groups.

CRITICAL READING AND CRITICAL LITERACY

What Is It?

Critical reading and critical literacy are closely related concepts. Critical reading, the intellectual forerunner of what is now called critical literacy, refers to skills such as judging the authenticity and authority of sources; recognizing an author's purpose; going beyond a literal understanding of text; distinguishing fact from opinion; evaluating the soundness of an author's argument; and recognizing bias and propaganda. Critical reading overlaps with the related concepts of critical and higher-order thinking, and is a mainstay of the traditional liberal arts education.

Critical literacy incorporates the idea of reading with a critical lens that goes beyond the literal interpretation of text but, in addition, takes a philosophical stance that assumes that texts—whether written, oral, visual, or multimedia—are imbued with implicit perspectives regarding gender, race, socioeconomic status, and other sociohistorical elements regarding issues of cultural equity and power. For example, rather than a simple, entertaining fairytale, "Cinderella" can be viewed as a social and historical text intended to teach that a good daughter/woman is obedient. Building on the work of Freire (1970), critical literacy has become synonymous with issues of justice and equity where literacy is seen as a tool for social justice. Critical literacy is the ability to move beyond taken-for-granted (Luke & Woods, 2009) cultural norms represented in text, to being able to critique and recognize the implicit social issues and to recognize *whose* knowledge as well as *what* knowledge is represented. A component of critical literacy is the belief that processes of critiquing and questioning text can lead to transformations of self or one's world (McDaniel, 2004). The role of critical literacy in education is thus coupled with notions of social change, social justice, and democratic citizenry.

What Do Teachers Need to Know?

Teachers need to know that both critical reading and critical literacy refer to active processes of inquiry and examination that need to be taught to students. In the Internet age, judging the authoritativeness of text has become absolutely essential even for young children. While we are fortunate to have easy access to far more texts than ever before in history; with no entry barriers to distribution many of those texts receive no expert review. Also, students who can discern an author's purpose and detect biases will be better equipped to understand and resist the ever-present marketing surrounding us.

Critical literacy, however, is not a set of techniques, but rather a philosophy or a way to view purposes of reading and writing (McDaniel, 2004). As such, it is important that teachers themselves are aware of, *and experience*, the purposes for and questioning nature of critical literacy. As in other literacy processes, to teach critical literacy it is important that teachers model, demonstrate, and promote the purposes and processes of critiquing and questioning the taken-for-granted aspects of text. Choosing texts or a set of texts that explicitly invite students to consider multiple perspectives on a topic can help students develop awareness of and sensitivity to other perspectives. Choosing texts with multiple levels of interpretation and helping students understand that they can relate to a text on multiple levels is another aspect of critical literacy as well as critical reading. Critical literacy demands opportunities for authentic dialogue and discussion in a classroom climate in which student perspectives are encouraged, valued, and validated. Finally, teachers adopting a critical literacy perspective need to provide students with opportunities to connect new awareness with concrete social experiences such as service learning activities.

ACTIVITY 3.8
Viewing Texts Critically
ELIZABETH DUTRO

Activity Type: In-class activity.

Materials: Video clips.

Duration: About 1 hour.

Professional Learning Focus:
- Media as text.
- Awareness of "taken-for-granted" contexts in texts.
- Critical comprehension instructional activity.

K–8 Student Learning Focus:
- Awareness of "taken-for-granted" contexts in texts.
- Critical comprehension strategies.

Standards Links

IRA Professional Standards:
2.2 Implement and evaluate instruction in each of the following areas: concepts of print, phonemic awareness, phonics, vocabulary, comprehension, fluency, critical thinking, motivation, and writing.

Incorporate traditional print, digital, and online resources as instructional tools to enhance student learning.

2.3 Guided by evidence-based rationale, select and use quality traditional print, digital, and online resources.

4.2 Provide instruction and instructional materials that are linked to students' backgrounds and facilitate a learning environment in which differences and commonalities are valued (e.g., use literature that reflects the experiences of marginalized groups and the strategies they use to overcome challenges).

Provide instruction and instructional formats that engage students as agents of their own learning.

Common Core State Standards: Reading Anchor Standards

Integration of Knowledge and Ideas
7. Integrate and evaluate content presented in diverse media and formats, including visually and quantitatively, as well as in words.

Rationale

This learning activity provides opportunities for teachers to develop awareness of media as text and explore the role that television and movies play in children's information and value formations. Furthermore, this activity allows teachers to surface "taken-for-granted" social contexts found specifically in children's television.

Description

This activity can be done in one class period.

1. Have teachers view a 5- to 10-minute clip of a current children's television show or movie, such as *Angelina Ballerina*, *Arthur*, or *The Incredibles*. Debrief with the whole class what they noticed.

2. Teachers view the clip again, but this time have them view with a particular focus, such as gender, race, socioeconomic status, and family roles. Each teacher will have one focus, assigned through random distribution of cards with the focus listed.

3. After the second viewing, teachers with the same perspectives meet and discuss in small groups what they noticed.

4. Debrief each group's findings with a whole-group discussion. Direct teacher focus to what is/isn't being "seen" in the clip. Make sure that the discussion includes connections to classroom practices not only in choosing texts but also in helping students to think critically about the sociopolitical contexts of the texts they read and view. Also, ensure that students understand the activity is not designed to demonize popular culture or to suggest that children and youth should not engage with (or be fans of) media texts. Rather, emphasize that the activity points to the power and subtlety of cultural narratives, the extent to which they can reinforce what counts as the norm (and, thus, what is positioned as outside the norm), and the power of focused critical analysis of all texts.

5. Follow-up can vary:
   - Individual written reflections as exit slips.
   - Creation of a T-chart to allow for compare/contrast of the values teachers learned in family/school/church settings and the values that they believe are perpetuated by popular media.
   - Debrief the chart.

Discussion

I have used this activity several times in various preservice and inservice contexts, including courses in writing methods (elementary and secondary), reading methods, teacher research, gender and literacy, content-area literacy, and education and film. Popular culture in the classroom often immediately piques interest and participants always enthusiastically engage in this activity. One of the satisfying aspects of this lesson is to see the nature of their engagement shift as the activity unfolds. In the first viewing, most are amused by the media clip. During the second viewing, however, as they look more closely, they inevitably start to write notes about 1 minute into the clip and continue steadily until the end. In small groups, they often express amazement at the difference between what they saw during the first and second viewings. In their written reflections after the activity, participants' comments have fallen broadly into three themes: (1) how their own engagement with media texts will change based on the activity, (2) how the activity helped them better understand how and why to engage in critical analysis, and (3) the value of this kind of activity for children and youth (and, if teachers, their desire to replicate a similar activity with students in their own classrooms). Based on student comments, I believe the activity can be eye-opening for many participants and provides an example of the power and importance of critical analysis, particularly of texts that can and do masquerade as neutral and benign.

Note from Susan Martin, Boise State University: I experienced this activity as a teaching assistant in Elizabeth's preservice literacy course. What an *aha* experience this lesson was for me! At the time, I was immersed in reading about critical pedagogy in my doctoral program, but never made connections to looking critically at media/text in this way. I hadn't yet taken a course specifically on critical literacy. I believe that teachers need models particular to practice to help them make connections and come away with teaching tools. Elizabeth didn't just have us read about and discuss these important issues around making meaning from text. We teachers saw the activity modeled while being immersed in doing it. Furthermore, I had not considered media as text: *new literacies* was not a term bandied about at the time. Although times have changed, I think that concepts to do with media literacy and media as text are new for most teachers.

Supporting Materials

Video clips can be found online. Go to the website for a particular TV program/ movie to see what video clips are available. Several programs can be found at *www.pbskids.org*, such as *Arthur*, *Word Girl*, and *Chuck Vanchuck's Explosion*. When you go *www.pbskids.org*, you will need to click on the picture of the show character (e.g., Arthur). That will take you to the screen for the character. Look for the word video and its icon. Click on this. A list of video titles should appear on the right-hand side that you can scroll through.

Videos that will work for this activity include:

- Word Girl video: *Oh Holiday Cheese.*
- Arthur Video: *Arthur's Perfect Christmas.*
- Angelina Ballerina Video: *The Best for You, Hip Hop Kid, Angelina's New School.*

CHAPTER 4

Writing Processes, Instruction, and Assessment

In this chapter we focus on writing and teacher practices specific to writing. We begin by highlighting issues of writing identity as central to lifelong, effective, and motivated writing. We then turn our attention to issues of composition processes, written genres, and teacher practices— each important for effective learning and teaching of writing.

WRITER IDENTITY

What Is It?

Having an identity as a writer is the ability to see oneself as a writer and envision purposes for one's writing. It also requires a sense of capability and confidence in one's abilities to put one's voice out into the world. A writer is someone who may recognize the challenges of writing processes, but can persevere and appreciate the unfolding of thoughts and ideas.

What Do Teachers Need to Know?

We are all writers! Many of us have misconceived images of a *writer* as someone who is a published author or for whom writing is easy. But texting, five-paragraph essays, lesson plans, journals, and math problems are examples of writing. Children need to recognize the multiple ways they engage in writing tasks in their lives to see themselves as writers.

To help students understand this, teachers must also view themselves as writers. In our experience, few teachers view themselves this way. Furthermore, years of academic-focused writing skews the way in which teachers view writing and its purposes (Martin, 2009).

Students (and teachers) need to understand writing as purposeful and meaningful to their lives. Writing must become something more than a school task done for an audience of one—the teacher. Students should engage in writing processes that allow for personal choices, decision making, and social purposes.

Finding one's voice as a writer requires digging deep (Edgerton, 2003) into personal thoughts and memories. Safe writing environments that explicitly foster risk taking, inviting of feedback, and social interactions are critical to these processes. Red-inked pages and feedback focused solely on conventions of writing are counterproductive to the development of students' selves as writers. For some students, hearing the teacher call them *writer* contributes to identity development.

ACTIVITY 4.1
Genre-Based Writing Portfolios
SUSAN D. MARTIN and SHERRY DISMUKE

Activity Type: In-class activity and assignments.

Materials:
- Guidelines for the project.
- Final products written over the course of the semester.
- Entry slips.
- Three-ring binders.

Duration: Multiple class times throughout the semester.

Professional Learning Focus: Creation of various written products through writing processes.

Standards Links

IRA Professional Standards:
2.2 Implement and evaluate instruction in each of the following areas: concepts of print, phonemic awareness, phonics, vocabulary, comprehension, fluency, critical thinking, motivation, and writing.

Common Core State Standards: Writing Anchor Standards
5. Develop and strengthen writing as needed by planning, revising, editing, rewriting, or trying a new approach.

10. Write routinely over extended time frames and shorter time frames

K–8 Student Learning Focus:
Creation of a variety of written
products through writing processes.

for a range of tasks, purposes, and
audiences.

Rationale

The report of the National Commission on Writing (2003) points out that few states require coursework in writing for elementary certification, thus many teachers are never taught how to teach writing (Dismuke, 2013; Pardo, 2006). Teachers have little opportunity to develop understandings of writing processes, what good writing looks like, or to "see themselves as writers—to experience the power and satisfaction of writing as a means of learning and self-expression" (National Commission on Writing, 2003, p. 23). This lack of understanding about writing and writing instruction is compounded by the fact that composition is an extremely complex and demanding task. Furthermore, as students, teachers spend several years writing research papers on topics they do not choose or on which they have little interest.

This genre-based portfolio activity serves several important purposes, but none more important than allowing teachers opportunities to write for themselves in a variety of formats that are not academic writing. Teachers are involved in decision-making processes that allow them choice and voice in their writing. As they are immersed in creating their pieces and portfolios, they are experiencing this learning activity from the perspective of the learner/writer, as well as seeing connections to the scaffolded instruction and social interactions that guide and support their efforts. As one of our experienced teachers commented at the end of the course: "How could I be expected to teach something that I don't do or understand myself!"

Description

In this assignment, teachers create several genre/format-specific written products over the term of a course (either preservice or inservice) focused on writing and writing instruction (see Figures 4.1 and 4.2). The genre/formats that we choose for the course—feature article interview of a classmate, cinquain, choice-of-format poem, memoir, and travel brochure in a content area—have been chosen specifically to be engaging to adult learners, while providing models of assignments that could be done in K–8 classrooms. We have also consciously chosen genres that will be different from what teachers typically experience, especially course research papers.

Writing the pieces is accomplished through teacher-guided lessons and as much socially interactive, in-class writing time as possible. Written products are developed across the stages of writing processes—prewriting, drafting, revision,

For this assignment, you will keep a portfolio/folder of the different forms/genres of writing that we explore this semester and personal samples of each. The purpose of the portfolio is to enhance awareness of the different forms and functions of writing in the classroom and encourage reflection on individual processes and needs in writing.

Evaluation: 20 points based on completeness of the portfolio. A checklist will be used. Your portfolio should be in a notebook or secured on the left-hand side. Please make a table of contents.

Your portfolio will need to include the following:

Written pieces—Final drafts (also include all of your earlier drafts, prewriting activity when possible)
- Interview.
- Cinquain.
- Another poem in a format of your choice.
- Memoir.
- Writing across the curriculum self-selected genre/collaborative piece.

Writing-to-learn products
- One response to readings.
- One graphic organizer.

Other pieces that you would like to include:

Entry slips: You will also complete **three portfolio entry slips** to be attached to particular pieces of your writing.
- Two of these will be different forms provided in class.
- One will be in graphic/pictorial form.
- **One of these forms needs be attached to a writing-to-learn piece.**

Reflection: Include a one- to two-page reflection on your portfolio contents and writing processes. You might want to address these questions. Use your first-day papers as a starting point.
- What did you learn about yourself as a writer?
- Have you changed as a writer?
- Have your perceptions of yourself as a writer changed?
- What are your thoughts about your pieces? Which do you like the best? Why?
- Which did you enjoy creating? Why?
- What did you learn about writing processes through your own experiences?
- What have you learned that you will apply in your classroom?

FIGURE 4.1. Writing portfolio assignment guidelines for students.

editing, and publication/presentation. Teachers are encouraged to think about planning for and creating one piece during the semester as a gift for someone in their lives.

Near the end of the course, teachers prepare their writing portfolios in three-ring notebooks. Portfolios must include all prewriting documents, rough drafts, and final products of the pieces. Additionally, two pieces of writing that are "writing-to-learn" products (e.g., responses to reading, graphic organizers) need to be included. Teachers can include other pieces of writing if they wish. They then complete reflective entry slips for three of their products. Entry slips (see Figure 4.2) provide opportunities for writers to note information about a specific piece (i.e., genre, purpose, audience) and reflect on it and their writing development (e.g., What do you like best about this piece? What does this piece show about what you are learning?). Finally, teachers must also include a one- to two-page reflection on their portfolio contents and writing processes. We provide prompting

---

Name of piece: _____

Date written: _____

Genre/form: _____

Purpose: _____

_____

Audience: _____

_____

Processes used/appropriate to the piece: _____

_____

What do you think is the strongest aspect of your piece?: _____

_____

What did you learn from writing this piece (about self/self as writer/writing/implications for writing instruction)?: _____

_____

FIGURE 4.2. Portfolio entry slip.

questions. Freewrites, focused on self as writer and completed the first week of the course, are returned to students. These serve as the starting point of the reflection. Teachers share their portfolios with one another on the last day of class.

Assessment for this assignment is meant to gauge teachers' engagement with and reflection on the learning activity—not to evaluate their written pieces or writing processes. Our focus in the classes is on teachers writing for themselves, not for a grade. Self-assessment, peer interactions, and modeled writing conferences with us are designed to provide specific feedback. Assessment of the portfolio assignment is thus accomplished with a checklist of the required elements: binding/cover, written pieces, attached entry slips, and quality one- to two-page reflective statements. This checklist mode of assessment and the self-assessment provide models of assessments discussed during the course. Positive feedback to teachers occurs liberally throughout the portfolios, as we read them. We also discuss the portfolio as an assessment tool in K–8 classrooms.

Discussion

We have found that creation of genre-based portfolios provides a central focus for the courses, around which development of knowledge regarding writing and teacher practices, as well as self as writer, occurs. These experiential learning opportunities place teachers in the roles of writer/learner that can serve to disrupt prior negative notions about writing and writing instruction, as well as misconceptions pertaining to learning to write. We believe that this complex, multifaceted activity is a high-leverage (Ball & Forenzi, 2009) writing teacher education practice.

Survey data from the preservice course over a 3-year period shows that the teacher-guided genre lessons and creation of a writing portfolio came out on top in candidate rankings of course activity. Sixty percent of the candidates rated the teacher-guided genre lessons as first, second, or third out of 11 possible teacher-guided activities that affected their learning. Seventy percent of candidates ranked the portfolio as first or second (out of five) in the category of major assignment/weekly reading. Clearly, teachers perceived this activity as quite influential on their learning experiences in the course. One portfolio reflection stated: "This portfolio is a representation of everything that I have learned over the last three months." Analyses of teachers' comments on the surveys suggest that experiential engagement in both the genre lessons and creating the portfolio appears to have provided opportunities for candidates to perceive change/growth to their identities as writers: "First of all, I am a writer; before I didn't really consider myself a writer." Comments also revealed deeper understandings of writing processes and written products; the personal, social, and emotional aspects of the writing/learning experiences; and knowledge specifically linked to teaching writing. As one teacher commented: "I don't remember ever having fun with writing, but learned this semester it can be fun. I hope to bring the joy of writing to my students. If they don't experience the joy early on, they may not ever get the chance to feel it."

References

Ball, D., & Forenzi, F. M. (2009). The work of teaching and the challenge for teacher education. *Journal of Teacher Education, 60*(5), 497–511.

Dismuke, S. (2013). *Examining influences of a university writing methods course on teachers' dispositions, knowledge, and literacy practices.* Unpublished doctoral dissertation, Boise State University, Boise, Idaho.

National Commission on Writing. (2003). *The neglected "R": The need for a writing revolution.* Retrieved from *www.host collegeboard.com/advocacy/writing/publications.html.*

Pardo, L. (2006). The role of context in learning to teach writing: What teacher educators need to know to support beginning urban teachers. *Journal of Teacher Education, 57*(4), 378–394.

COMPOSITION PROCESSES

What Is It?

Composition processes are those cognitive, physical, social, and affective processes and tasks that result in a written product. Writing is a matter of mind, hand, and heart (Pritchard & Honeycutt, 2007).

Composition has commonly been referred to as *the* writing process, which includes stages of writing (Murray, 1982) such as planning/prewriting, drafting, revision, editing, and presentation/publication. Each of these stages involves the writer in complex tasks. For example, planning involves gathering of relevant information and decisions about topic, audience, and purposes.

What Do Teachers Need to Know?

Writing Processes

There is no singular *writing process.* Instead, writing processes will vary by genre, purpose, and individuals' preferences for strategic approaches to writing. For instance, creating a list will not involve the same processes as composing a research report. Some writers prefer to use visual graphic organizers for planning; others prefer to plan through drawing, freewrites, creating lists, or in conversations with friends.

Writers, especially developing writers, need to have clear understandings of and practice with the discrete processes and tasks of planning, drafting, revising, editing, and presentation to be purposeful and strategic while composing. In our experiences, even adult students seem unclear about writing processes and their purposes. One teacher commented that in an undergraduate composition course she deliberately put errors into her rough drafts, so that she would have something to revise and could show the instructor her revisions.

Teachers, however, also need to understand that effective writers move through the stages of writing in fluid and recursive ways. Experienced writers edit and revise as they draft, they return to prewriting if they need to gather more information, and audience awareness affects their planning processes.

Skills and Strategies

Writing depends upon the foundational skills of spelling, handwriting, keyboarding, and language conventions. Automaticity in these processes frees working memory space in the brain for focus on ideas and strategic language choices. Each of these skills is difficult to learn, requiring a good deal of practice in order to develop fluency and automaticity. Skills are not ends in themselves—they serve communicative purposes. However, lack of fluency in foundational skills affects motivation and quality of written products.

In addition to skills, problem-solving strategies are fundamental to writing processes (Graham, 2006). Writing strategies are tools that help writers tackle the challenges of writing processes and tasks. For instance, generating a list of topics is a strategy that can help writers with decisions of what to write about. Use of a Venn diagram during planning is a strategic way to generate and organize ideas when one needs to compare and contrast two items. Inviting feedback from a colleague on a particular aspect of a draft can even be thought of as a strategy.

Affective Processes

Motivation, perseverance, and self-regulation are also integral to writing processes. The complexity and challenges of writing indicate that attention to motivation is an important component of effective writing instruction. Teachers can foster motivation by providing relevant and meaningful writing experiences for children, encouraging communicative and social interactions around writing, and giving students challenging tasks, such as learning about and writing across a variety of genres (Boscolo & Gelati, 2007; Bruning & Horn, 2000).

Beginning Writers

Teachers working with emerging and beginning writers may wish to focus just on planning and drafting processes as children learn to create individual pieces. Use of shared or interactive writing procedures, in which the teacher is the scribe for students' ideas, can aid in teaching elements of revision and editing that may be beyond the students' current developmental levels in foundational and other writing skills.

Linking Process and Product

Composition processes and tasks are linked to the written products that are being produced. For instance, planning will occur differently when generating ideas for an expository report than it will for writing a journal entry. In one case, the writer must take time to research and find necessary information in books and other sources; in the other, the writer may use strategies to jog memories or prioritize what will be written. Revising and editing a poem may require a different focus than revision and editing of a persuasive essay. Some products, such as reading notes, do not require revision or editing processes.

Traits of writing—ideas, organization, voice, word choice, sentence fluency, conventions, and presentation—typically associated with quality of written products, are also dynamic aspects of composition processes (Culham, 2003). Effective writers are strategic in generating and organizing ideas during the planning stages of writing. Voice, word choice, sentence fluency, and conventions are considered during drafting or as tools for revision processes.

Writing and Thinking

Writing processes are intertwined with thinking processes. Writing can extend and distribute memory through the creation of lists. Writing can be used to demonstrate knowledge and ideas, as in the organization and syntheses apparent in research reports. Importantly, writing can also be used to foster thinking. The act of writing often generates new ideas and understandings. Even elementary students are capable of understanding these writing outcomes. A fourth-grade student once remarked, "It [writing] kind of makes you know more. . . . How it makes you know more is you're writing things down, and like between those things you find something new that you may have not known until you actually write it down and look at it and read it and think it over."

ACTIVITY 4.2

Composing and Decomposing:
Understanding the Complexities of Writing Processes
with Play-Doh and Other Visual Representations
SUSAN D. MARTIN and SHERRY DISMUKE

Activity Type: In-class activity.

Materials: A container of Play-Doh for each student; chart paper/pens.

Duration: One class period/1 hour.

Professional Learning Focus:
Teachers develop knowledge of and engage in writing/composition processes of planning, drafting, revising, editing, and publication.

K–8 Student Learning Focus:
Knowledge of and engagement in writing/composition processes.

Standards Links

IRA Professional Standards:
2.2 Implement and evaluate instruction in each of the following areas: concepts of print, phonemic awareness, phonics, vocabulary, comprehension, fluency, critical thinking, motivation, and writing.

Common Core State Standards: Writing Anchor Standards
5. Develop and strengthen writing as needed by planning, revising, editing, rewriting, or trying a new approach.

Rationale

This activity engages teachers in decomposition (Grossman et al., 2009), the examination of the various aspects of a process, such as writing. It also models classroom practices and provides an opportunity to develop conceptual understandings and instructional tools. Susan was first inspired to develop this activity several years ago after reading a newspaper article that highlighted a local high school writing teacher. In the article, both she and her students described the benefits of the Play-Doh composition activity. We still show the news article in our classes and talk about how teachers find good ideas for lessons in many places!

Description

In preparation for this activity, teachers will have read about the stages of process writing and filled in a writing process graphic organizer (see Figure 4.3) with their notes before coming to class. We have used Chapter 1 from the text *Teaching Writing: Balancing Process and Product* by Gail Tompkins (2011) as a reading on this topic.

	Writing Process/Task				
	Planning	Drafting	Revision	Editing	Publication/ Presentation
Key points					
Implications for instruction					

FIGURE 4.3. Writing processes graphic organizer for teachers to fill in while reading.

1. We first give teachers a package of Play-Doh and ask each to compose a pencil holder that needs to be functional. We also informally discuss what qualities one would pay attention to in composing in this medium. They create their pencil holders.

2. We ask teachers to smash these products and compose another version. We ask them to do this again.

3. They choose one version and construct a "rough draft" product. They share their products with one another. We encourage noticing elements that they like and may want to add to their own pencil holders.

4. Then a series of instructor-given prompts helps them to revise and edit. Prompts may ask them to add a visual artistic element such as *texture* to their product. Additionally, they may be asked to add one additional element to their object and/or to remove one.

5. Teachers create their final products and display them on their desks/tables.

6. The class does a gallery walk viewing all the final pieces (see Figure 4.4).

7. We unpack their composing experiences in a group discussion that focuses both on processes and implications for doing this activity with children.

8. The Play-Doh composition activity serves as a preliminary task to further decomposition of process writing. Drawing on course readings and using their individual graphic organizers, teachers meet in small groups to discuss what processes and tasks writers use in stages of planning, drafting, revision, editing, and presentation, as well as implications for instruction. Additionally, the groups are jigsawed so that each group will create a class chart for one stage of process writing with the implications for instruction noted.

9. These jointly constructed charts are put on the wall (see Figure 4.5). A group discussion occurs in which the instructor and teachers further decompose issues of writing processes, such as recursiveness, self-regulation, and strategies.

FIGURE 4.4. Play-Doh pencil holder.

FIGURE 4.5. Process chart at end of semester.

These charts are kept up throughout the course. (We later include writing traits and focus lesson opportunities on the charts.) The joint construction of the chart is then linked to a video clip for the accompanying CD for *Teaching Writing: Balancing Process and Product* (Tompkins, 2011) with elementary students discussing their process charts.

Discussion

This rich, multitask lesson has worked well for us in preservice and inservice courses, as well as in professional development workshops. Data from surveys of teacher candidates taken over a 3-year period suggest that these visual representations have impacted students' understandings of the writing process. Teachers love seeing the Play-Doh set out for them! Inevitably, the final products are far more interesting than the first drafts. This activity lends itself to discussion about multiple aspects of writing processes, instruction, and product outcomes. The resulting process chart is a great way to model students' engagement in creating classroom charts—rather than the teacher going to a school supply store and buying a writing process chart that is put up on the wall and ignored by students. Some of the teachers have talked about referring back to it themselves while writing in the course. Furthermore, we add notations to the charts when we learn about and discuss the 6 + 1 traits as dynamic aspects of writing processes. For example, we add the term *ideas* to the planning, drafting, and revision processes of writers, but then discuss where teacher-led focus lessons and scaffolding for ideas would best occur as students engage in writing processes.

References

Ball, D., & Forenzi, F. M. (2009). The work of teaching and the challenge for teacher educa-tion. *Journal of Teacher Education, 60*(5), 497–511.

Grossman, P., Compton, C., Igra, D., Ronfeldt, M., Shahan, E., & Williamson, P. W. (2009). Teaching practice: A cross-professional perspective. *Teachers College Record, 11*(9), 2055–2100.

Tompkins, G. (2011). *Teaching writing: Balancing process and product.* New York: Allyn & Bacon.

WRITTEN PRODUCTS

What Is It?

The written products we can accomplish through engagement in writing processes vary greatly by form and purposes. Following Bakhtin's (1986) use of the term *speech genres*, we use the word *genre* to reference various forms, formats, and types of written representations. For instance, math word problems and persuasive posters are both unique genres. Each has key features that distinguish it, as well as distinctive social and personal purposes. Some products are intended to extend memory (to-do lists) and/or prompt reflection (personal journals).

What Do Teachers Need to Know?

Written Genres and Formats

Written products occur in a wide range of genres—across content areas and occupations. Marilyn Chapman (1997) has listed more than 100 genres or types of written representation ranging from *acrostic* to *zigzag book*. A close look at many written products suggest that they are hybrid in form and purpose. For instance, a travel brochure is a product that relies on graphics, color, and font, as well as written language. Its purposes are both informational and persuasive. Technology is rapidly changing the look and nature of written products in K–12 settings. New genres are appearing as writers interweave music and pictures with written words. PowerPoint, Digital Storybook, and Animoto are all computer programs that can be used by students to represent their knowledge and ideas.

The CCSS focus on three broad *types* of writing: narrative, expository, and argument. Children, however, need to develop knowledge of and experience with the key features and purposes of a wide range of specific written formats used for various social purposes. For example, understanding the general features of narrative writing is not sufficient for writing an effective fable. Additionally, writing in formats that serve personal purposes, such as journals and poetry, are important for developing motivation to write, a love of language, and an identity as a writer. These genres should be an important part of a K–8 writing program.

Writing to Prompts

We have noticed a focus on writing prompts in K–8 classrooms. In many cases this appears to be a response to high-stakes assessments. Other times, it appears that teachers have no other understandings of writing instruction. Writing to a prompt is a particular genre that serves specific social purposes. Students can benefit from learning how to write to prompts effectively (Angelillo, 2005). However, prompt-driven writing instruction does not provide for the needs of beginning writers and cannot be the only type of writing that students encounter in their classrooms. Writing to a prompt or a teacher-selected topic does not allow students to develop proficiency in some planning processes. Choosing a topic can be particularly challenging for students who struggle in writing (Martin, 2002).

Content-Specific Genres

Knowing about and being able to write in content-area genres is critical in K–12 settings. Knowing how to write scientific hypotheses and observations goes hand in hand with experimentation. The CCSS seek to underscore the importance of students learning to write for *authentic* purposes for work and study beyond K–12 settings.

Genres and Traits of Written Products

Attention to general traits of written products—ideas, organization, voice, word choice, sentence fluency, conventions, and presentation (e.g., Culham, 2003)—contributes to quality outcomes. Traits, however, vary by genre. Punctuation and capitalization conventions for free-verse poetry are quite different from those of a personal narrative. Some traits are more central to one genre than another. Word choice, though important in most genres, is especially critical in genres like haiku poetry, where a few words convey a depth of meaning. Likewise, voice may be central to a first-person narrative, but organization of well-reasoned ideas may be the key feature of an argument.

Units of Study

Well-integrated units of study, centered on specific written formats and genres, can provide opportunities for students to explore both written traits and writing processes in authentic, genre-focused contexts. Genre studies that engage students across writing processes can be a helpful way to conceptualize curriculum in the elementary classroom. Writing in genres and formats that they teach will enable teachers to more deeply understand both the key feature and composition processes central to that genre.

EFFECTIVE WRITING INSTRUCTION

What Is It?

Effective instructional practice fosters students' abilities to become strategic, knowledgeable, and motivated writers (Graham et al., 2007). Effective instruction allows plenty of time for students to engage in learning and practicing writing processes, strategies, and foundational skills. It provides opportunities for students to compose in multiple genres for varied purposes and audiences. Additionally, effective instruction involves active teachers who scaffold and guide students, in part, by providing them with tools to promote independence and self-regulation (Pressley et al., 2007; Troia, Lin, Cohen, & Monroe, 2011).

What Do Teachers Need to Know?

Learners need ongoing opportunities to practice writing processes and tasks. The foundation of writing workshop, as an instructional approach to writing, is an opportunity for extended engagement in written composition.

Scaffolding and modeling proactively across all composition processes and tasks are critical to writing instruction, as students are capable of more when guided. Gone are the days of thinking that if students just *write, write, write* development will happen. Students need to be given explicit knowledge about and purposes for skills and strategies if they are to be applied generatively and purposefully.

Given the challenges of writing, motivation needs to be central to planning and guidance of writing activity. Effective instruction can foster a can-do attitude in students (Graham et al., 2007). In our interviews with children, we have found that final products, in which children take pride and want to share with others, can motivate and help them persevere through difficult tasks.

Social interactions with peers are a critical aspect learning to write. Interactions provide motivation and important feedback to writers. The sharing of ideas—reading one's work to others—needs to occur throughout all stages of writing—not just at the end with publication processes.

CLASSROOM-BASED WRITING ASSESSMENT

What Is It?

Classroom-based writing assessment provides the foundation for gathering data that helps teachers provide feedback critical to students' writing development and to plan appropriate instruction.

What Do Teachers Need to Know?

Along with observation of and conversation/conferences with students, teachers can use interest inventories, checklists, rubrics, and portfolios as assessment tools for writing (see Tompkins, 2011). Assessing students' processes, beliefs, and attitudes is as important as assessment of written products. We feel that this holistic assessment of students is vital to effective instruction and nurturing students' writing development. Some interest inventories are specific to writing (e.g., Kear, Coffman, McKenna, & Ambrosio, 2000; Rhodes, 1993); writing interviews can focus on ascertaining students' beliefs about writing (e.g., Rhodes, 1993). These tools can help teachers identify understandings that may interfere with students' writing development or shed light on ways to motivate and engage students in writing. Portfolios allow for assessment of engagement in writing processes, as well as development over time.

The emergence of written text provides a visible focus for teacher and student attention. Face-to-face conversation or conferencing with students is a critical feature of effective writing assessment and instruction. The goal of conferences, whether long, short, formal or informal, individual or small group, is to provide writers feedback on texts that will help them develop and move beyond what they are already able to accomplish on their own. Feedback to students should include "words to glow and words to grow."

The traits of written products (e.g., Culham, 2003) can provide a common vocabulary for teachers and students to think about when discussing issues of composition. Understanding the traits can help teachers assess and provide feedback to students in multiple ways—not just on conventions, which are easiest to know. More formal rubric assessments, focused on one or more of the six traits (Culham, 2003), are valuable for teachers to understand how to assess and provide specific feedback on students' processes and products.

Self-assessment, while important in all areas of literacy, is critical to the learning complexities of writing processes and genres. Student-friendly versions of checklists and rubrics, as well as portfolio entry slips, can help students' awareness of their strengths and needs in the writing process.

ACTIVITY 4.3
Writing across the Curriculum: An Integrated, Multigenre Project
SUSAN D. MARTIN and SHERRY DISMUKE

Activity Type: Assignment

Materials: List of genre options; books in the topic area.

Duration: 3-4 weeks depending on the degree of in-class collaborative writing and planning desired by the instructor.

Professional Learning Focus:
- Create product in self-selected genre.
- Research about and focus on content-area topic.
- Collaborative writing.
- Collaborative planning and designing assessment rubric for a unit of study.

Standards Links

IRA Professional Standards:
2.2 Implement and evaluate instruction in each of the following areas: concepts of print, phonemic awareness, phonics, vocabulary, comprehension, fluency, critical thinking, motivation, and writing.

Common Core State Standards: Writing Anchor Standards
1. Write arguments to support claims in an analysis of substantive topics or texts, using valid reasoning and relevant and sufficient evidence.

2. Write informative/explanatory texts to examine and convey complex ideas

K–8 Student Learning Focus:
- Learn to write in a variety of genres.
- Research and write in content areas.
- Write collaboratively.

and information clearly and accurately through the effective selection, organization, and analysis of content.

3. Write narratives to develop real or imagined experiences or events using effective technique, well-chosen details, and well-structured event sequences.

5. Develop and strengthen writing as needed by planning, revising, editing, rewriting, or trying a new approach.

8. Gather relevant information from multiple print and digital sources, assess the credibility and accuracy of each source, and integrate the information while avoiding plagarism.

10. Write routinely over extended time frames and shorter time frames for a range of tasks, purposes, and audiences.

Rationale

This is a complex project in which teachers are immersed as readers, writers, presenters, and listeners as they research a topic, represent their knowledge in a self-selected genre, present their products, and listen as classmates share their work completed on the same topic but through another genre. Engagement in these roles provides opportunities for teachers to experience the cognitive, social, and motivational aspects of this assignment firsthand. Additionally, teachers are expected to set learning targets, design planning organizers, and create assessment rubrics for their students. This project thus serves multiple purposes.

We designed this assignment to provide opportunities for teachers to understand the importance of *teaching*, not just expecting writing in content areas. We also want teachers to understand and be able to plan for the guidance and scaffolding of students as they research topics and present their learning through writing. Almost all teachers with whom we have talked lament the lack of curriculum materials for writing. Personally, we feel that writing and accompanying foundational skills are too complex for a set curriculum, especially if writing is situated in content areas. We feel this activity gives teachers an opportunity to understand how to put together an integrated writing unit.

Furthermore, we think it critical to issues of fostering motivation and individual voice both in writing and content areas, for teachers to learn that students can represent their learning in multiple ways—not just the five-paragraph essay or some variation of it. Last, social interactions and collaboration around writing, as well as use of technology, are ways to provide students with motivating and challenging tasks (Boscolo & Gelati, 2007).

Description

1. We go over the assignment guidelines/assessment in class (see Figure 4.6). Although we choose a broad content-area topic for teachers such as the solar system, they are responsible for selecting the specific topic(s) of their piece (e.g., Mars and Venus, asteroids). Teachers also select a partner to work with and a genre from among several choices. A range of genres that have worked well and been fun for teachers include travel brochure, Readers Theater script, advertisement, fractured fairytale, fable, informative booklet, song/rap, simulated journal, business or personal letter, phone text, tall tale, persuasive poster, two-voice poem, newscast script, myth, and recipe. We pass around a sign-up sheet in class. Because of the complexity of this assignment, we have found it saves us all a good deal of grief to provide them with a Writing across the Curriculum Report Form (see Figure 4.7). The form is filled in electronically and when completed, it is shared on our BlackBoard site. We also discuss the rubric assessment for the assignment (see Figure 4.8), as well as provide a checklist self-assessment (see Figure 4.9).

2. For the next class meeting, we focus on genre and genre instruction. Teachers bring in information about their genre that they have gathered from courses, texts, and/or the Internet. They also must locate a mentor text or other genre model of their genre that could be used with K–8 students. Working collaboratively they record information on their report form. In addition, they prepare a digital anchor chart for the genre—with purposes, key features, typical audiences, and other pertinent information listed. These anchor charts can serve as models for what can be developed with students in a classroom. Teachers also begin the processes of thinking through what specific kind of graphic organizer they could use for themselves and with their students to aid in strategic planning processes. For example, a concept web may be useful for a travel brochure, but a Venn diagram will aid in planning for a two-voice poem. The graphic organizer will also be recorded on the form.

3. For the next part of the assignment we focus on content and writing processes. Teachers bring in information that they have gathered around the topic. We bring in children's books on the topic from the local library. Using the graphic organizers that they have developed, teachers begin to gather data for their pieces.

For this assignment you will work with a partner to explore and write in a self-selected genre in a science content area. You will be responsible for sharing information about the genre and your final product with your classmates. You will need to post your products on a BlackBoard site, so that people can view and download your work.

This assignment has multiple purposes. You will engage in learning about integrating writing in content areas. You will also engage in activities that provide opportunities for you to gain understandings of informational, argument/persuasive, and/or narrative text formats and purposes. Furthermore, this assignment is designed to immerse you in practices central to teachers' work, such as planning for instruction, creating a mentor text, and designing an assessment that matches your learning targets. You will need to draw on and integrate your understandings of writing processes, strategies, genres, traits of writing, and instructional practices to complete this project. In essence, you will be designing curriculum consistent with Common Core State Standards for writing and language arts. At the end of our class sharing, you will have specific tools for your toolbox.

We will work on this assignment over a 4-week period. Some of it will be done in class and some will be done for homework.

Preparation for Instruction
1. Learn about the chosen genre.
2. Find mentor texts/models for the genre.
3. Design/select a graphic organizer that would help with finding and organizing information for this particular genre.

Creating a Model for Students
1. Decide on a graphic organizer(s) to use.
2. Gather information about the subject matter using your graphic organizer(s).
3. Collaboratively write about the topic in the chosen genre to create a product/mentor text.

Linking to Learning Targets—*What do you want your students to learn?*
Generate a list of five learning targets for your students. Two of the learning targets need to be specific to the CCSS anchor standards for writing. Learning targets need to include at least one associated with the traits of writing (not conventions) and one associated with conventions/language arts. Additionally, you will need to have one content goal.

(continued)

FIGURE 4.6. Guidelines for writing across the curriculum: Integrated, multigenre project.

Planning Instruction across Stages of Writing—*How will you provide learning opportunities so your students reach the learning targets? How will you guide and support them?*

1. Think through what you will want students to be doing at each stage of the writing process. Complete the process chart using bullets.
2. Think through about how you will guide/support them. For example, teach a focus lesson, conference/monitor, and provide feedback. Complete the process chart using bullets.

Assessing for Your Learning Target—*How will you know that your students have achieved the learning targets that you established for this unit?*

1. You will need to create a rubric assessment linked to your learning targets using the form provided.
2. Numbers will be used.
3. Points will be "weighted" so that important features of the assignment have more value than others.

Presenting in a Professional Learning Community

1. Presentations will be Week 15.
2. You will display your mentor texts and genre anchor chart in class.
3. You will share your piece with your classmates orally.
4. You will turn in the completed Writing Across the Curriculum Report Form.
5. A copy of your genre product will be entered into your writing portfolio.
6. Send an e-copy of your written products to _____ for posting on BlackBoard.

Reflection/Self-Assessment

Complete the reflection and self-assessment checklist individually.

What Else?

You may add anything else to your project that you feel would be relevant to you for future teaching.

Assessment

- Checklist self-assessment.
- Rubric assessment by the instructor.

FIGURE 4.6. *(continued)*

Names _____

Genre/Format _____

Mentor/Model Texts _____

Genre Chart

Purposes/Audiences/Key Features

Graphic Organizer

(continued)

FIGURE 4.7. Writing across the curriculum report form.

Learning Targets

1. Writing (CCSS)	
2. Writing (CCSS)	
3. Six traits	
4. Conventions	
5. Content	

Instruction across the Stages of Writing

	Prewriting	Drafting	Revision	Editing	Publication/Presentation
Students					
Teacher					

FIGURE 4.7. *(continued)*

(continued)

133

Assessment Rubric

FIGURE 4.7. *(continued)*

Once they have gathered the needed information in planning, they move to collaborative drafting, revision, editing, and publication processes and tasks. This final product is not included on the form. It must, however, be created or recorded digitally for sharing on our BlackBoard site.

4. When they have completed their genre piece, teachers shift back into instructional roles. Using the guidelines provided, they must create learning targets for their genre/content lesson, detail what students and teacher will be doing across the writing processes, and construct a rubric assessment that aligns with the objectives. These are all recorded on the project form. We model construction of rubric assessments through thinking aloud how we will assess this project. We deal with issues of weighting certain aspects of the assessment, and expect our teachers to do the same (see the rubric assessment in Figure 4.8).

5. Teachers share their genre charts and products during class time.

6. They then reflect individually and collaboratively on this project and what they learned.

7. Assessment for the project is achieved through the project rubric.

Discussion

This is a complex assignment that we are still developing to maximize learning for teachers. The addition of the project form was something we added to create less confusion. Nevertheless, this is one of those projects that is sometimes too "ambiguous"—especially for preservice teachers. We have had to make it clear that the work of teachers *is* ambiguous and requires problem-solving efforts!

We also found that teachers were invested in their written products and spent far more time than we expected on them. We are still thinking about how to rein in the time spent. We have given projects like this in the past that were done mostly outside of class time, in a jigsawed manner. We wanted to provide class time for collaborative writing and for opportunity to collaborate on the teacher planning as well.

The outcomes were incredible—the presentations were quite engaging! Several pairs used technology for their products, even though we did not require it. Inservice teachers, in particular, seemed to be surprised by the presentations. Feedback included comments like "I never knew that there could be so many ways for students to present their knowledge on one topic."

We feel that this rich project is well worth the class time.

Reference

Boscolo, P., & Gelati, C. (2007). Best practices in promoting motivation in writing. In S. Graham, C. S. MacArthur, & J. Fitzgerald (Eds.), *Best practices in writing instruction,* (pp. 202–221). New York: Guilford Press.

Name _____

	3	2	1
Written piece/ model for students	• Clearly demonstrates key features/format/organization of the genre. • Thorough ideas—uses five to eight content facts or concepts. • One or no convention errors. • Written collaboratively.	• Mostly demonstrates key features/format/organization of the genre. • Mostly thorough ideas—uses four ideas or concepts. • Two to three convention errors. • Written mostly collaboratively.	• Somewhat demonstrates key features/format/organization of the genre. • Thorough ideas—uses three ideas or concepts. • Four to five convention errors. • Written somewhat collaboratively.
Mentor texts	XXXXX	XXXXX	Title/author of model or name of the model.
Genre chart	XXXXX	Thorough listing of key features, purposes, and audiences of this genre.	Somewhat thorough listing of key features, purposes, and audiences of this genre.
Planning organizer	• Very specific to genre. • Supports collection and organization of ideas.	• Somewhat specific to genre. • Some support for collection and organization of ideas.	• Minimally specific to genre. • Minimal support for collection and organization of ideas.

FIGURE 4.8. Rubric for the writing across the curriculum assignment (20 points total).

(continued)

	3	2	1
Learning targets	• Five targets. • Two writing targets are connected to the CCSS. • One appropriate trait target. • One appropriate conventions target. • One appropriate content target is listed.	• Not all five learning targets of the required targets are listed. • The learning targets may be only somewhat appropriate to the genre.	• Not all five learning targets of the required targets are listed. • The learning targets may be only minimally appropriate to the genre.
Instruction across writing stages	• Thorough/clear understandings of what students will do. • Clear noting of teacher-directed focus lessons, conferences, or providing feedback, etc.	• Somewhat thorough/clear understandings of what students will do. • Some noting of teacher-directed focus lessons, conferences, providing feedback, etc.	• Minimal understandings of what students will do. • Little or no noting of teacher-directed focus lesson, conferences, providing feedback, etc.
Assessment rubric	• Appropriate breakdown, clearly linked to learning targets. • Numbers are used. • Points are weighted.	• Appropriate breakdown, somewhat linked to learning targets. • Numbers are used. • Points are weighted.	• Appropriate breakdown, minimally linked to learning targets. • Numbers are used. • Points are not weighted.
Checklist and reflection	XXXXX	• Checklist is completed. • Reflection is thoughtful and thorough.	• Checklist is completed. • Reflection is somewhat thoughtful and thorough.

FIGURE 4.8. *(continued)*

_____ Written piece (a mentor text for students)

    _____ Key features and format of the genre are evident.

    _____ Content includes five to eight concepts or facts about the chosen topic(s).

    _____ Piece was cowritten with team members.

    _____ We have edited and have no convention errors.

_____ Title/author of mentor text is listed.

_____ Genre chart

    _____ Key points of genre.

    _____ Purposes of this genre.

_____ Planning organizer

    _____ Helps students gather information/develop ideas.

    _____ Helps students organize information.

_____ Learning targets

    _____ One writing target from CCSS anchor standards.

    _____ One traits target.

    _____ One convention learning target.

    _____ Content learning target.

_____ Instruction across the writing stages

    _____ Clear bulleted notation of what students will do at each stage.

    _____ Clear bulleted notation of focus lesson, conferencing, feedback, etc.

_____ Assessment rubric

    _____ Rubric is clearly linked to learning targets.

    _____ I have worked on weighting categories.

    _____ Expectations for students are clear/includes numeric information.

Reflection: Please write a one- to two-page typed self-reflection addressing the following prompts:

1. What did you learn about planning writing integrated with a content area?
2. How did writing in the content area help develop/deepen your content knowledge?
3. What did you learn about writing collaboratively?
4. What did you experience that you will use in your classroom? Why?

FIGURE 4.9. Checklist self-assessment for writing across the curriculum.

CHAPTER 5

Creating Learning Environments
That Support Literacy Learning

The creation of supportive learning environments is crucial to the development of children's abilities to read and write. A literate environment provides children the opportunity to use, appreciate, and create meaningful acts of literacy both in the classroom and beyond (International Reading Association, 2010). Effective learning environments support individual development within the social contexts of a community of literacy learners. Establishing a literate learning environment that meets the needs of diverse learners is complex work. Teachers must synthesize multiple factors into a cohesive whole that shifts over time and with changing contexts. In this chapter we explore three interconnected aspects of the literate learning environment: the physical learning environment, the social learning environment, and structures and routines that support literacy learning.

PHYSICAL ASPECTS OF THE LITERATE
LEARNING ENVIRONMENT

What Is It?

The arrangement of classroom space and availability of literacy materials comprise the physical aspect of an environment designed to support literacy learning. Ideally, the environment is print rich (Dowhower &

Beagle, 1998), with word walls, class-constructed charts and schedules, children's work visible on the walls and shelves, and classroom libraries filled with books. Writing supplies and tools, including computers, are easily accessible. Desks, chairs, and tables are organized to promote students' interaction with one another around text, as well as teachers' free movement throughout the classroom to support student learning.

What Do Teachers Need to Know?

Physical Environment

Planning for the physical layout of the classroom typically occurs before the school year begins. Teachers turn a conglomeration of furniture and bare walls, within a given floor space, into a teaching and learning environment. Teacher and students will spend several hours together each school day in this space. Thoughtful consideration of how to best organize it for learning is important.

Several factors need to be taken into account for literacy learning, including instructional activities and available materials. Teachers may need to ask themselves questions such as "Do I need a space for all students to sit on the floor in a group when we read and write together as a class?" "Will I need a carpet?" "Where can I place big chart paper?" "Where can I put tables for small-group instruction and interaction?" and "Do I have a bank of computers in the classroom?"

Additionally, needs and interests of students must be considered. Co-construction of charts and bulletin board displays, and joint decision making over displays of student work is an acknowledgment of the fact that the classroom is a place for all, not just the teacher.

In our experiences, we have seen class bulletin boards where each student has a space to post work that he or she would like viewed. We have also seen anchor charts in which students have not only shared in the creation and recording of concepts, but also created the visuals to support these concepts. We have noticed student-made monthly class calendars, rather than commercially produced versions.

The way that a classroom is organized affects the social interactions of the children, as well as they way they interact with print. For example, materials organized so that children can easily access them, such as a center with various types of writing materials, support children's independent writing development. An effective learning environment will have comfortable and inviting places for children to read to themselves or with a buddy. Sofas, beanbag chairs, and even bathtubs serve these functions in classrooms. Having some workspaces available free of visual distraction helps children who have difficulty staying focused. Such spaces can be created with inexpensive folding screens or even three-sided poster board.

Literacy Materials

Perhaps the most enduring symbol of classroom environments in our society is the presence of literacy materials—books, pencils, and paper. Today, of course, teachers may use smartboards instead of chalkboards; children may be reading on e-readers and composing on computers. No matter what the form, literacy materials are central to learning and teaching in our schools.

Availability of a wide range of literacy materials in the classroom is critical to literacy learning. For reading, this may range from picture books to comic books, to charts of poems and songs, and to comprehensive literacy programs, to reading on the Internet. Books that have been written by students in the class—either during a shared writing activity or independently—are often popular choices. Tangible evidence of the value placed on literacy in many languages is shown by the presence of books and other materials written in the students' home languages. Pencils, colored markers, and digital composition tools are each important as writing tools. Variety and opportunities for choice are important, as the texts that students read, as well as those they compose, affect literacy learning and motivation. For some students, discovering and reading graphic novels may well be the door to reading fluency and enjoyment. Likewise, using computers to integrate visual features with written text may captivate a reluctant writer.

Careful organization of the classroom library enables students to self-select appropriate and interesting texts—a key to developing independence in reading. Although organizing classroom books by level can be instructionally helpful to teachers and students, books organized in other ways—by genre, author, or topic, for example—help students learn to choose books that they love. In some classrooms, children have book boxes on their tables, or book bags on the back of their chairs that are filled with books that are at their appropriate reading level. They read these books during a "just right" reading time, and books chosen on the basis of interest at a second independent reading time. The second independent reading time supports the social aspects of literacy, as children read and discuss books with their friends, and is often highly motivating. Some teachers buy several copies of popular books to support this practice.

Teachers can also draw on this variety of materials to plan effective literacy instruction. Understandings of educational and literacy purposes for a range of materials, particularly the components of comprehensive reading programs, can be coupled with knowledge of learners to provide the foundations for thoughtful instructional decision making and modification of materials in response to students' needs or interests.

ACTIVITY 5.1
Evaluating the Quality of Digital Books
ELIZABETH DOBLER

Activity Type: In-class activity.

Materials: E-reader device (i.e., iPad, Nook, Kindle, smartphone, laptop); access to the Internet to download free books.

Duration: Two 60-minute sessions.

Professional Learning Focus:
- Identify e-reader devices and sources for accessing free and for-purchase digital books.
- Become familiar with the various ways digital books are published, including independent publishers, e-publishers, and traditional publishers.
- Identify elements of high-quality digital books.
- Evaluate the quality of free and for-purchase digital books using quantitative and qualitative criteria.

Standards Links

IRA Professional Standards:
2.2 Incorporate traditional print, digital, and online resources as instructional tools to enhance student learning.

2.3 Build an accessible, multilevel, and diverse classroom library that contains traditional print, digital, and online classroom materials.

6.2 Promote student appreciation of the value of reading traditional print, digital, and online resources in and out of school.

Common Core State Standards: Reading Anchor Standards
7. Integrate and evaluate content presented in diverse formats and media, including visually and quantitatively, as well as in words.

10. Read and comprehend complex literary and informational texts independently and proficiently.

K–8 Student Learning Focus:
Students will be presented with quality literature in digital format for use during independent reading, center time, or whole-class shared reading.

Rationale

The idea for this activity stems from a connection I formed between two coinciding events. After several years of teaching language arts and reading methods, I eagerly embraced the opportunity to teach children's literature to elementary education teachers. Around this same time, members of our elementary education faculty each received an iPad. Although technology and literacy is an area of research and interest for me, I was a bit unsure of how I would use the iPad, until I discovered all of the free children's books available through the app store and the iBookstore. I soon learned of the free digital books also available for the Kindle, the Nook, smartphones, and laptops. As I began exploring these resources, I noticed the varying levels of quality of digital books available for children. Many digital books for children are credible works of literature and may include interactive illustrations, a read-aloud feature, a highlight of key words, or an internal dictionary. Yet, my eyes soon opened to issues of poor quality in some digital books, such as basic spelling, grammar, and punctuation errors, and inappropriate language and topics. The ease of sharing books through mobile devices has also prompted an ease of publishing and a loosening of the publication standards held for traditional print books.

I wanted to help the teachers in my children's literature course become aware of the many free children's digital books available for mobile devices, along with providing a tool, the Digital Book Evaluation Rubric (see Figure 5.1) to help them determine quality when selecting digital books to use with the children in their future classrooms. My colleague Daniel Donahoo and I developed the Digital Book Evaluation Rubric to assess the quality of children's digital books on any platform.

Description

Session 1

In the first session I introduce the Digital Book Evaluation Rubric and model its use with a high- and a low-quality digital book. I use *Axel the Truck* by J. D. Riley as a high-quality anchor book and *The Case of the Missing Banana* by Matthew Ryan as a low-quality anchor book. Both are available in the iBookstore. If an iPad or iPhone are not available, browse Amazon or Barnes and Noble for free children's books to be downloaded to a Kindle, Nook, or other e-reader. In the first session it is necessary for all teachers to view the same two digital books.

	Robust Quality	Adequate Quality	Limited or Weak Quality
Reading Options	Readers can choose options for reading, listening, viewing, or interacting with the text.	A limited number of reading options are presented, but the reader has no choice (i.e., audio and text).	Reader has no choice of options beyond reading the text and viewing the illustrations.
	Children can adapt the way this digital book is read, depending on their reading needs and interests. If a choice cannot be made, at least several options are available (read, view, listen).	*Children can read and listen to this digital book but cannot choose between the two.*	*Children only have the option of reading this digital book.*
User Friendliness (if special features are available)	Various prompts are provided, such as arrows or sounds, for accessing special features (i.e., turning pages, moving objects). Guides the reader towards interaction with the text.	A limited number of prompts are provided for accessing special features.	No prompts are provided for accessing special features. The reader must dig to discover the features.
	Children can easily understand how to access all of the bells and whistles available in this digital book.	*Children can find the special features of this digital book with some exploring.*	*Children have to search to find the special features of this digital book and even then an adult may not find them.*

(continued)

FIGURE 5.1. Digital book evaluation rubric. Created by Elizabeth Dobler and Daniel Donahoo.

	Robust Quality	Adequate Quality	Limited or Weak Quality
Appropriateness	The text (vocabulary and ideas) and illustrations are appropriate for the age level of the intended audience. *This is an appropriate digital book that a teacher or parent could share with children.*	One or two questionable elements are present in the words and/or illustrations. *A teacher or parent should provide an explanation prior to sharing this book with children.*	The topic, language, and/or illustrations are not appropriate for the age level of the intended audience. *A teacher or parent should give serious consideration before sharing this book as some content is inappropriate for certain age levels.*
Polished Appearance	The text has been carefully edited for spelling, grammar, and punctuation. No errors are present. The illustrations are placed near the appropriate text. *This digital book can be recommended to children with an assurance of high quality.*	One or two small editing errors are present in the entire digital book, and these do not detract from the text. Illustrations are placed close to the appropriate text. *A miniscule number of editing errors are found in this book, but the value of the digital book provides a balance.*	Numerous spelling, grammar, and punctuation errors are present in the text. Illustrations are repeatedly not placed near the text. *The many editing errors in this digital book provide an inappropriate model for children.*

FIGURE 5.1. *[continued]*

1. I begin the activity by sharing one higher-quality and one lower-quality free digital book with the teachers. For this first step, the two suggested books may be substituted with two other digital books of similar quality. We first discuss the general quality of the two anchor books and I ask teachers what they notice after reading each book as a class. Through discussion, we make some comparisons between the digital books. I encourage the teachers to comment on both the literary quality and the digital features of the books.

2. I introduce the Digital Book Evaluation Rubric by describing the elements of the rubric, discussing terms, and giving specific examples from the high-quality anchor book to help explain ideas. When possible, I link back to the points teachers brought up in the previous discussion. Together we assess the high-quality book.

3. Teachers then work in pairs or small groups and use the Digital Book Evaluation Rubric to evaluate the low-quality anchor book. I monitor discussions and provide further explanations as needed. After all groups finish, I invite the teachers to share their impressions and concerns about the lower-quality digital anchor book and make comparisons to features of the higher-quality digital book.

Session 2

1. Teachers should have previously located and downloaded two to three free digital books appropriate for children onto their computers or other devices. This avoids Internet issues from interfering with the activity. Teachers can work alone, in pairs, or in small groups, and only one device would be needed for each combination. I provide teachers with blank copies of the Digital Book Evaluation Rubric. We review the main categories of the rubric, then have teachers evaluate the quality of their digital books.

2. Upon completion of the evaluation tool with two or three books, I invite teachers to share with the entire class notable strong or weak elements of a specific digital book or observations about digital books in general.

3. We discuss how the Digital Book Evaluation Rubric helps a teacher determine the quality of digital books for children and why this process is important. I remind teachers that once they become familiar with the elements of the Digital Book Evaluation Rubric and the wide range of digital children's literature available, an intuitive sense of quality will develop, and careful evaluation using the Digital Book Evaluation Rubric may no longer be necessary.

Discussion

As with any time one teaches with technology, it is important to have a backup plan. The teacher should find two to three digital books, in addition to the anchor books listed above. If Internet access during Session 2 becomes an issue, then share the additional books with the class as a whole, and have teachers evaluate the books individually or in small groups; however, the best experience for teachers is to locate and choose the digital books themselves, as they would do in their own future classroom.

Anecdotal evidence from teachers leads me to believe that many were not aware of the free digital books available for children and had not considered issues with quality and the impact of little or no formal publication standards for digital books. In the concluding discussion during my class session, teachers revealed many of their own personal feelings about digital books, both pros and cons. Some lamented the loss of the traditional book, while others expressed excitement for the accessibility of digital books on mobile devices. This discussion itself is of value, as we all are grappling with the changing nature of text. Our discussion led the group as a whole to conclude that both digital and print books can and do coexist, and we, as teachers, must help students learn how to gain knowledge and entertainment from each.

ACTIVITY 5.2
Creating a Scene with Text Sets
MAGGIE CHASE and EUN HYE SON

Activity Type: Assignment.

Materials: Models of texts around a topic; guidelines.

Duration: 3–4 weeks in-class explanation and instruction, 3–4 weeks outside-of-class preparation, 1–1.5 hours in-class presentations.

Professional Learning Focus:
- Use multiple sources of information to guide instructional planning to improve reading achievement of all students.
- Incorporate traditional print, digital, and online resources as instructional tools to enhance student learning.
- Build an accessible, multilevel, and diverse classroom library that contains traditional print, digital, and online classroom materials.

Standards Links

IRA Professional Standards:
1.1 Explain the research and theory about effective leaning environments that support individual motivation to read and write (e.g., choice, challenge, interests, and access to traditional print, digital, and online resources).

2.3 Guided by evidence-based rationale, select and use quality traditional print, digital, and online resources.

5.1 Design the physical environment to optimize students' use of traditional print, digital, and online resources in reading and writing instruction.

Common Core State Standards:
Reading Anchor Standards
7. Integrate and evaluate content presented in diverse media and formats, including visually and quantitatively, as well as in words.

K–8 Student Learning Focus: Read
and comprehend a variety of resources
on a single topic or issue.

Rationale

There are teachers we know in our local school district who could easily be dubbed
the "book whisperers of Boise" (Miller, 2009) because of the emphasis, joy, and
near reverence they give books in their classrooms. When you walk into their
classrooms, your eyes are immediately drawn to the attractive displays they have
set up in their rooms to feature great books. Nearly always, though, the backdrops
are there, but the table or shelves are empty because the students have already
grabbed the latest "must reads," or they've taken the books on a particular topic
to their desks to explore in more depth. We want our preservice teachers to leave
our children's literature courses with the same passion for getting children excited
about reading, while giving a nod to the importance of aesthetics.

For a number of years, we have asked the teachers in our children's literature
courses to develop a text set on a particular theme, topic, or issue of their choosing. We feel it is important for them to consider the vast array of engaging, rich
resources now available in book and digital formats for use in the classroom, while
taking into consideration the range of reading skills and interests inherent in the
makeup of a typical elementary class. When using review sources, various data-
bases, bibliographies prepared by professionals, and their own developing senses
of determining what is appropriate for specific grade levels, teachers build relevant

FIGURE 5.2. An aesthetically pleasing display.

text sets around self-selected topics or themes. Text sets must include a mix of nonfiction/informational, poetry, and fiction, including picture books and chapter books. Themes have been wide ranging and included topics such as friendship, change over time, world religions, and bullying. A variation we do on this assignment involves having groups of teachers research aspects of a particular kind of diversity, such as Arab or Asian Americans.

We stress the importance of aesthetics and inviting children into the world created by the text set theme or topic. By this, we mean that it's not enough to just gather resources, but one must also consider the target audience and the aesthetic appeal of an alluring display. Most children cannot resist the siren call of a text set on an enticing topic, when displayed beautifully with the addition of a few props, an attractive backdrop, and activities that lure them into engaging with the materials (see Figure 5.2).

We end this assignment with a book fair, asking teachers to invite any and all children they know to come for the presentations. We feel this assignment prepares teachers to successfully demonstrate ways for teachers to access and engage with the resources they have collected.

Description

First In-Class Day

1. We ask teachers to bring to class three to five nonfiction books on the same topic. This alone can be a difficult task for some teachers because it requires them to narrow down the myriad choices available in the children's section of a typical public library. As the instructors, we do the same, bringing books that have good examples of text features such as a table of contents, an index, and illustrations/photos with captions. We also bring in great nonfiction books that may not have any of these features, but are still valuable resources on a topic, such as the journal-like book about grizzly bears called *Searching for Grizzlies* by Ron Hirschi.

2. During class, we hand out a Checklist for Evaluating Nonfiction Trade Books (see Figure 5.3) to the teachers and go over all the components to take into consideration when selecting nonfiction resources for a unit of study (see Figure 5.4). As we share our model texts, we ask them to look for these same features in the books they have brought. We ask them to determine if their books offer a range of reading levels and to analyze whether each offers enough text features to support a student's use of the book for learning more about the topic. Taking the perspective of a particular age child when analyzing a book's usefulness can be difficult for teachers, but their heightened awareness of the many features to consider aids in developing this perspective.

3. We also brainstorm with the teachers a long list of topics and themes. Teachers then sign up for one to pursue and work outside of class for 3–4 weeks on this assignment.

Author: _____

Title: _____

Theme/topic: _____ Target age/grade level: _____

Publisher and copyright date: _____

If part of a series, what is that series? _____

3 = meets all or most criteria   2 = meets some criteria   1 = meets few criteria
(Check off individual criteria that are present in the book.)

Accuracy

_____ Information about author expertise/experience given.

_____ Information about photo credits given.

_____ References cited throughout text or bibliography provided.

_____ Information is current and accurate.

Organization and Layout (Circle all that are present in book.)

Table of contents	Summaries	Page numbers	Illustrations
Index	Glossary	Charts/diagrams	Graphs
Timeline	Maps	Chapter and section headings	

What is the predominant pattern (structure) of organization (see next page)? _____

_____

_____

_____

Is the visual layout uncluttered and appealing? _____

_____

_____

Are there captions for the visual elements? _____

_____

_____

(continued)

FIGURE 5.3. Checklist and criteria for evaluating nonfiction trade books. Adapted from Farris, Fuhler, and Walther (2004). Copyright by Pamela J. Farris. Adapted by permission.

Cohesion of Ideas

____ Major ideas are logically connected throughout the text.

____ Sentence-level ideas are logically connected to each other (i.e., does not require reader to make a lot of inferences).

____ Accounts for reader's probable background knowledge.

____ Appropriate conceptual load for target age.

____ Avoids irrelevant details.

____ Provides good model of expository writing.

Specialized Vocabulary

____ Defined as it is introduced.

____ Defined in pictures, captions, labels, or clarified visually.

____ Defined in glossary.

____ In bold lettering.

Reader Interest

____ Has aesthetic appeal.

____ Has colorful illustrations or photos.

____ Uses appropriate format (i.e., page and print size).

____ Has positive role models with respect to gender and ethnicity.

____ Activities and/or experiments within text are motivating and age appropriate, if present.

Overall

Is there something unique, riveting, inspiring, or engaging about this particular text? If so, describe that feature here: _____

_____

_____

_____

_____

_____

_____

_____

FIGURE 5.3. *(continued)*

The following criteria should be taken into account when selecting and evaluating nonfiction books.

- Is the information accurate and up to date with current research data (with no significant omissions)?
- Is the content organized in a logical sequence to lead the reader from the familiar to the new?
- Is the text clear and interesting, containing appropriate vocabulary for elementary children?
- Is there a glossary with concise definitions of specialized terminology or are terms explained clearly in text?
- Does the author clearly distinguish among fact, theory, and opinion?
- Are both text and illustrations free from stereotypes?
- Is there evidence of careful research, such as bibliography, references, and endnotes?
- Are appropriate reference aids included, such as headings, index, and recommended additional readings?
- Is the visual format uncluttered and appealing?
- Are there full-color visual aids, such as photographs, illustrations, maps, charts, graphs, diagrams, original documents, and reproductions of artwork?
- Are the visuals and their captions accurate, and do they clarify and extend the text?

Typical Nonfiction Text Structures/Organization:

- **Description:** The author gives the characteristics of the topic (e.g., *Spiders* by Gail Gibbons).
- **Sequence:** The author lists items in order, usually chronologically or numerically (e.g., *How to Make a Chemical Volcano and Other Mysterious Experiments* by Alan Kramer).
- **Comparison:** The author juxtaposes two or more entities and lists their similarities and differences (e.g., *The War on Terrorism: Opposing Viewpoints* edited by Karen F. Balkin and *Crocodiles and Alligators* by Seymour Simon).
- **Cause and Effect:** The author states an action and then shows the effect, or result, of this action (e.g., *Blizzard: The Storm That Changed America* by Jim Murphy).
- **Problem and Solution** (also referred to as question and answer): The author states a problem and its solution or solutions (e.g., *Understanding the Holy Land: Answering Questions about the Israeli–Palestinian Conflict* by Mitch Frank).

FIGURE 5.4. Criteria for evaluating nonfiction. Based on Lynch-Brown (2007).

Second In-Class Day

At least 2 weeks prior to the book fair, we share photographs of displays—some good, some poorly executed—and develop criteria with the teachers for what makes an engaging, inviting display of books. We also ask the teachers to invite any children they know (usually their own, relatives, or neighbors) to come to the fair.

Third In-Class Day

On the day the project is due, teachers bring all materials and set up their exhibits. It works best if you can arrange to use a room with tables. If a class meets several times per week for shorter duration, you can schedule teacher presentations over more than one class meeting. Half the teachers stand at their displays while the other half browse (see Figures 5.5 and 5.6). Everyone who is browsing the displays, even the children, complete Feedback Sheets (see Figure 5.7).

Discussion

There are many things that preservice teachers can learn from creating text sets. First, this helps them to realize that there are good-quality curricular resources available other than textbooks. This assignment opens their eyes to different options, alternatives, and ideas for presenting, reinforcing, and explicating a topic

FIGURE 5.5. Child interacting with the text set via an activity.

FIGURE 5.6. Preservice teacher interacting with children who visit her display.

or theme. Using the text sets, they can delve deeply into a topic or theme and start to explore a variety of perspectives on the topic. Creating a text set also gives them a hands-on experience of locating, identifying, and evaluating materials, including trade books and digital materials (e.g., video clips, e-books, websites). Examining and analyzing the materials, they consider readability, intertextual connections across texts, text complexity, and purposes that the books can serve to meet students' goals, interests, and needs.

Creating text sets also enables preservice teachers to switch roles between readers and teachers. In teaching children's literature classes, we often witness preservice teachers taking a teacher-centered approach to seeing books (i.e., how to use books in the classroom), overlooking the possibility that many books offer the chance to explore a topic for pure enjoyment. A focus on efferent reading only (Rosenblatt, 1978) may hinder aesthetic responses and the opportunity to ignite a passion in children for a particular topic. We believe this text set assignment reminds preservice teachers to simply enjoy the books without a teacher's hat, and balance the two perspectives as a reader and teacher when they select books. Furthermore, by setting up the display and interacting with an audience, especially with children, teachers experience and learn how important an aesthetically pleasing and literature-rich environment is in attracting students to books and motivating them to read.

We've noticed many will change or refine their topics once they begin their search for materials appropriate for the targeted age/grade level. They discover their topic is too broad or that the materials available for a particular grade level are not extensive or appealing. At this point in the semester, the teachers have

	Absolutely	Somewhat	Really???
Name of Evaluator: _____			
Topic: _____			
Presenter: _____			
The theme or topic of the set of books is obvious.			
The display is attractively arranged.			
The display has something other than the books to draw the reader in.			
The activity(s) is directly related to the topic or theme.			
The presenter could talk about the books in the collection.			

Comments/Suggestions: _____

_____

_____

_____

_____

_____

_____

_____

_____

_____

_____

_____

_____

_____

FIGURE 5.7. Presenter feedback form.

already learned how to write an annotated bibliography and have explored characteristics of quality picture books, fiction, and poetry; this assignment pushes them to consider the literary dimensions of a topic or theme by considering how a poet or the author of a fictional account might handle a particular subject.

By setting up the display and interacting with an audience, especially with children, teachers experience and learn how important an aesthetically pleasing and literature-rich environment is in attracting students to books and motivating them to read. The excitement and energy children bring to the event is what makes all our students' work worthwhile. They immediately see a purpose for why we have stressed aesthetics and engagement; it's an important but hard lesson when the teachers look on while children flock to some displays, while avoiding others. The children ask good questions as they browse and they love completing the evaluation forms. By inviting children to the event, teachers gain motivation, an authentic audience, and a purpose. The reflections we ask the teachers to write after the event reveal the important lessons they've learned from this activity, but by far the most prevalent comment we receive is having children attend provides the final, most important piece of the scene.

References

Farris, P., Fuhler, C., & Walther, M. (2004). *Teaching reading: A balanced approach for today's classroom.* Boston: McGraw-Hill.

Lynch-Brown, C. (2007). *Essentials of young adult literature.* Upper Saddle River, NJ: Pearson Education.

Miller, D. (2009). *The book whisperer: Awakening the inner reader in every child.* San Francisco: Jossey-Bass.

Rosenblatt, L. M. (1978). *The reader, the text, the poem: The transactional theory of the literary work.* Carbondale: Southern Illinois University Press.

SOCIAL AND AFFECTIVE ASPECTS OF THE LITERATE LEARNING ENVIRONMENT

What Is It?

Although reading and writing are often conceptualized as solitary activities, they are actually essentially communicative, social activities. Writing exists to be read. Readers develop deeper understandings when they discuss their interpretations of text. Social engagement around literacy provides important opportunities to learn with others and is highly motivating for many students.

What Do Teachers Need to Know?

Effective learning environments for literacy learning are language rich, as well as print rich. The nature of social interactions can provide support for literacy learners (International Reading Association, 2010). However, establishing social interactions that promote rich, supportive interactions is not an easy task. Creating a classroom community with standards for interaction that support literacy learning requires thoughtful attention to teacher–student and student–student interactions, as well as the patterns of interaction during whole-class and small-group engagement in a learning focus. Social interactions in these various contexts have the capacity to enhance or inhibit learning for each student.

Teacher–Student Interactions

Knowledge of learners and subject matter, and positive teacher dispositions such as high expectations for all students, provide the foundation for interactions with individual students that enhance literacy learning. Teachers' interactions with students can scaffold and guide reading and writing. Conversations provide feedback that promotes a positive sense of self or pushes students to greater abilities. In one observed writing conference, we heard a third-grade student express new awareness about the uniqueness of his biliterate writing abilities, after his teacher provided him such feedback. Teachers' words and interactions can build an environment of trust and risk taking. In our classroom observations, we have noted that often the exact words of teachers come back through their students. For instance, one third-grade urban teacher used the word *challenge* frequently with her students during writing workshop—in ways that suggested she knew they could achieve these challenges. Not surprisingly, students talked about how they liked undertaking challenges in their reading and writing.

Student–Student Interactions

Social activity with peers increases student engagement and motivation and has the potential to increase student learning. As Vygotsky (1978) noted, learning first happens as a result of interactions among people and then is later individually internalized. In classroom activity among 25–30 children, the "knowledgeable other" is often a peer. For example, pairing two readers at approximately the same level in a "buddy reading" situation may provide an optimal learning environment as the two readers operate together in the zone of proximal development to solve learning challenges. Student conversations of reading content may open up new perspectives for each of them. When students know that they are writing for a valued audience such as their peers, for example, motivation to write is higher: students care about their writing, and the writing tends to be of higher quality. Student interactions and collaborations at the computer screen are central to tenets of new literacies (Leu, 2002).

Small-Group and Whole-Class Interactions

Social interactions that promote deep engagement in literacy activities depend on a psychologically safe environment. Teachers must teach children how to treat one another with kindness and support, and set clear, firm classroom expectations for positive interactions. Building a sense of diverse and inclusive community can be established through teacher guidance in whole-class literacy activities, such as author's chair/writers' share or group presentations. The words teachers' model, as well as explicit expectations for interaction in such situations, can set the tone for more independent student–student interactions.

We have noted a tendency for novice teachers to plow through a lesson plan with the typical teacher–student–teacher–student (IRE) conversational interaction. In effective large-group settings, group interactions and engagement through strategies such as choral responses, authentic questioning, or turn-to-an-elbow partner are regular instructional features.

ACTIVITY 5.3
Setting the Foundations
for a Community of Writers and Learners
SUSAN D. MARTIN

Activity Type: In-class, part of one or two sessions.

Materials: Yarn ball; 3" × 5" cards.

Duration: 1.5 hours depending on size of group.

Standards Links

IRA Professional Standards:
5.2 Model and teach students routines for establishing and maintaining positive social environments.

Professional Learning Focus:
- Experience explicit attention to setting standards at the beginning of the school year.
- Experience student involvement in setting standards.
- Develop an understanding of the teacher's role in establishing a diverse, inclusive, and respectful learning environment.
- Reflect on own experiences with and attitudes toward writing.

K–8 Student Learning Focus:
- Engagement in a community of learners.
- Develop respect and appreciation for classmates and teacher.
- Reflect on own experiences with and attitudes toward writing.

Common Core State Standards: N/A.

Rationale

I explicitly attend to and model practices at the beginning of each course that set norms and standards for social interactions that foster a learning community. In my writing courses, however, this is imperative, as teachers are very much pushed out of their comfort zones and are expected to share personal writings with one another. Some teachers are terrified about sharing.

In this course, teachers are involved in a number of roles, and thus will engage in a variety of overlapping communities as learners, writers, and teachers. They will also engage with one another a good deal of the time either one-on-one or in small groups. Setting the standards explicitly in the whole-class setting establishes the foundation for the type of interactions that are expected in all the social configurations.

Description

Day 1 of Class

1. Introductions, with a slight twist, begin this course. I first introduce myself as a teacher and a writer. I share several ways that I write in my life–especially e-mail. Teachers then freewrite to prompts that ask them to reflect on their senses of self as a writer and their histories with writing. When the freewrites

are completed, they are asked to share something about themselves as writers or something to do with their writing history.

2. We move our chairs into a large circle/oval, as each teacher introduces him- or herself into the community and shares. I begin, and I make sure that I share a negative experience with writing, so they will feel free to respond honestly about their experiences. I use a ball of yarn to facilitate this sharing. Once a person has shared, he or she tosses the ball across the circle to another person, but he or she holds on to the yarn. What occurs is the development of a yarn web (I like to use multicolored yarn) that provides a visual and tactile metaphor for the connectedness of our group. We debrief everyone's comments (What did you notice? Any commonalities?). Some talk about what a relief it was to hear that other teachers also have problems with writing. Typically there will be a wide range of attitudes toward writing and self as a writer. This provides an opportunity for me to mention that their future classrooms will also have such diversity. We also debrief the web metaphor, and I share how I used this activity to begin the school year in my elementary classroom. I am sure to point out that this is only a foundational activity that our community will continue to develop over the semester.

3. After the teachers are all back at their seats I have them introduce themselves to their tablemates and give them some time to talk about what social norms we need to have in place to feel comfortable discussing readings and sharing their writing with others. We debrief as a whole class and I record their statements.

Day 2 of Class

1. At our second meeting, I present our course norms and standards. I have categorized what they have put forward around these four principles (Gathercoal, 2004):

- We all belong: inclusive classroom community.
- We all have relevant perspectives: respecting diversity within the community.
- We all want to learn and grow: discussion and activity are purposeful, collaborative, and social.
- Engagement in writing/learning-to-write activity: Creating safe environments for writing.

A sample of a completed norms list can be found in Figure 5.8. I typically will have added in a few bulleted items of my own. I ask the teachers if they can live with these standards and/or if anything is missing. We all agree to abide by them and I post them on our class website.

2. When this is done, I ask the teachers to set a social participation goal for the course. I pass out index cards for them to record at least one participation

goal. I typically allot several points in the course for participation, since the course is very interactive. I tell the teachers that they will self-assess for one-quarter of those points (e.g., 5 out of 20) based on their social goal. I usually provide a couple of ideas for them. For example, speak out more—if you are very quiet in class; be an active listener to classmates—if you tend to dominate conversations, and complete all reading in advance of class discussions so that rich conversations that push everyone's thinking can occur.

Last Day of Class

1. I discuss and model closure to the school year during the last class. This is usually a fun class in which we engage in bookmaking. For our last activity, we sit in a circle and pass the yarn ball again. This time it simply goes around the circle from one teacher to the next. When they share this time, they briefly discuss one thing they have learned about themselves as a writer and/or one idea about writing or writing instruction that they will take with them into their practices. When all have shared, I also share what I am taking away from our time together. I then go around the circle with a scissors and cut the yarn so that each of them will be able to take away a piece of the yarn as a visual reminder that, although our community is breaking up, they are taking with them many new ideas from our experiences together and, in some cases, new friends.

2. I pass the goal cards back to the teachers and they self-assess. They must give themselves a score and write a sentence or two that explains their self-assessment.

Discussion

This activity has really worked well for the teachers and me. After a master's-level first weekend class, one of the teachers wrote in a reflection: "I can't believe how we really did create a sense of community in such a short time." It does take up a good chunk of time, but just as in elementary classrooms, that upfront time spent establishing social norms is time well spent. I also think the activity provides important modeling for students, both at the beginning and end of the semester.

Self-assessment is important in learning, especially, I think, in writing, so this activity fits in well with my goals. Students seem to value this opportunity to self-assess part of their course grade. Sometimes they are much harder on themselves than I would be! A few students may have a hard time understanding what a social participation goal is, even with the models. They can get stuck on setting academic goals instead.

To support one another's learning and writing, we agree to these social norms in our class:

We all belong: inclusive classroom community.
- Show respect to others.
- Get to know people in your group and class—including on a personal level.
- Let others know about you.

We all have relevant perspectives: respecting diversity within the community.
- Encourage others to participate and share their ideas. Be open-minded and curious about others' ideas, opinions, and perspectives—ask questions.
- Be willing to take risks. Share your ideas and perspectives with others.
- Give others the benefit of the doubt—ask for clarification.
- We will not always agree, but keep discussions positive and issues focused.
- Be respectful of others' feelings.

We all want to learn and grow: discussion and activity are purposeful, collaborative, and social.
- Be an active and attentive listener to others—be in the moment.
- Be aware of nonverbal communication that can shut people down or hurt their feelings.
- Have a high level of expectation for yourself and others.
- Contribute your share to discussions and collaborative activities.
- Be proactive in your own learning—be willing to contribute, take risks, and move out of your comfort zone.
- Be prepared for class discussion and activity by doing the readings and assignments.

Engagement in writing/learning-to-write activity: creating safe environments for writing.
- Respect the work and learning of others.
- Provide constructive feedback positively and gently.
- Be open to feedback/suggestions on your writing—invite feedback from others.
- What is written or shared in class stays personal.

FIGURE 5.8. Sample class norms and standards.

ACTIVITY STRUCTURES AND ROUTINES
IN LITERACY LEARNING ENVIRONMENTS

What Is It?

Structures and routines refer to the ways in which teaching and learning activities are socially, physically, and temporally organized in the classroom. Effective literacy instruction engages children in a variety of social settings including teacher-led whole-class, small-group, and one-on-one settings. Additionally, students regulate their own learning when in student-led individual, partner, and small-group settings. Within each of these structures, distinct responsibilities for teachers and students, along with norms of social interaction, are established. Instructional routines are those structured activities that occur repeatedly within the classroom—such as read-aloud or journal writing.

What Do Teachers Need to Know?

Varied structures serve different learning purposes. For example, a whole-class, teacher-directed lesson may be appropriate to introduction of and modeling of literacy strategies. On the other hand, conferencing one-on-one with a student to discuss and provide feedback on his or her text facilitates the individual types of interactions necessary for writing development. Or, teacher- or student-led small-group discussion may be the most appropriate organizational format to maximize text comprehension. Teachers make decisions about which activity setting best matches particular learning goals and student needs.

Fostering students' abilities to read and write independently is an important goal of literacy education. It is not just a matter of teaching students to work in nondisruptive ways. Children need to develop abilities to self-regulate, persevere, problem solve, and make decisions. Explicit and proactive teacher guidance supports children as they take responsibility for and engage meaningfully in literacy tasks. It also provides the foundation for successful independent, partner, and small-group work.

By bringing consistency and continuity to learning tasks, daily and weekly routines promote student independence and responsibility. The security and predictability of routines enable students to focus their attention on learning. Routines set norms of social interaction that allow students to self-regulate and be partners in their own learning processes.

Reading and writing of connected text is the most important literacy activity in a classroom. As a result, the routines and norms of a classroom should be designed to allot extended periods of time for these activities. Routines also need to be modified to meet students' changing needs. For example, the amount of time students can read independently will grow over the course of the school year.

ACTIVITY 5.4
Centers as an Instructional Approach in a Teacher Education Classroom
SUSAN D. MARTIN and MARY ANN CAHILL

Activity Type: In-class activity.

Materials:
- Varying materials for each center.
- Pocket chart/name cards/center cards for rotational centers.
- Signs/rationales for each rotational center.

Duration: Vary to suit your schedule: 30 minutes for menu centers, 12–15 minutes for each rotation of rotational centers.

Professional Learning Focus:
- Engage in small-group instruction and social interactions.
- Practice with literacy concepts.

K–8 Student Learning Focus: Practice with literacy skills.

Standards Links

IRA Professional Standards:
5.4 Use evidence-based rationale to make and monitor flexible instructional grouping options for students.

Model and scaffold procedures, so students learn to work effectively in a variety of classroom configurations and activities.

Use various practices to differentiate instruction.

Common Core State Standards: Reading Standards: Foundational Skills

Phonological Awareness
2. Demonstrate understanding of spoken words, syllables, and sounds (phonemes).

Phonics and Word Recognition
3. Know and apply grade-level phonics and word analysis skills in decoding words.

Rationale

Using centers or stations in our own elementary classrooms was a favorite instructional approach when we were teaching elementary school. It allowed us an opportunity to interact more individually with students to get to know them better, motivate learning, and to differentiate instruction to suit their needs.

Using centers in our literacy courses provides an opportunity for teachers to develop understandings of this instructional approach and of the important role of social engagement in learning. Additionally, the content fosters development of concepts related to literacy topics (phonological awareness, phonics, fluency, morphology), as well as practice with instructional tools and teacher planning. Planning, organization, and managing of centers can be modeled and discussed. Resource materials, such as *Guided Reading and Writing* (Fountas & Pinnell, 1996), can be demonstrated. Participating in centers gives us a common learning experience that can be discussed from the teachers' perspective. We do not think many preservice teachers see this model of instruction in school settings—especially in the upper grades.

Description

Center-based instructional activity engages teachers in a variety of small-group activities focused on particular learning tasks. We typically use two models of center-based instruction during a term.

Menu Approach to Centers

One type of center-based instruction is a menu approach in which all tasks focus on one concept. We facilitate centers focused on phonological awareness. Teachers select which center activities to do and the social configurations for engagement in the activity. They typically work in groups of two to four. Menu-approach activities are typically accomplished during one course period in a 30-minute block of time. Center activities are simple and include tasks with picture cards (beginning sound sorts, syllable sorts), clap–snap–tap activities, singing, and use of toy objects. Using a simple half-sheet form, the teachers record activities and note what aspect of phonological awareness the center focuses on (see Figure 5.9).

Rotational Approach to Centers

Centers can also be organized so that small groups rotate through the activities in a particular sequence. This allows classroom teachers to work with a small group of students. We set up learning tasks during rotational centers for exploration of and practice in elements of literacy development as well as instructional practices that support prospective teachers' development in these areas. We use a pocket chart to provide and model organization for the rotations. We put up signs for the centers with the name and rationale of the activity. All necessary materials are available at each center. There is usually an individual or group recording form at each center.

We have set up rotational centers for exploration and review of phonics and morphology, as well as worthwhile instructional activities in those areas. Specific centers we have used include:

Name: _____

Activity Name and Number	Phonological Concept Practiced
_____	_____
_____	_____
_____	_____
_____	_____
_____	_____
_____	_____
_____	_____
_____	_____
_____	_____
_____	_____
_____	_____
_____	_____
_____	_____
_____	_____
_____	_____

FIGURE 5.9. Recording sheet for phonological awareness centers.

1. Read Around the Fifth Floor: a vocabulary activity adapted from "Read Around the Room" (Fountas & Pinnell, 1996). Cards with pertinent vocabulary (e.g., instructional-level reading, phoneme, diphthong) are placed on the hallway walls outside our classroom. Students must use the words to fill in an accompanying worksheet—descriptive sentences with blanks. Use of the reading wand is optional, but our students love it!

2. *Starfall.com*: online exploration of a specific literacy website (*www.starfall.com*).

3. Big Book Shared Reading: engagement in making and justifying decisions about choosing an appropriate Big Book for K–1 shared reading. After selecting the book, the group decides on an accompanying phonics lesson. Students record their decisions as a group on a worksheet.

4. Morphology Potpourri: choice to create a base word tree (*Words Their Way*, Bear, Invernizzi, Templeton, & Johnston, 2008) or a picture showing multiple-meaning words/homonyms.

5. Fluency Fun: opportunity for students to read/reread short texts, poetry, and/or a play script to explore various tools to make rereading engaging for children. Tools include masks, inflatable microphone, phonics phone, and "voice dice." On each side of the voice die, directions for how to read are given (e.g., read rapidly; read in a big, giant voice).

Each rotation typically goes from 12 to 15 minutes. These centers usually occur at the end of two or three class periods.

Debriefing

A critical part of engaging prospective teachers in a centers-based approach to literacy learning is the discussion afterward. We facilitate a group discussion about the advantages and challenges of utilizing this instructional approach in elementary classrooms. We use *Guided Reading* (Fountas & Pinnell, 1996), videotapes of a kindergarten classroom, and our own experiences as elementary teachers to foster this conversation.

Discussion

Preservice teachers enjoy this change of pace to their instruction in college classrooms! As one candidate stated, "I loved the centers. I learn best with a hands-on approach, therefore it was good for me to see these activities come to life. I also can really see myself using this in my own classroom." One semester, we were thrilled when a first-year middle school teacher tried centers with her students after she had experienced them in a course. She reported that her students were very motivated to work in centers-based learning activities. Two years later, she again commented on her use of centers in her classroom.

We enjoy the centers too! We have modeled working with one group, but typically, teachers appreciate the opportunities to be in charge of their own activity. So, we wander and interact with the teachers. We also make sure that they understand what the teachers' role would be in a K–8 classroom setting.

Frankly, getting centers planned, together, and set up can be time-consuming—just as with elementary teachers. Mary Ann, for instance, spent much time setting up all the materials and activities for the phonological awareness menu centers and the fluency activities. However, we keep these materials in a kit that several instructors use each semester. The time is well spent and worth the effort!

References

Bear, D. R., Invernizzi, M., Templeton, S., & Johnston, F. (2008). *Words their way.* Upper Saddle River, NJ: Pearson Education.

Fountas, I. C., & Pinnell, G. S. (1996). *Guided reading: Good first reading for all children.* Portsmouth, NH: Heinemann.

CHAPTER 6

New Literacies

LEE ANN TYSSELING

In the last 30 years our lives have been transformed by the digital revolution. The changes in work and daily living habits during this revolution have been as dramatic as those that occurred during the Industrial Revolution. Video streaming, digital cameras, smartphones, the Internet, and tablet computers present a dizzying array of possibilities and promises for literacy learning and literacy demands. The digital universe has fundamentally changed the way individuals and groups communicate and collaborate. As we live through the digital revolution it can be hard to get a fix on the horizon, to know what direction to head, and which tools and techniques will be useful. However, one thing is certain; holding on to the past will be self-defeating. The teachers we work with live in the digital world and must be prepared to use and teach about new literacies effectively.

As an emerging concept, the term New Literacies (also called digital literacies, information communication technology [ICT], and many other terms) refers to the now pervasive multimodal means of electronic communication including the Internet. As Leu (2010) describes them, New Literacies include the new skills, strategies, dispositions, and social practices that are required by new technologies for information and communication. New Literacies are central to full participation in a global community (Leu, 2010), yet because the digital landscape changes on an almost daily basis, it is challenging to keep up with the skills and potential of recent innovations. Because the digital revolution has so fundamentally changed the world, every discipline is affected.

It may be helpful to look at the impact and implications of technology as three tiered. The first tier can be viewed as basic technology-based tools that all literacy users can benefit from using (e.g., word processing features and tools, including online file sharing and collaboration). The second tier is the addition of a wide range of new language practices that make for new genres or require new literacy skills (e.g., Animoto, PowerPoint, Prezi, and Internet searching or reading comprehension). The third tier is the fundamental change in the ethos (Lankshear & Knobel, 2011) of language arts in the world at large including cyberspace (e.g., wikis and Machinima). The tiers are not intended to represent a hierarchy of value—rather a level of complexity. One way we can help teachers deal with the onslaught of ICTs, teaching ideas, and new sets of standards is to demonstrate the close links that can be forged between the unfamiliar technologies and familiar language arts skills and strategies. As Leu and his colleagues (2009) emphasize, "Educators, researchers, and policymakers must begin to recognize the Internet as a reading comprehension issue, not simply as a technology issue" (p. 173).

READING IN DIGITAL ENVIRONMENTS

What Is It?

Reading printed words now takes place on electronic screens as well as on paper. Digital text is also much more than just reading printed words. Competent reading in a digital environment requires the development of new reading and research strategies and skills.

What Do Teachers Need to Know?

Reading in the digital environment and online shares much with traditional linear reading of books, stories, and articles. The reader must still make meaning of the written form of language. But there are important differences as well. Digital text typically is multimedia rich. Including images and videos is inexpensive and has resulted in the expectations of readers/ viewers that these visual elements will be included (Haskell, 2012). Additionally, in digital environments there can be instantaneous access to tools to support word recognition and comprehension. In addition to embedded dictionaries and audio pronunciations in digital text, maps, images, encyclopedias, and other sources are readily available to assist comprehension when reading on a device with full Internet access. Of course, as with reading in the paperbound environment, the reader must be sufficiently engaged and motivated to take advantage of the available supports. Readers also need enough metacognitive awareness of their own comprehension to be aware of their need to use these resources and the strategic knowledge to access them.

However, reading in the unbounded space of the Internet poses challenges beyond those found in paper-based, linear text. Reading online can require more inferring and synthesizing than reading in the paperbound environment (Coiro & Dobler, 2007; Hartman, Morsink, & Zheng, 2010). Researchers continue to refine our understandings of the specific skills and strategies needed by readers when online (Coiro, 2011a). The following are findings of research studies to date on the specific literacy skills and strategies demanded when working in the online environment. In some cases, when reading informational text on an electronic device, the reader cannot flip through a text scanning the headings to gain an overview of the entire text or a section within (Coiro & Dobler, 2007). Even when navigation panels are present in digital text, readers need to be aware of their presence and have the skills and strategies to use them. More frequent synthesizing of information is needed when reading online than paperbound reading because information is split across multiple pages within and across websites. The linked and layered nature of reading online (Coiro & Dobler, 2007) calls for greater use of skimming and scanning. The online reader must also be able to switch nimbly from the skimming and scanning required to *find* information to close, high-concentration reading when *within* a relevant, longer text. In addition to interpreting the printed information found in multiple locations, reading in the Internet environment more frequently calls on skills in interpreting nonprint sources of information—photographs, drawings, maps, graphs, videos, and audio recordings. Finally, much Internet reading is question or problem driven, requiring greater reliance on goal setting and self-regulation than reading for other purposes. After observing skilled adolescent Internet users seek answers to questions through Internet search and reading, Coiro and Dobler (2007) concluded that each reader literally constructs his or her own text through the particular set of sites, documents, images, charts, or other features that he or she visits and reads.

The ability to locate relevant information on the Internet can be viewed as a prerequisite skill for reading comprehension in the online environment (Kuiper & Volman, 2008). Navigating to find a relevant piece of information requires locating a useful website and then navigating within it. This usually demands rapid scanning and evaluation based on just a few words. Internet readers must also evaluate the likely reliability of the information they seek, first through an understanding of the website address system, and then when reading within a site through critical analysis, as in print reading. Finally, knowledge about how search engines and websites function is used to make the needed inferences. Readers on the Internet who do not possess the requisite prior knowledge in any of these areas will experience difficulty locating relevant information, and can easily end up feeling lost and confused (Coiro & Dobler, 2007).

ACTIVITY 6.1
Modeling Reading within a Webpage
Using a Think-Aloud Protocol
DEBORAH G. LITT

Activity Type: In-class activity.

Materials: One or two answerable questions; a website suitable for upper elementary students that answers the question(s).

Duration: 30–45 minutes.

Professional Learning Focus: Skills for reading on the Internet.

K–8 Student Learning Focus: Skills for reading on the Internet.

Standards Links

IRA Professional Standards:

2.2 Incorporate traditional, print, digital, and online resources as instructional tools to enhance student learning.

Common Core State Standards: Reading Anchor Standards
7. Integrate and evaluate content presented in diverse media and formats, including visually and quantitatively, as well as in words.

Writing Anchor Standards
8. Gather relevant information from multiple print an digital sources, assess the credibility and accuracy of each source, and integrate the information while avoiding plagiarism.

Note. Inspired by Coiro (2011b).

Rationale

Being a proficient reader today encompasses reading online, and, as with all aspects of literacy learning, we cannot assume that all children will figure out how to navigate websites without assistance. So, teachers need to be prepared to help children learn this critical skill. I work with some teachers who are so comfortable with the Internet that they have no conscious awareness of the special reading skills they are using to scan the components of a site and to evaluate the likelihood of information located in different places to be relevant to their purposes. I work with other teachers who are just beginners in using the Internet as a source of information. Teachers in either group could have difficulty recognizing what their students need help with to be effective online readers or in explaining the tasks to the students. By observing and then practicing a think-aloud of each step of an ongoing Internet reading for information activity, the teachers gain (1) an appreciation of the complexity of decision making in the online environment, and (2) skill in conveying an efficient decision-making process to their students.

Description

Preparation

In advance, I choose a question or two to which upper elementary students would be likely to be seeking answers. I also find a website containing relevant information that is appropriate for children. Most recently I used "What causes global warming?" for my demonstration question and the U.S. Environmental Protection Agency's website for students on global climate change: *http://epa.gov/climat-echange/kids/index.html*.

Pair–Share (3 minutes)

First, I ask teachers to brainstorm with a partner about what they do when using a website to find information in answer to a question. The groups share out loud, and I make a master list of all the actions mentioned.

Instructor Modeling and Think-Aloud

With the homepage "A Student's Guide to Global Climate Change" showing on the screen so everyone can see it (see Figure 6.1), I use the mouse to indicate where my eyes are focused and explain what I am thinking as I scan the page and decide where to click. For example, I will point to the large block on the top left that says, "Learn the Basics" and say, "Well, I think I'll probably find something on what causes global warming here because that's probably a basic idea of climate change, but before I click let me just see what the other possibilities are." Then I read aloud the other major headings and make comments about their likely usefulness.

FIGURE 6.1. Home page: A Student's Guide to Global Climate Change. Available at *http://epa.gov/climatechange/kids/index.html.*

I also point to the headings in black print across the bottom of the page and note that I might find the answer to my question in the "Frequently Asked Questions" section because I think my question is probably asked a lot. The home page of this website includes a video titled "Climate Change Basics." I will explain that the video might have the information I'm looking for, too, but since *my* preference is to get information from printed text, I will try one of the other links first, although other people would probably try the video first.

Finally, I click on the link and read the information that comes up and comment on whether or not it answers my question. I then wonder aloud whether I would have found out the answer using the Frequently Asked Questions or the video link and try those, too.

Teacher Modeling and Think Aloud

I ask the group to generate some additional questions about climate change or global warming that they think elementary school children might have and write them down. If enough teachers have brought their own laptops or tablets to class, I have them work in groups of two or three to practice modeling their own process of navigating a website in search of specific information. While one person works on the computer, the others observe and note what the searcher does. The observers are encouraged to ask the searcher to explain his or her choices and decision making.

Debriefing

After the demonstration and practice, we debrief the experience beginning with some very general questions and proceeding to some more specific ones:

> "What did you notice? Did anything you saw in this activity surprise you?"
> "How is reading a website different from reading informational text in a book or article?"
> "What did you or the people you observed do when working with the website that is different from what you usually do?"
> "Think of the children in your classrooms. Would all of them be able to find the answer to the questions on the website? If not, what would be the stumbling blocks for them?"

Discussion

Although the personal computer did not exist until I was well into adulthood, I have embraced the convenience of computers and the Internet in my own life. (In fact, much of this book was drafted and revised using Google Sites.) Nevertheless, in my teaching I have neglected online reading until very recently, unsure of how to approach it. However, after reading articles, especially Coiro (2011) and Coiro and Dobler (2007), and attending conference sessions on the subject, I recognized that by mostly ignoring the new literacies—and the specialized reading skills involved—I was doing a disservice to the children my preservice teachers would be teaching, especially since a high proportion of the teachers I work with teach populations dependent on school for this kind of information.

During the debriefing portion of the session, teachers note that they perform searches with such ease that they hadn't previously thought about the barriers children might encounter. They say they tend to assume children know how to conduct a search, but they really don't, yet they hadn't figured out how to help them. Several teachers told me they had not previously realized how critical vocabulary and background knowledge was for judging where to go within a website—if children didn't know that *impacts* and *effects* mean the same thing, then they wouldn't know to click on the "See the Impacts" button to find the answer to their question about the effects of global warming. Teachers find this activity very helpful both for understanding where the breakdowns might be for children, and as a model for what they could do in their classrooms to help children successfully navigate within a website.

References

Coiro, J. (2011). Talking about reading as thinking: Modeling the hidden complexities of online reading comprehension. *Theory Into Practice, 50,* 107–115.

Coiro, J., & Dobler, E. (2007). Exploring the online reading comprehension strategies used by sixth-grade skilled readers to search for and locate information on the Internet. *Reading Research Quarterly, 42*(2), 214–257.

RESEARCH ON THE INTERNET

What Is It?

Conducting research using the Internet rather than paper-based sources.

What Do Teachers Need to Know?

Reading and research on the Internet are closely bound. The most common reason for reading on the Internet is to find something out—it is question driven (Leu, Leu, & Coiro, 2004). We all turn to the Internet to answer our everyday questions about sports, celebrities, food, weather, fashion, news, and politics, but serious academic research is also conducted through the Internet. Research on the Internet requires all of the same components as research in the pre-Internet era—formulating a good question, locating information, evaluating the reliability of sources, evaluating the accuracy of information, selecting relevant information, keeping track of sources, and synthesizing information from multiple sources. However, some of these components require different techniques in the Internet environment that are more challenging to perform than in the paperbound world. For example, while locating information is much faster now than in the days of card catalogue searches, that ease produces its own problems—too much information to read all of it, and information of dubious quality. Students can be overwhelmed by the number of choices returned when they type their topic into a search engine. Many do not know how to select the sites most likely to help them (Coiro, 2005). More so than paperbound readers, reader–researchers on the Internet must keep their goals clearly in mind at all times to avoid distractions and from following links deeper and deeper into a rabbit hole.

Coiro (2005) identified four skills researchers in today's digital environment must possess: knowing which link to follow, knowing how to navigate within a website, evaluating the validity of information found on a website, and synthesizing information from multiple sites without plagiarizing. Because anyone can post anything on the Internet, learning to evaluate the accuracy of information takes on greater importance, and, because elementary-age children are using the Internet for research, must be taught to younger children than in the pre-Internet days.

ACTIVITY 6.2
Reading and Evaluating Internet Search Results
DEBORAH G. LITT

Activity Type: In-class activity.

Materials: Printout of a screen shot of an Internet search; graphic organizer for recording answers to questions.

Duration: 30 minutes.

Professional Learning Focus:
- Skills for reading on the Internet.
- Skills for researching on the Internet.
- Conscious awareness of criteria for evaluation of website utility.

K–8 Student Learning Focus:
- Skills for reading on the Internet.
- Skills for researching on the Internet.
- Conscious awareness of criteria for evaluation of website utility.

Standards Links

IRA Professional Standards:
2.2 Incorporate traditional, print, digital, and online resources as instructional tools to enhance student learning.

Common Core State Standards: Reading Anchor Standards
7. Integrate and evaluate content presented in diverse media and formats, including visually and quantitatively, as well as in words.

Writing Anchor Standards
8. Gather relevant information from multiple print and digital sources, assess the credibility and accuracy of each source, and integrate the information while avoiding plagiarism.

Rationale

Evaluating the returns of an Internet search is the gateway skill for research on the Internet. If a reader does not know which sites are most likely to contain the information he or she is seeking, his or her search will be unproductive and frustrating. For most teachers, their own reading of search engine results is so automatic that they are unaware of the parts of the page they are reading, and the criteria by which they make their decisions. I use this activity adapted from Coiro's (2005)

Note. Adapted from Coiro (2005). Adapted with permission from ASCD.

work with adolescents to help teachers become more aware of the skills children need to become proficient interpreters of Internet search results.

Description

1. Prepare a graphic organizer with three columns: Question/Answer, How do you know? and Why is it important to know? (see Figure 6.2). The rows will contain your questions. Some of the questions can be asked of any web search: "How many websites were found in this search?" and "Which site(s) are likely to be unavailable in 6 months?" Other questions should be particular to your search. For the Martin Luther King, Jr., search, I asked, "Which site would provide you with photos?" and "On which site would you find the texts of his speeches?"

2. Make copies of a screen shot of your search or project it onto a screen (see Figure 6.3). Participants should not view the search on their devices because you do not want them to click through the sites.

Question/Answer	How do you know?	Why is it important to know?
Which site would provide you with photos of him?		
How many websites were found using this search?		
Which site is likely to be unavailable in 6 months?		
On which site would you find the texts of his famous speeches?		
Which site will have the most "trustworthy" information (unbiased)?		
Which site may have "untrustworthy" information (biased)?		

FIGURE 6.2. Graphic organizer for reading and evaluating Internet search results (used with a search for Martin Luther King, Jr.).

3. Participants complete the graphic organizer.

4. Debrief.

Discussion

While the teachers are completing the chart, I hear them saying, "Children wouldn't know that" and that children don't bother to read the description found below the hot link. Many say that until they were doing this exercise they never considered whether or not a website would be available in the future. During the debriefing period, as teachers share the reasoning they use to determine which websites they would go to, their background knowledge about website structures and reliability emerges. They bring up the difference between URL addresses ending in .org, .gov, .net, and .com, and the reliability of Wikipedia. They discuss the need to explain that the order of sites is determined by the frequency of visits, not their relevance to a student's question or the site's quality. Since the search I used most recently was on a topic (Martin Luther King, Jr.) many had researched before, some teachers shared knowledge about specific websites they had previously visited such as the Nobel website. The teachers recognized that they use their extensive background knowledge about the information certain websites

FIGURE 6.3. Google search results for Martin Luther King, Jr. Google and the Google logo are registered trademarks of Google Inc.

contain—information that is not necessarily provided in the description and would not be known by children—in deciding which websites visit.

The activity not only brings teachers' unconscious knowledge about Internet searches to the surface, but also persuades them of the need to explicitly teach children how to interpret search results. In addition, it provides them with a model of how they might teach how to read a search result page. In fact, the most recent time I used this activity, one of the teachers asked for a blank copy of the chart to use with her daughter who had "learned" from the Internet that wearing a bra 24 hours a day could cause breast cancer.

Reference

Coiro, J. (2005). Making sense of online text. *Educational Leadership, 63*(2), 30–35.

COMPOSING IN DIGITAL ENVIRONMENTS

What Is It?

Just as in reading, writing has taken on new dimensions with the advent of digital tools, the Internet, and social media. On one hand, the innovations to digital composing have simplified writing. For instance, the ability to *cut-and-paste* sections of text with the computer has significantly altered the ease of revision processes, especially when the writer is considering whole-section or whole-document organization. On the other hand, both written products and writing processes have become more complex. Powerful digital compositional tools, such as PowerPoint, Prezi, and Animoto, provide the capacity for the writer to interweave written text with graphics, photos, music, sounds, and speech to create multimodal products. Multilayered composition processes are central to the creation of these products. Gathering information in precomposing processes may require use of tools such as digital cameras and the Internet, as well as traditional methods used in prewriting. Drafting and revision processes may include attention to how text, visuals, and sound interact for richer depth of meaning, as well as issues of organization or vivid word choice inherent to written text.

Digital environments are also shifting the landscape of social environments for writing. The Internet has opened up new possibilities for publication venues and audiences. The use of computer screens, rather than paper, provides more easily viewed products with ensuing social interactions in classroom environments (Leu et al., 2008). Likewise, the use of Internet sites such as wikis and Google Drive facilitate collaborative drafting, revision, and editing processes.

What Do Teachers Need to Know?

Educators use explicit materials and instruction to teach students how to use pencil/paper technologies and handwrite in both print and cursive fonts. Students need to be as well prepared to use new technological tools for writing—beginning with keyboarding skills that need to become automatic through practice. Modeling and explicit instruction around digital tools that are used strategically are important as well—for example, How does music enhance the mood of a particular text? Where should this photo be placed in relation to the text? Many children are quite proficient in using some digital tools and programs for their own purposes. But we can't assume that these digital competencies transfer to tools used in academic settings, or academic uses of tools they know. Simple skills such as knowing how to access fonts and make font selections strategically may need to be explicitly modeled and taught. Even first graders can create complex PowerPoint presentations when they are guided and scaffolded on tool use.

Composition with new digital technologies is not only important for students' futures but can serve to motivate classroom writing. Authentic purposes and audiences provided by the Internet, along with opportunities to create multimodal products that suit a broader array of personal interests and talents, can inspire children's composition. For example, a student who loves to work with visual representations may persevere in composing products that include photos or graphics.

Engagement in writing oneself is important to understanding composing processes, skills, and strategies specific to particular written products (Pritchard & Honeycutt, 2007). This is particularly important for digital products that are multimodal, as these genres may contain processes, skills, and strategies that are new and unfamiliar to those who have composed only in traditional written genres. It is hard to teach what you don't know. Teachers need to have experiential understandings themselves to help scaffold student learning (Martin & Dismuke, 2013).

ACTIVITY 6.3
Engaging Educators in Multimodal Composition Using Animoto
SHERRY DISMUKE

Activity Type: Assignment.

Materials:
- Computer access for all students.
- Establish an educators account at *animoto.com*.
- Colored craft feathers.
- Chart paper or document camera.

Duration: 2 weeks.

Professional Learning Focus:
- Develop an understanding of digital writing processes.
- Identify key features of a specific digital product.
- Learn to compose and produce poetry in Animoto video format.
- Experience the motivational factors involved in composing in a digital format.

K–8 Student Learning Focus:
- Strengthen writing skills in organization, word choice, presentation, and voice.
- Increase student confidence, and motivation to write.
- Develop digital literacy skills.

Standards Links

IRA Professional Standards:
2.2 Implement and evaluate instruction in each of the following areas: concepts of print, phonemic awareness, phonics, vocabulary, comprehension, fluency, critical thinking, motivation, and writing.

Common Core State Standards: Writing Anchor Standards
5. Develop and strengthen writing as needed by planning, revising, editing, rewriting, or trying a new approach.

6. Use technology, including the Internet, to produce and publish writing and to interact and collaborate with others.

10. Write routinely over extended time frames and shorter time frames for a range of tasks, purposes, and audiences.

Rationale

Animoto is a software platform that allows the writer to create a multimodal product that uses photographs, sound, and written text. This is an exciting presentation platform that increases motivation to write, as it provides writers with authentic purposes and audiences for demonstration of content-area knowledge (Bruning & Horn, 2000).

Because Animoto requires users to express themselves in a limited text format, developing word choice skills and content-area vocabulary are essential. A few well-placed words make all the difference. The addition of music and pictures to support the text requires that authors using this platform consider tone, mood, and prosody. This helps the author develop voice. Composition in Animoto happens frame by frame. This requires students to join text and pictures in support of one idea at a time, in a linear progression. This process acts as an organizational tool.

Writing in Animoto can also relieve stresses of transcription for English language learners and others. Additionally, slide-by-slide production scaffolds both planning and organization processes. Animoto can allow students with a variety of learning disabilities to "show what they know" without the roadblocks of a lengthy essay.

Composing in Animoto provides teachers an opportunity to experience first-hand the motivational factors, organizational scaffolding, and ease in which teachers can provide differentiated content-area writing experiences. In this activity, teachers are immersed in their own digital composition processes while creating a frame-by-frame presentation. Teachers make composition decisions and become more aware of their own writing processes while composing in a digital medium. Using pedagogical approaches that engage learners in applying their own processes make those processes explicate and therefore easier to teach (National Staff Development Council, 2011).

Description

In preparation for this activity I first composed two pieces using Animoto: a cinquain poem and an informational product on weather. Using Animoto for different purposes helped me better understand my own composing processes. I took note of the barriers I faced to composing that were unique to creating these digital products—for example, downloading music from an outside source, adjusting the pace and music to create mood, and expressing myself with limited text. Understanding my own processes was the first step in preparing to explicitly teach and scaffold the teachers through their own composition processes.

This activity happens over several class sessions as follows:

Day 1

I engage the teachers in a guided writing lesson focused on cinquain. A cinquain is a five-line poem with this format:

- Line 1: Topic.
- Line 2: Two adjectives.

- Line 3: Three verb participles (*-ing* endings).
- Line 4: Simile.
- Line 5: Synonym word or phase for the topic.

The particular lesson I use is a lesson adapted from Marjorie Frank (1987), in which teachers experience interactions with colorful craft feathers. For example, during prewriting, teachers blow the feathers back and forth to each other, watching them move, then generate lists of possible verbs participles for the third line of the cinquain. I model and engage the teachers in prewriting activities, as well as focus lessons for revision. During revision we focus on word choice and the way in which a simile can create a mood or tone for the poem. By the end of this lesson, the teachers have handwritten drafts of a cinquain. They are welcome to further revise at home.

Day 2

1. We are ready to continue revision and editing processes, as well as focus on presentation/publication processes. I share a variety of models of Animoto compositions completed by past teachers, elementary school students, and me. Together, the teachers and I view and discuss the models. We inductively look for commonalities across the models and discuss what we believe are the key features, purposes, and implications for teaching this presentation format. I record the teachers' ideas on a class chart.

2. I add to the group chart by highlighting the necessity to purposefully integrate written text with images and sound. I provide additional examples of how these elements of written, visual, and auditory composition work together to create the final product.

3. I give a brief demonstration of Animoto and its features. I provide explicit instruction on navigating the tools, such as how to insert images and select music. Teachers are provided a short lesson on using music selection to convey tone and voice. This helps them more carefully consider their choice of music and the role it plays in connecting to their audience.

4. The teachers begin to transfer drafts into the Animoto platform. They enter into digital revision processes as they prepare their poetry for presentations. They spend approximately 45 minutes in writing workshop composing collaboratively in Animoto. They are encouraged to confer with one another as they brainstorm ideas for supporting, elaborating, and enriching their meaning with pictures and music.

5. While we are in workshop, I occasionally stop to ask the teachers to share effective techniques or point out powerful word choice. After receiving collaborative support in workshop, teachers are asked to finish working on their products at home.

Day 3

1. We share our digital products in class. Peers provide specific feedback on which features of the shared digital compositions were most effective. The teachers are learning from one another what makes a digital presentation strong. I stress that ideas are meant to be shared and teachers are encouraged to go back and apply what they have learned through our decomposition of models to further revise their own products.

2. After the presentations, the teachers complete freewrites on their experiences composing and viewing an Animoto. Additionally, they write about how they could use Animoto with a specific group of students or in content areas like science or social studies. This is followed by a whole-class discussion to debrief the experience.

Discussion

The cinquain has been a good entry point into working in Animoto. Use of an existing handwritten text aids composition processes in a new medium, as does the brevity of the text. The mood or tone of the simile and inherent attention to movement of a feather provide a foundation for selecting appropriate music and visuals to accompany the written text. I do not assess this written product in my courses, as I want the teachers to write for themselves and simply experience use of the digital tools. Feedback for writing development comes through self-assessments and invited peer interactions.

Teachers have been very enthusiastic about using Animoto for their own writing and in the classroom. I have collected freewrites from my graduate-level writing course. One hundred percent of teachers reported that they planned to implement some form of digital presentation choice during the next school year. This activity had a role in changing teachers' dispositions about using technology as a presentation choice for their students, including English language learners. They commented on students' motivation, opportunities to develop and present content information, and development of writing identities. As one teacher noted, "I can guide them through the prewriting, drafting, revision, and editing processes, but in the end, for the product I will let them make it creative and special to their lives. I will show them my product (Animoto) before they present in order for them to understand there is no limit in how to create their final form."

I have been able to follow several preservice teachers into the field and observe their use of Animoto in the classroom. Teachers have taken their experience composing poetry in Animoto and extended it to other subject matter areas. One student teacher has gained a reputation for his use of Animoto in creating content-area research projects. His mentor teacher commented that "Through partnering with his students on projects, Jeff has discovered how to break the projects up into pieces that the students can understand. After that, he turns it over to them and they can do projects on their own." After viewing many of the students' products, I was further convinced that Animoto provides the students with the motivation to persevere through the complex task of writing to produce videos that contain evidence of both content-area knowledge and writing skills.

References

Bruning, R., & Horn, C. (2000). Developing motivation to write. *Educational Psychologist, 35*(1), 25–37.

Frank, M. (1987). *Complete writing lessons for the middle grades.* Nashville, TN: Incentive Publications.

National Staff Development Council. (2011). *Learning forward: Standards for professional learning.* Retrieved July 19, 2011, from *www.learningforward.org/standards/learning-designs/index.tcfm.*

COLLABORATIVE WEBSITES: COMMUNITIES OF INQUIRY

What Is It?

Collaborative websites are spaces in the digital universe that allow individuals to work with partners or groups in a wide range of media (Tysseling & McCulley, 2012). The digital universe offers unprecedented opportunities for this type of collaborative work. Collaborative websites can support discussion, research, writing, multigenre work, and multimedia projects. Wikis, comments on blogs, book reviews on sites like Amazon or Goodreads, document-sharing services like Google Drive or DropBox, video-sharing sites like YouTube, and fan-fiction sites are all examples of digital spaces available in which affinity groups or readers/writers may meet to collaborate.

What Do Teachers Need to Know?

Readers and writers can interact in many ways and in many time frames through the Internet. These collaborations demand new sets of literacy skills, strategies, conventions, and registers. For example, collaborative websites or e-mails in a school or workplace context demand a more formal register than is found in informal social networks like those in Facebook, but use less formal language than traditional essays or reports.

A second important issue for teachers within a social networking context is that of attribution (or plagiarism). Twenty-first-century citizens have a dramatically different value system for the use of intellectual property (Gabriel, 2010). They have revised the ideas of copying or plagiarism and have recast them using the terms *remix, mash-up,* and *fanfiction* to describe their practices (Lankshear & Knobel, 2011). Clarifying the accepted standards for attribution in different situations needs careful attention in this changing social context. Even at the college and graduate-school level, it is important to explicitly teach the academic world's requirement for attribution of any and all ideas that do not originate with the writer.

ACTIVITY 6.4
Wikis in Literature Circles and Interdisciplinary Studies
LEE ANN TYSSELING

Activity Type: Unit—in-class activities and out-of-class work; can be used in online courses.

Materials:
- Children's or young adult novel selected by instructor.
- Computer access.
- Wiki shell.
- Model wikis.
- Project guidelines and grading rubrics.
- Short expository reading passage related to the topic of the novel.
- Research worksheet (Coiro, 2005).
- Professional articles on use of wikis, Web 2.0, and research skills/strategies.

Duration: six 60- to 90-minute class sessions.

Professional Learning Focus:
- Use of Web 2.0 for collaboration and discussion.

Standards Links

IRA Professional Standards:
2.2 Incorporate traditional print, digital, and online resources as instructional tools to enhance student learning.

2.3 Guided by evidence-based rationale, select and use quality traditional print, digital, and online resources.

Common Core State Standards: Reading Anchor Standards
7. Integrate and evaluate content presented in diverse formats and media, including visually and quantitatively, as well as in words.

Writing Anchor Standards
6. Use technology, including the Internet, to produce and publish writing and to interact and collaborate with others.

7. Conduct short as well as more sustained research projects based on

- Fostering literature discussions.
- Structuring interdisciplinary studies.

K–8 Student Learning

- Online literature discussions.
- Web 2.0 writing conventions.
- Research skills and strategies.
- Synthesis of information from multiple resources.
- Writing processes: publication.

focused questions, demonstrating an understanding of the subject under investigation.

9. Draw evidence from literary or informational texts to support analysis, reflection, and research.

Rationale

The CCSS are placing a renewed emphasis on research and writing skills as well as small-group projects and reporting. This unit is designed to introduce teachers to the use of wikis, which can be used to support group work for all kinds of discussions or projects. Perhaps the most famous wiki is Wikipedia, but wikis are also used in many businesses and research groups as a platform for collaboration. Allowing for asynchronous group work, wikis are a valuable digital tool when time pressures make it difficult for small groups to meet during a class period.

In this activity, a wiki serves as a digital resource for an integrated thematic unit. It is a tool that can be used with book discussion groups, as well as a workspace for research groups. In this situation, naturally quiet teachers find a place to voice their thoughts without the social pressures of face-to-face discussions and every teacher responds—not just the most eager ones. Finally, online discussions seem to help keep the discussion group "on topic."

The wiki also is a perfect workspace for small-group projects in integrated thematic units. In the activity featured here, I use online discussion for literature circles, and wikis for a small-group research project related to the book discussed in the literature circle. An illustration of this is a recent book study of *Peak* by Roland Smith in which students in a content literacy course also researched and posted (published) their findings about Buddhism, HAPE (high-altitude pulmonary edema), the geology of the Himalaya Mountains, the history of climbing on Mt. Everest, and sherpas.

Description

First Meeting

During this meeting I introduce a children's or young adult novel to the teachers, create novel discussion groups, and assign homework related to the novel and discussion. I also introduce the concepts of interdisciplinary study to the teachers.

An important aspect of the first meeting is an overview of the wiki (template) I have prepared. (For an example of a completed wiki visit *https://sites.google. com/site/peak544bsu*.) Internet access and a short (perhaps 15-minute) orientation to working in a wiki are required to begin. Only minimal technology skills are needed; most activities require only knowledge of the writing/editing tools found in all word processing programs. Adding graphics, video, and sound take a little more technical skill, but 95% of the teachers in my classes quickly discover how to insert these objects. This activity models ways in which teachers can make digital tools accessible to students. At this first meeting I emphasize the discussion portion of the wiki.

The essential pieces of the wiki shell are as follows:

- *Home Page:* Description of the novel, explanations of wikis, videos of "how tos" for the wikis, a navigation bar with links to the other portions of the wiki, and messages/announcements
- *Discussion Groups Parent Page:* Assignment requirements and grading rubric listed (see Figure 6.4), with links to small-group discussion pages.
- *Research Projects Parent Page:* Assignment requirements and grading rubric listed (see Figure 6.5), with links to an example research project page.
- *Team Page:* Biographies of the class members are posted. (I do this early in the year when teachers are not yet familiar with one another.)
- *Calendar.*
- *To-Dos.*

Note: An advantage of using Google Sites is that you can copy an old wiki and edit the pages instead of having to build wikis from scratch.

Second Meeting

After a discussion about the strengths and weaknesses of online discussion, I begin an explanation of the thematic research projects. Small groups will pick a topic of interest and complete individual research from at least three different digital or paper resources, and collaborate in the composition of the summary about the topic to be posted on the wiki. I also demonstrate adding a page to the wiki. (There are easy-to-follow videos on YouTube or the providers' websites on how to perform all of these tasks.)

Third Meeting

Continue the conversation about strengths and weaknesses of online discussion. Demonstrate research skills such as question generation, summarization, clarifying, note taking, attributions, and other research skills you typically teach. I have

Introduction: We will divide into five groups. You may read at your own pace, but need to finish (title of book) by (date). That will leave us 1 week to focus exclusively on the disciplinary research projects. I have assigned you to a group so that you will work with others who have different interests than your own.

Schedule: Because having our discussion online means that we don't all have to read at the same pace, I have set up "chunks" for discussion. You must (but are not limited to) post at least three entries for each chunk. I place an emphasis on discussion rather than "post and run." We will cover how to manage and participate in small-group discussions during class. You do not need to summarize—but some (enough) details from the book are helpful to assure me that you've read the complete book. I have divided each discussion page into the three chunks, but you can add other topics or sidebars. For example, if you want to add a separate "topic name" discussion section, you could put it at the bottom of the page or in a side column. As you get used to wikis and Google site features, you'll find the "insert" pull-down menu at the top left of your editing page useful. I've added a side column here as an example of what you might do on your discussion page.

Edit Page: Please use the edit page function to add to the discussions (rather than the comment option). This allows for asynchronous (without specific time boundaries) discussions. Add your name and date to each entry. I have added an example at the beginning of each of your discussion pages.

Grading Rubric: In our first meeting we will discuss the grading of discussions. I am posting a rubric here that one of my classes used in the past. We will discuss and edit it during our first class meeting.

Grading Rubric—Discussion		Professional (90–100%)	Developing (80–89%)	Needs attention (0–79%)
Timing (1 point)	A minimum of nine posts spread out over time (three in each chunk). • Participates promptly.			
Substance (3 points)	Postings will help carry the discussion forward and provide some evidence that the author is engaged with the reading. • Mindful discussion. • Proofreading.			
Interaction (1 point)	You listen carefully to others and respond to their contributions. You also help move the conversation forward. • Respectful. • Don't dominate. • Be open-minded.			

FIGURE 6.4. Discussion group instructions and grading rubric (posted on Discussion Groups Parent Page).

Research Group: You will need to begin the research process by identifying a topic, joining a group, and formulating a research question. Good research is always question driven. Post your topic title and the question on your group research page. You may modify and adjust your question(s) as you go but your group should work from a shared question(s). The final page will be due after class on Monday (date). You will need to work together to develop a research summary page that combines your research across all your readings. Try not to repeat resources. (You may subdivide "big" resources. For example, Wikipedia may have four or five big subsections. Each of you may choose one.) On (date) your group will present your topic to the class.

Personal Research: You will each read a minimum of three resources related to your research project and post the notes/summary/synthesis for each resource as a subpage linked to your topic page. Create a new page and attach it to the topic page for each source. Paste a copy of the Coiro (2005, p. 35) worksheet on each page and fill in each section as you work with the resource. Name each page with "(your name) research 1" ["(your name) research 2" and "(your name) research 3"]. These will be cumulative; your worksheet for resource 2 should include some thinking about how the new information adds to or changes your thinking from resource 1 and how resource 3 adds/changes your thinking after 2 and 1. Create a separate search summary page for each resource. Remember, you should approach this as one of your students would.

Citing Sources: Record just the URL if you are working from a website. If you are working with an online article, essay, or encyclopedia record both the URL and appropriate APA or MLA citation. You may also use paper resources. In that case, use the appropriate APA or MLA citation format.

Grading Rubric—Research

Total: 10 points		Professional (90–100%)	Developing (80–89%)	Needs attention (0–79%)
Worksheets (3 points)	A "professional" approach to this will demonstrate that you have built knowledge and thinking over the three sources (your work is cumulative). The summary of each resource is connected to the research question your group has established. The entries will demonstrate higher-level thinking, as well as accurate summarization.			

(continued)

FIGURE 6.5. Research connections instructions and grading rubric (posted on Research Parent Page).

Total: 10 points		Professional (90–100%)	Developing (80–89%)	Needs attention (0–79%)
Research summary on wiki (5 points)	A "professional"-level page will show evidence of collaboration (I can see from your worksheets that everyone has contributed to the content of the page), is well written, and is appropriate for a K–8 school audience.			
Media or graphics (2 points)	Appropriate for the content of the page, that they support the content of the page, and they contribute to learning.			
Citations (1 point; included on Research Summary Page)	Model appropriate citations for K–8 students.			

FIGURE 6.5. *(continued)*.

found a worksheet created by Julie Coiro (2005, p. 35) to be very helpful here. Most teachers are expert researchers and it is important to remind them our goal is to explore strategies that will be useful for less sophisticated readers and researchers. Each resource should be summarized on one worksheet.

Fourth Meeting

Continue the conversation about the strengths and weaknesses of online discussion. Allow 30–40 minutes of workshop time to begin the group research projects. Each group should complete the following:

- Add topic pages to the research project parent page.
- Add individual research pages to the group's topic page. The format of the individual research pages may vary. Require or urge group members to select different research resources.

Fifth Meeting

Have a summary conversation of the strengths and weaknesses of online discussion. Check in on the research projects and discuss any online research problems.

You may wish to introduce additional search engines for research. Many users rely exclusively upon Google searches. In doing so, often they encounter a great deal of repetition of information. More specialized search engines such as ProQuest, the Science Information Search Portal (*www.scirus.org*), the American Memory Project (*http://memory.loc.gov/ammem/index.html*), or e-books, such as those found in the Gale Virtual Reference Library, may help identify resources that go into more depth than resources found through Google.

Allow workshop time for research groups to begin planning and writing summaries. Emphasize that their work should be original rather than "cut-and-paste." They may choose to include poetry, images, sound, or other multimedia on their summary page. I generally suggest some time limits for out-of-class work. Usually 1–2 hours of outside research and another hour to complete the summary page should be adequate. During the workshop time the group should also make a brief plan for how to present their research to the whole class.

Final Meeting

Research groups make a 5-minute presentation to the whole class on their research topic. I also guide a summary discussion about the use of a wiki for small-group research projects.

Discussion

Most of the teachers with whom I complete this activity are now relatively comfortable with computers and the Internet. However, each semester I have a few teachers who are very uncomfortable with technology or a wiki. These teachers will require some additional support that their classmates, our university student technology lab assistants, or I provide for them. Additionally, many of the literacy skills and strategies that are introduced in this unit deserve additional elaboration. I like to use this activity near the beginning of the semester because it provides a vision, creates enthusiasm, and helps formulate working groups.

The selection of an appropriate novel is critical. Books selected must have multiple interdisciplinary links. Titles that I have used recently, in addition to *Peak*, include *The Beekeeper's Apprentice* and *O' Jerusalem* by Laurie R. King (crossover adult books for secondary teachers), and *The Maze* by Will Hobbs. I try to stay away from books that are typically used in classrooms to avoid cognitive conflict caused by teachers' expert knowledge of commonly used novels.

An important part of the wiki is that it be socially constructed. Using a wiki for this kind of study should involve a rather dramatic change in "ownership" for both the reading of the novel and the small-group research projects. Many teachers have difficulty resisting the impulse to "mediate" the relationship between reader and author. Literature discussion groups and small-group research projects are typically designed to give more agency to K–12 students than is typical in teacher-directed novel study. Using a relatively unfamiliar novel helps create a workspace that allows teachers the joy of finding and exploring new intellectual horizons on their own.

I prefer wikis to blogs whenever the activity involves group work. Blogs are good platforms for individual work. Wikis are designed specifically for collaboration. There are many different "brands" of wikis, including PBworks, Wikispaces, Google Sites, and Wetpaint. Almost all are free. YouTube has some helpful videos to get users started. Many K–12 schools' firewalls will block most wikis because they are considered "social media." I have found that Google Sites usually gets through the firewall. Many universities, as well as K–12 schools, have wikis available within their course management systems, but I usually use an external service because it allows teachers to retain access to the material in the wiki for as long as I keep the site. You can delete sites, but most services allow you to leave them up indefinitely.

Reference

Coiro, J. (2005). Making sense of online text. *Educational Leadership*, 63(2), 30–35.

CLASSROOM DISCUSSIONS UNBOUNDED FROM TIME AND PLACE

What Is It?

All language arts teachers value discussions. We want students to share their thinking in a variety of contexts: partners, small groups, and large groups. Digital platforms now make it possible for us to explode the four walls of our classrooms, and eliminate part of the pressures of time by including digital discussion opportunities in our courses.

What Do Teachers Need to Know?

Face-to-face discussion provides important learning opportunities in classrooms and aids in developing the habit of collegial interactions for teachers. Opening discussion up to the digital universe provides expanded opportunities for teachers to interact and can extend in-class work. Students, who otherwise would be hesitant to talk, often are motivated to contribute to digital discussions. Digital discussion forums allow students to have voice and present themselves using a modality with which they are comfortable, or want to explore. Offering this as an option in some or all discussion activities will build on the community that instructors have already worked hard to create in their classrooms. I have also found that digital discussion helps students who have difficulty with staying on topic in a classroom discussion, or have a tendency to make inappropriate comments, remain focused on the topic.

The CCSS will create even greater need for the inclusion of digital spaces for discussions. The standards are quite clear that oral communication and presentation skills are important. Inclusion of digital opportunities to develop these skills can help teachers move toward those goals.

When working on comprehension or understanding of either specific written text, or big ideas in a classroom, digital discussion spaces have some great advantages. Individuals have the luxury of time to think about ideas and events instead of having to produce their ideas on the spot. They also have the opportunity to be a bit more thoughtful or reflective in their responses to the contributions of their classmates. How many of us have finally "thought of" what we really wanted to say in a circumstance just after everyone has left the room? Digital discussion spaces eliminate the boundary that time has forced on our responses. Participants can return to the discussion more than once to add to their initial response, comment on or add to the responses of others, and add new ideas. It has the additional advantage of offering opportunities for deepening the thinking of participants over time. Discussions are no longer one-time events bounded in space. Instead they can become threads that weave through time, bringing our community of inquiry back to important ideas for weeks or longer.

ACTIVITY 6.5
VoiceThread
Erica Bowers

Activity Type: Collaborative online activity.

Materials:
- Computer access.
- An instructor site at *www. voicethread.com*.
- Tutorial PowerPoint for online courses.
- Project guidelines and grading rubrics.

Standards Links

IRA Professional Standards:
1.1 Recognize major theories of reading and writing processes.

2.3 Incorporate traditional print, digital, and online resources as instructional tools to enhance student learning.

Duration: Six online assignments.

Professional Learning Focus:

- Use discussion to build understanding of the definition of reading based on research and how your personal definition influences your teaching/assessment of reading.
- Explore an Internet communications tool that is also used in K–8 classrooms.

K–8 Student Learning Focus:

- Use discussion and collaboration to build understanding of content-area topics.
- Navigating online texts.
- Critically evaluating information.

Common Core State Standards: Reading Anchor Standards

7. Integrate and evaluate content presented in diverse media and format, including visually, quantitatively, as well as words.

Speaking and Listening Anchor Standards

1. Prepare for and participate effectively in a range of conversations and collaborations with diverse partners, building on others' ideas and expressing their own clearly and persuasively.

5. Make strategic use of digital media and visual displays of data to express information and enhance understandings of presentations.

Rationale

VoiceThread (VT) is a powerful application enabling users to share information in many modes. VT is a free service, although it does offer individual and site licenses with increased capabilities. VT encourages discussion and commentary on work posted on the central canvas that is the center of each screen, as noted in Figure 6.6.

Images, documents, presentations, and videos can all be uploaded to be shared for group discussions. Visitors to a VT view the page or pages in the thread and have the option of leaving a comment in five different ways: microphone, telephone, webcam, text, or by uploading an audio file. Like a wiki, VT requires Internet access and a short orientation to understand how to participate.

Teachers are now using VT as a way to differentiate instruction, offer peer responses to student writing or artwork, and respond to brief video segments. It also offers possibilities for pre- and postreading comprehension activities. VT conversations that have been designated *Open for Sharing* enable users to view examples of excellent ways to use VT in both the K–12 classroom and for higher education.

VT can be especially useful when trying to create a sense of community—whether it is in an online college course, in the K–8 classroom, or communicating with parents. When teaching an online college course I prefer VT to a blog or discussion board as each teacher has an avatar, similar to Facebook. A VT conversation is easy to embed into a wiki or on a college online platform.

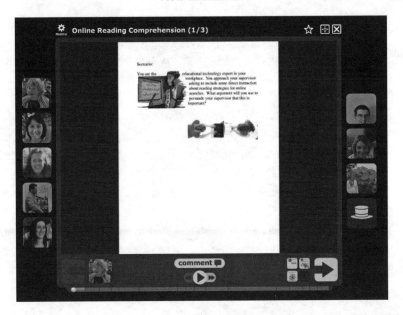

FIGURE 6.6. Sample screen shot of VoiceThread. Reprinted by permission.

Description

The purpose of this assignment is to have students refine their personal definition of reading by reviewing what researchers throughout history have described as the act of reading. Discussion around defining reading occurs in digital environments.

Week 1: Providing the Technical Groundwork

As this assignment occurs in the first course of an online graduate program, many preservice teachers need support in using some of the technology. To provide a scaffold, the week before we begin using VT for substantive discussions, the teachers are provided with a video tutorial that I made, which shows how to access and use VT. In face-to-face courses, instructors could demonstrate this during class time. We then have the teachers participate in a low-stress, introduce-yourself activity where they use some of the capabilities of VT; uploading a document to the VT, adding voice or typing a comment, and using the doodle tool.

Week 2: Surfacing and Building on Prior Knowledge

1. The teachers begin by writing their personal definition of reading. They then post their definition on their group's wiki page. A BlackBoard discussion site would also serve the purpose.

2. During the following week the teachers read their group members' definitions and revise their original definition. They add their new definition to the group wiki, including a reflection on how their group members' definitions influenced their revised definition.

Week 3: Establishing a Definition of Reading Based on Research

1. During Week 3, the teachers use VT to view various research-based definitions of reading. They post comments on the definitions that resonate the most and the least with them. The post should include a rationalization for their choice.

2. Also during this week, the teachers post how the activity aided in the refinement of their definition.

3. Finally, the teachers go to the final slide of the VT and post their final definition of reading.

I assess the assignment using the rubric in Figure 6.7.

Discussion

What I have noticed about this activity and other discussion activities in the online environment is that you actually get to "hear" all of the voices in the class. Many times when teaching a face-to-face class you have students who dominate the conversations and others who are happy to sit quietly and not participate. The online discussion requires everyone to have a voice. VT, in particular, does an excellent job of building community in an online environment as you and your students get to "hear" and "see" one another. In addition, I find it's important to guide teachers during the early conversations. When teachers are just beginning an online class they need to be coaxed to add more deep thought and to support that thought with citations and research. To do this, I highlight portions of teacher comments that exhibit deep thought, demonstrate strong support from research or the text, and include proper use of citations and APA format.

Working in VT gives teachers a chance to learn the technology and experience its strengths and weaknesses. I also share with them ways to use VT in K–8 settings.

Criteria	0	1	3	4
Quality	The teacher did not contribute at all.	The teacher was underprepared and contributions suggest readings were not completed.	Contribution to the dialogue was minimal, did not further the dialogue, or help push thinking. Several parts of the activity were omitted or the teacher only contributed basic facts, did not back up opinions with examples and/or references when applicable, or did not integrate comments/ implications from others. Postings suggest surface thinking about the topic of the discussion, materials, and concepts.	The teacher responded to all parts of the activity, backed up opinions with examples and/ or references when applicable, and integrated comments/ implications from others. Postings suggest deep thinking about the topic of the discussion, materials, and concepts, and they help further the dialogue and push thinking.
Timelines	One or more of the required posts is more than 72 hours late.	One or more of the required posts is between 25 to 72 hours late.	One or more of the required posts is between 1 to 24 hours late.	All required posts are made on time.
APA and grammar, mechanics, and spelling	Mistakes in APA, spelling, grammar, and mechanics are excessive.	Mistakes in APA, spelling, grammar, and mechanics detract from the meaning of the message.	Minimal mistakes in APA, spelling, grammar, and mechanics.	No mistakes in APA, spelling, grammar, and mechanics.

FIGURE 6.7. Rubric for VoiceThread discussion activity.

CHAPTER 7

Differentiation for Diversity

Celebrate diversity! Yes, it is a cliché, but the variety of experiences and ways of viewing the world embodied in our children bring richness and energy to our classrooms. Meeting children wherever they are in their literacy learning journey, and helping them to grow from that point forward is the challenge faced by all teachers. Embracing diversity and the inclusive classroom can provide rich learning experiences for all children and teachers (Peck, Galluci, & Staub, 2002). This is a difficult, yet deeply satisfying task for educators. In this chapter we address ways in which teachers can vary tasks, texts, levels of support, and other aspects of the instructional environment to meet the needs of the variety of learners in their classrooms. We also include information that we think teachers would find particularly helpful about language learning and motivation.

DIVERSITY OF LITERACY LEARNERS

What Is It?

In much of the discourse about public education, diversity is shorthand for children who are different in some way from what is considered mainstream—that is, white, middle-class, English speakers with typical learning abilities. Children meeting that profile no longer constitute the majority in most U.S. cities, yet the majority of teachers are white, middle-class females (Hollis & Guzman, 2010). Differences between teachers and their students along the dimensions of race, culture, language, social class, and ethnicity can affect children's response to instruction, particularly when these differences produce misunderstandings and miscommunication.

We broadly define diversity to include differences in ethnicity and culture, as well as differences in experiences outside of school, in dispositions, individual preferences, and current levels of achievement—additional types of diversity that affect literacy learning.

What Do Teachers Need to Know?

Today, when standards are higher than ever before, while children living in poverty and children from historically marginalized groups continue to perform at far lower levels than middle-class white children, it is essential that all teachers have the knowledge and skills to reach students from traditionally marginalized groups, and those with literacy learning difficulties. Teaching reading and writing effectively to diverse students is the job of today's literacy teacher. Students will differ on many dimensions even in classrooms that appear homogeneous.

A child is more than the sum of his or her labels. The relationships among children's outward appearance, internal identity, home experiences, and in-school learning is complex. Teachers must be wary of stereotyping and overgeneralizing, but should not ignore racial, ethnic, and cultural differences. Some white teachers follow a social convention that considers open acknowledgment of skin color to be impolite. On the contrary, acknowledging such differences allows all children to be visible (Paley, 2000).

All children in our schools are English language learners; a central purpose of education is to foster further oral and written language development. We use the term *English language learners* to refer to those children adding English to the language they acquired at home. English language learners are not a uniform group. Some students were born and raised in the United States, while others have spent years in foreign refugee camps. Some are literate in their home language, while others may not have ever held a pencil or seen a print version of their language. Children who are already literate in one language will have an easier time learning to read and write in English.

Native-English speakers are not uniform, either. Some native-English speakers have had rich and/or school-like language experiences at home, and others have not. They bring dialect diversity to our classrooms. Dialects that vary from Standard English, such as Appalachian or African American Vernacular English (AAVE), are often stigmatized as improper or inferior English. However, professional linguists do not consider these varieties inferior because they conform to consistent rules, and speakers are fully able to express ideas using the dialect. Nevertheless, conscious or unconscious dialect prejudice is widespread, even among individuals who speak the variation.

ACTIVITY 7.1
Diversity Graffiti Wall
SUSAN D. MARTIN

Activity Type: In-class activity.

Materials: Poster paper/pens, previously read articles, book chapters.

Duration: About 1 hour.

Professional Learning Focus:
- Teachers develop knowledge of children's diversities as they relate to literacy and literacy instruction.
- Immersion in an instructional approach that they could use with students.

K–8 Student Learning Focus: N/A.

Standards Links

IRA Professional Standards:
4.1 Recognize, understand, and value the forms of diversity that exist in society and their importance in learning to read and write.

Demonstrate an understanding of the ways in which diversity can be used to strengthen a literate society, making it more productive, more adaptable to changes, and more equitable.

Demonstrate an understanding of the ways in which the various forms of diversity interact with reading and writing development.

Common Core State Standards: N/A.

Rationale

Although our undergraduate and graduate teacher education programs include courses dedicated to development of understandings regarding children's diversities in classroom settings, I consider it important to explicitly address issues of diversity as they relate to literacy learning in my courses. In this activity, I hope to foster dispositional responses and deeper senses of responsibility toward meeting the various needs of all their students. Discussion about many aspects of diversity from a variety of perspectives aids in achieving this goal. In addition, the opportunity to choose their own topics for more in-depth reading increases my preservice teachers' engagement and knowledge development.

This activity fits into the section of lessons in my writing courses that focus on writing development and the need to know our learners. We first look broadly at how writing typically develops, and then home in on what might be going on with specific students—what factors can influence individual development.

Description

1. This activity begins with reading assignments prior to class (see Figure 7.1). I have all students read two powerful and moving short selections: "Two Languages in Mind, But Just One in the Heart" by Louise Erdrich, a novelist of Native American heritage found in *Writers on Writing: Collected Essays from the New York Times*; and "Education from an Autistic Perspective" (Section 8) from *Teaching Hope: Stories from Freedom Writer Teachers* by Erin Gruwell. One is a first-person description of experiencing issues of culture and language, and the second is a teachers' personal depiction of living with autism. I also have teachers read about issues of motivation (e.g., *Best Practices in Promoting Motivation in Writing*: Boscolo & Gelati, 2007).

Teachers also self-select an article from an available set focused on a particular issue such as learning differences, language, race, special needs, or gender. I try to find articles that are research based and practice focused, with practical ideas for teachers. Articles focused on writing have been hard to find, but are becoming more common. A list of readings used in this activity can be found in this activity's reference section.

2. Teachers are also asked to write a personal response to the articles, which provides them with an opportunity to reflect on and connect these ideas to prior understandings (see guidelines in Figure 7.1).

3. In class, teachers meet in small groups based on the self-selected topics. I hope that teachers have opted to read from the range of articles, as they are meant to complement one another. Each group constructs a chart that lists key points from their articles including strengths to build on in the classroom, challenges to teaching, and implications/ideas for teacher practices.

4. Once the charts are completed, they are hung together on a whiteboard with their sides touching. This provides the foundation for our graffiti wall. We gather as a group around the wall.

5. Teachers are instructed to read and respond to the ideas on the wall without talking. They may (a) add comments, (b) ask questions, and/or (c) draw lines connecting ideas across the charts. They are required to make three entries on our graffiti wall. Extra space on the whiteboard can be used as well. I have many markers available.

This week we will continue our focus on issues of knowing our students and begin delving into issues of our students' diversities and differentiating for instruction.

READING FOR ISSUES OF DIVERSITY

All the readings for this topic are in the Diversity Readings link in the left-side bar on our class home page.

Everyone: Read the first three brief selections: *Two Languages in Mind, But Just One in Heart*, Section 8 from *Teaching for Hope*, and *Best Practices in Promoting Motivation for Writing*.

Jigsaw: Choose an area of interest: second language learners, special education learners, or gender differences in writing. Once you have identified your area, read the abstracts to figure out which *one* article you would like to read. You will be responsible for being able to *discuss* these points with a small group:
- What characteristics do these students bring to writing learning opportunities in classrooms?
- What benefits/challenges do these characteristics bring to their teachers?
- What are the implications for effective instruction for these students? Think especially about issues of motivation.

Not every article will address these specific questions. Do what you can.

Respond: Write a one-page, personal response for all the selections you read (overall concepts, not each article one by one).

GUIDELINES FOR A PERSONAL RESPONSE

What: A reading response is a particular type or genre of writing.

Purposes: To communicate how you've connected with and understood the reading. To provide an opportunity for you to think more about and *connect* with the content of reading. To prepare you for lively and thoughtful discussion.

Audience: Your instructor, yourself.

Key elements: An informal and personal type of writing (*conversation*) that may communicate and *discuss* one or more of these elements:
1. What have you learned from *these* articles (*What made me say "Aha!"?*)?
2. How have ideas in this article connected with your prior understandings, experiences, readings from the text, and/or our discussions in class (*What other thoughts/images came to mind as I read?*)?

(continued)

FIGURE 7.1. Guidelines for reading and response: Diversity.

3. What questions did the reading cause you to think about (*What is confusing for me?*)?

4. Do you agree/disagree with the author's ideas and why (*I can really agree/disagree with this idea because. . . .*)?

5. How might you use the ideas in your future (*How might I use these ideas in my future classroom? What does this mean for how I'll teach writing?*)?

These responses are not summaries or regurgitation of the information.

FIGURE 7.1. *(continued)*

6. Once everyone has had a chance to participate, including me, we begin to debrief what we notice. For example, typically issues of motivation, scaffolding, and relationships are noted on every chart and are very clearly linked on the graffiti board. Other issues, such as code switching, stand alone. I make sure that all questions have been answered. I highlight important points or add any that were missed. The resulting product is typically very interesting, and definitely looks like graffiti! (See Figure 7.2 for an example.)

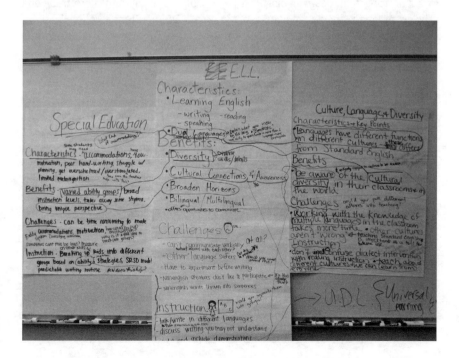

FIGURE 7.2. Example of a diversity graffiti wall.

7. I follow this activity up with a short video clip of a teacher conferencing with a second-language learner about his written piece. It clearly depicts differentiated feedback that supports this child's writing and use of code switching. This is my own video clip from classroom research, but there is a DVD that accompanies *Teaching Writing: Balancing Process and Product* (Tompkins, 2011) that depicts teachers and students in classrooms involved in writing conferences.

8. Teachers then engage in a summarization/reflection activity. Depending on time, I have either small groups or individuals create a list of teacher practices that will help support and differentiate learning in the classroom. I ask teachers to make pledges to themselves of what they will do in classroom practice.

Discussion

Although I have used the graffiti wall in a course focused on writing and writing instruction, it could be easily adapted to any literacy courses, depending on the reading selections. This activity provides a foundation for other activities in the course that focus on specific differentiation strategies such as choice, scaffolding, and building on students' strengths and interests.

Based on teachers' oral and written feedback, this is a powerful activity for influencing attitudes. Reading first-person pieces along with more traditional articles on learning and teaching seems to create an important emotional impact, especially for teachers who have not yet experienced the emotional attachment to students. I am always impressed with the summaries and pledges for practice.

I have lately been considering limiting choices in my undergraduate courses just to issues of language learners and children with special needs. Many of the teachers opt for the articles on gender differences. I am not sure why, but I do not think they have understandings yet of the complexities they will face in classrooms with English language learners and struggling writers.

I have listed a few articles in Figure 7.3; they vary in length and complexity. Some are more appropriate for inservice teachers. It is also possible that you will want the teachers to do their own searches for articles on the topics that are of interest to them—set within particular guidelines. I typically write a brief blurb for each article on our course web site where they are available to teachers.

References

Boscolo, P., & Gelati, C. (2007). Best practices in promoting motivation in writing. In S. Graham, C. S. MacArthur, & J. Fitzgerald (Eds.), *Best practices in writing instruction* (pp. 202–221). New York: Guilford Press.

Tompkins, G. (2011). *Teaching writing: Balancing process and product.* New York: Allyn & Bacon.

Writing and Second-Language Learners

Gersten, R., & Baker, S. (2000). What we know about effective instructional practices for English language learners. *Exceptional Children, 66*(4), 454–470.

Shaugoury, R. (2009, March). Language to language: Nurturing writing development in multilingual classrooms. *Young Children, 64*(2), 52–57.

Writing and Race/Ethnicity

Delpit, L. (1998). The silenced dialogue: Power and pedagogy in educating other people's children. *Harvard Education Review, 58*(3), 280–299.

Writing and Gender

King, K., & Gurian, M. (2006). Teaching to the minds of boys. *Educational Leadership, 64*(1), 56–61.

Writing and Students with Special Needs

Troia, G. (2006). Writing instruction for students with learning disabilities. In S. Graham, C. S. MacArthur, & J. Fitzgerald (Eds.), *Handbook of writing research* (pp. 324–336). New York: Guilford Press.

FIGURE 7.3. Readings used for graffiti wall activity.

DIFFERENTIATING INSTRUCTION

What Is It?

Not all children in a class need to read the same texts, perform the same tasks, or receive the same level of support from the teacher. Each student should be working at an appropriate level of challenge to make progress.

What Do Teachers Need to Know?

Differentiating for children's literacy learning can be challenging. At times, this means developing new attitudes and learning ways of working in the classroom. Knowledge of practical strategies and approaches is critical to successful differentiation as well.

By considering each child's interests, background knowledge, skills, motivation, attention span, and independence when designing instructional tasks, teachers differentiate their instruction to reach all of their students. The techniques and principles that follow enable teachers to connect to all the children in their classrooms and provide them with instruction at an appropriate level of challenge.

Knowing and Valuing Your Students

When teachers respect and appreciate students' home languages, and understand how norms of communication differ in their students' home cultures, they are in a better position to use examples that are familiar to children, and to bridge incongruities between home and school settings. Children are more open to school learning when they feel valued and understood. Small gestures such as learning a few words of the languages children speak, and bringing representative artifacts from their cultures into the classroom go a long way toward establishing a welcoming, supportive environment. To learn about the cultures represented in their classrooms, teachers can invite community members into the classroom, make home visits, shop or otherwise spend time in the community(ies) their children live in, read books or watch movies made by individuals well versed in the culture, and, of course, ask their students about their lives. Establishing an environment where children feel psychologically safe trying out their developing English language skills is also critically important.

Children derive a special satisfaction when they see people like themselves in texts and school curricula. Teachers may need to make a special effort to find such texts for their students, yet should be careful not to limit them to such texts. We also think teachers need to look beyond outward characteristics such as skin color, gender, and family origin when seeking such matches that help children connect to text.

Choice

The second strategy, *choice*, is perhaps the easiest strategy to implement. When students select the book they are reading or the topic of the composition they are writing, they are more likely to be invested in the activity and motivated to complete it. Teachers can place boundaries on choice by leaving some dimensions open to student discretion while designating others closed—for example, the teacher chooses the genre of a composition, while the student chooses the topic or specific audience. All students benefit from having choice, but this strategy is especially important for students who are disaffected or discouraged. Having some choice gives meaning to a task and a sense of control to those readers who struggle, supporting their persistence through difficult work. This strategy can also encourage advanced readers and writers to select texts or tasks with appropriate challenge.

Scaffolding and the Gradual Release of Responsibility

Scaffolding is an action or factor that makes an instructional activity more accessible for a learner. Teachers, tasks, and/or materials can provide scaffolding. Selecting a cumulative text such as *The Napping House* (Wood & Wood, 2000) for fluency development is an example of scaffolding through the choice of material. Tasks can also scaffold learning. For example, shared reading, where the teacher and the students are reading together, offers more reading support for students than guided reading, where the teacher guides the student through a selected text. Providing a framework for writing with the words *first, then, next,* and *finally* makes writing a simple summary attainable for many children. Likewise, explicit teaching of planning strategies—such as use of a particular graphic organizer that aids students in gathering and organizing ideas—supports students' writing processes.

Some literacy activities are designed for the teacher to adjust support according to the amount children require, such as sharing the pen in writing activities (interactive writing), where the student(s) and teacher write together (McCarrier et al., 1999). With the gradual release of responsibility model, teachers provide less support over time as the students become more competent with practice, until children become fully independent with the task.

Gersten and Baker (2000) recommend adjusting the language expectations for English language learners according to the cognitive load of a task. If a task is demanding, demands for language performance need to be decreased. Similarly, when cognitive demands of a task are low, demands for language productivity and usage can be increased. When learning a new language, learners move back and forth between the languages or codes, sometimes even within a single sentence. Allowing use of both languages (code switching) in this manner during informal discussion or informal or first-draft writing is one method of reducing the language demand on the children.

Multiple Entry Points

Providing *multiple entry points* to a task is another strategy favored by some teachers who work to meet all students' needs. In this strategy, the teacher uses open-ended questions to provide opportunities for students to participate at different levels. For example, a first-grade teacher who is writing and reading a "morning message" on chart paper might ask his or her students "What do you notice?" This open-ended question gives children a range of possible answers from such things as "I see three letters B" to "I see the word *the* three times," to " 'Sarah' is the name of my dog." Open-ended questions without a defined right answer provide the opportunity for children to be successful in many different ways.

Flexible Grouping

Flexible grouping affords the efficiency of small-group instruction without the attendant issues of negative self-worth, often associated with static groups, particularly in reading. Flexible groups may be built around a level of text complexity, a learning objective (diagraphs), topic (frogs), a genre (mysteries), or student interests. They may also be invitational, in which a teacher selects specific students for the group and also invites any other children in the class to choose to join as well.

Build Language, Especially Academic Language

No matter their age, children need regular exposure to texts with more complex ideas and a richer, more varied vocabulary than those they can read independently. The texts that beginners or children performing below grade expectations can handle on their own do not contain those complex ideas and rich vocabulary. Without a steady input of more complex text, children lose critical opportunities to build the background knowledge, language structures, and implicit text structure knowledge needed to understand these texts. Critical thinking with complex text can be approached through read-alouds and shared reading, even with primary-age children.

Vocabulary development has always been part of a reading/language arts teacher's job, but for obvious reasons it is particularly important for English language learners and children who come to school with limited vocabularies. Extensive use of gesture, photographs, real objects, and video have been recommended for English language learners, but are powerful aids in helping all children understand new words and concepts. If a child's home language has English cognates—words that have similar roots in two languages (*comprende* in Spanish and *comprehend* in English, for example)—teachers can use the similar words when speaking to make their own language more understandable and show children how many of the words they know in their home language (cognates) can help them learn English. We recommend dedicated time for vocabulary development, perhaps as a component of interactive read-alouds. Well-supported approaches to building vocabulary are described in Chapter 3.

Academic writing is more abstract and includes more dense and complex sentences than those used in conversational language (Townsend & Lapp, 2011). Formal and academic language CALP (cognitive academic language proficiency; Cummins, 1981) takes English language learners about 8 years to develop and requires explicit instruction, whereas conversational English—BICS (basic interpersonal conversational language)—is typically developed through experience within 2 years. It is important to provide explicit instruction that assists in understanding academic vocabulary and to identify the structures and conventions that mark the academic register to children who have limited exposure to formal English. For example, teachers can show students how to connect clauses using signal words (e.g., *because, so, as a result*) or help them deconstruct and reconstruct complex sentences.

According to linguists, everyone speaks a dialect. An individual's home dialect is his or her home language, a part of his or her culture, and tied closely to his or her identity. American standard English is one dialect (actually there are many varieties of standard English), the variety of English spoken in Appalachia is another. Mastery of standard English and the academic register of standard English is a prerequisite for entry into higher education and many occupations, so it is incumbent upon teachers to help children gain control of standard (formal) English as an additional dialect. However, constant correction of students' home speech and writing patterns in the attempt to help them gain control over standard/formal English can result in students "reject[ing] the school's language and everything else it has to offer" (Delpit, 2002, p. 47) when they repeatedly experience such devaluing of their home language. Corrections of dialect-influenced pronunciation differences from standard English significantly interfere with a child's ability to focus on meaning while reading, and also undermines the child's confidence in him- or herself as a reader.

Contrastive analysis, a technique borrowed from teaching additional languages, is a highly effective technique for helping speakers of varieties of English understand and gain control over the features of standard English (Townsend, & Lapp, 2011; Wheeler & Swords, 2004, 2010). With that approach children become adept at code switching, selecting and using the dialect appropriate to a situation: informal for a skit about kids on the playground, formal for a letter to the principal. Students can practice formal English with tasks that lend themselves to rehearsal and practice such as formal debates, speeches, podcasts, or Readers Theater (see Activity 7.3). When writing, children have time to edit their first drafts to conform to formal English syntax and conventions. An important reason for the greater effectiveness of contrastive analysis and code switching over the more familiar correction approach is that children see their home dialects and accompanying cultures valued rather than dismissed as illegitimate and unworthy.

ACTIVITY 7.2
Multimodal Vocabulary Cards
SUSAN D. MARTIN

Activity Type: In-class activity.

Materials: 4″ × 6″ index cards, list of vocabulary words, previously written "story" containing vocabulary words.

Duration: 30 minutes.

Professional Learning Focus: Experiencing an interactive and multimodal vocabulary activity.

K–8 Student Learning Focus: Experiencing an interactive and multimodal vocabulary activity.

Standards Links

IRA Professional Standards:
2.2 Use appropriate and varied instructional approaches.

As needed, adapt instructional approaches and materials to meet the language-proficiency needs of English learners.

Common Core State Standards: Reading Anchor Standards
4. Interpret words and phrases as they are used in a text.

Rationale

One of the misconceptions about vocabulary development that I have noticed is the belief that children need *skill-and-drill* vocabulary activity. One of the activities I use to disrupt this way of thinking is multimodal vocabulary cards, a variation of *word cards* (Fisher, Brozo, Frey, & Ivey, 2011). This activity involves the teachers in developing personal word understandings (Alvermann, Swafford, & Montero, 2004) and provides opportunity for multiple exposures to words in engaging ways. This activity allows teachers to personally experience activities that involve discussion around word meanings, and that allow students to establish connections through visual and kinesthetic activity.

Many of the preservice teachers I teach will work with English language learners. The visual and kinesthetic elements of this activity are especially useful to second-language learners.

Description

1. I provide each small group of teachers a 4″ × 6″ index card and their vocabulary word. For this activity, I use the words actually used in a second-grade classroom: *amazing, clustered, wandered, raced,* and *gathered.*

2. Then I ask them to agree on and draw a picture that helps them make a personal connection with the word on the other side of the index card, and to come up with a motion that represents the word. I give them 10 minutes or so to work as a group.

3. Each group then presents their word, definition, picture, and movement to the rest of the class. Everyone practices the motions during the presentations.

4. I give them a little time to practice going back and forth between word and motion. Then I read a previously prepared paragraph that contains all of the words. As they hear me read the word, teachers need to stand up and do the relevant motion.

5. We then debrief the activity from both the perspective of the learner and the teacher.

Discussion

In my elementary content literacy course, teachers learned many strategies for teaching vocabulary. They were most enthusiastic, however, about this activity. They loved participating in the visual, kinesthetic, and social aspects of multimodal cards. Since I had observed and brought this activity directly from a second-grade classroom (thank you, Lili Saum, Joplin Elementary, Meridian, Idaho), I shared my perceptions that the second graders were equally engaged. I also described how this was an activity designed to provide practice with and personal linking to the words, as teacher and students had delved into definitions earlier. This link to an actual classroom perhaps added to teachers' enthusiasm for the activity. I have thought it would be interesting to try this activity with vocabulary words from our courses as well.

When we debriefed the activity, I tried to make sure that teachers understood the minds-on, as well as hands-on aspect of this activity. We talked about other possible uses for this activity, for example, use of either movement and visuals could also be used to help students understand distinctions between closely related words such as *walk, amble, stroll,* and *strut.*

References

Alvermann, D. E., Swafford, J., & Montero, M. K. (2004). *Content area literacy instruction for the elementary grades.* New York: Pearson.

Fisher, D., Brozo, W. G., Frey, N., & Ivey, G. (2011). *50 instructional routines to develop content literacy* (2nd ed.). New York: Pearson.

ACTIVITY 7.3
Circle Reading and Readers Theater with Folktales
SUSAN D. MARTIN

Activity Type: In-class activity.

Materials: Enough short scripts for several small groups of students.

Duration: About 45 minutes for circle reading; 30–45 minutes longer for Readers Theater presentations.

Professional Learning Focus:
- Immersion in activity to understand its purposes.
- Use of folktales from different cultures as content for Readers Theater.

K–8 Student Learning Focus:
Rereading for expression, language patterns, reading fluency, and comprehension.

Standards Links

IRA Professional Standards:
2.2 Use appropriate and varied instructional approaches, including those that develop word recognition, language, comprehension, strategic knowledge, and reading–writing connections.

4.2 Use a literacy curriculum and engage in instructional practices that positively impact students knowledge, beliefs, and engagement with the features of diversity.

Common Core State Standards:
Reading Standards: Foundational Skills
Fluency
4. Read with sufficient accuracy and fluency to support comprehension.

Speaking and Listening Anchor Standards
6. Adapt speech to a variety of contexts and communicative tasks, demonstrating command of formal English when indicated or appropriate.

Rationale

Circle reading (Walker & Plant, 1990) and Readers Theater—informal readings and performances of scripts—provide opportunities for authentic rereading of text. Readers Theater can be motivating and engaging for students, even for resistant readers (Worthy & Prater, 2002). Readers Theatre and circle reading—a less formal version of Readers Theater—offer opportunities for those who are learning the patterns, sounds, and words of English to practice reading and speaking. Furthermore, to speak with intonation within the persona of a character requires understanding of both the action and the character, thus fostering comprehension. I have seen a small third grader use her whole body to convey the sense that she was a massive water buffalo—to great effect!

By engaging themselves in circle reading and Readers Theater, teachers experience what their students would be thinking and doing. I model the teacher's role in supporting this instructional approach.

Description

1. Before class, the teachers will have previously read a short selection, "I Thought about It All Night": Readers Theatre for Reading Fluency and Motivation (Worthy & Prater, 2002), which explains the rationale for using Readers Theater in classrooms.

2. I have copied and prepared groups of short scripts to equal the number of students in the class. I use several from the book *Multicultural Folktales for the Feltboard and Readers Theater* (Sierra, 1996). This book contains scripts from cultures around the world that are funny and engaging for adults as well as children. I have also found published scripts and scripts online. Lois Walker's website (*http://scriptsforschools.com*) is a good website to find scripts and resources on teaching circle reading and Readers Theater.

3. In class, we begin with a short discussion about Readers Theater, and the more informal and less time-consuming variation, circle reading. I discuss folktales and give a rationale for using this genre. I model how to think about the character you are and how to read for expression.

4. Students meet in small groups. I provide them with a copy of Lois Walker's "Eight Steps to a Successful Circle Reading" (Walker & Plant, 1990):

- Step 1. Duplicate classroom scripts for your readers.
- Step 2. Ask your readers to silently read through the entire story.
- Step 3. After all the readers have read the story silently, gather readers into a large circle. Include yourself in the circle, if possible.
- Step 4. Next, begin by asking the reader on your left to read the first reader's part in the script, the next person to read the second reader's part, and so on. No individual parts are assigned at this point. Each reader reads in turn around the circle. Teachers can join in on the reading too.
- Step 5. When the circle has completed the story, take time to discuss the reader parts. What does each character look like? What kind of personalities do they have? How might they sound? How would each character stand or sit? What might each character wear?
- Step 6. Discuss the importance of the narrator. Explore how the narrators introduce the story, fill in all the details, set the proper mood for the story action, and help the character readers set and keep the right reading pace.
- Step 7. Review meanings and pronunciations of any difficult words.
- Step 8. Now, ask your readers to volunteer for specific reading parts.

Ask each volunteer to underline his or her lines, then read the script aloud again. Swap parts and scripts around the circle and read again. Continue until interest lags or time runs out.

5. During this time I go around and model giving feedback for oral expression and fluency.

6. We debrief the experience. I then explain the elements of Readers Theater performance. I also discuss the need for teachers to be engaging in front of a group of people. Groups practice in corners of the room for 10 minutes or so.

7. Teachers present their folktales to the class.

8. We debrief the activity, both from the perspective of the learner (What happened when you had to reread? How did it feel getting up in front of the class?) and from the perspective of the teacher (What did you notice about this activity as a teacher?). I also discuss how teachers could have older students write their own Readers Theater scripts by adapting stories.

Discussion

I find this activity to be a great way to develop a sense of community in the college classroom. The preservice teachers are always very engaged and enjoy themselves. We laughed heartily when one group cast a male teacher in the role of Senorita Ant, quite a flirt. Another time teachers placed their chins on the back edge of a table and spoke their lines as the cabbage chorus in an African tale. Just as any classroom teacher, I find that I learn about the teachers from watching these presentations. Some of their abilities really take me by surprise. It reminds me that even in college courses "kid watching" (Goodman, 1985) can be crucial to knowing one's students.

The conversations around this activity are always rich, and I share my own experiences engaging and watching children involved in both circle reading and Readers Theater. I explain how, for example, when I was running an after-school tutoring program, I happened to walk by a tutor who was involved in a circle read with her students. She was reading with great expression. I complimented her on expressive reading and how it sounded just like the character would. Immediately, the children reading began to read more expressively as well. I also make sure to stress how easy it is to engage children in informal circle reading and how it does not take up as much time as preparing to read to an audience. This would be an instructional approach that practicum and student teachers could easily implement.

References

Goodman, Y. (1985). Kid watching: Observing in the classroom. In A. Jagger & M. Smith-Burke (Eds.), Observing the language learner (pp. 9–18). Newark, DE: International Reading Association.

Sierra, J. (1996). *Multicultural folktales for the feltboard and readers theater.* Phoenix, AZ: Oryx Press.

Walker, L. J., & Plant, R. (1990). *Readers theatre in the elementary classroom: A take part teacher's guide.* North Vancouver, BC: Take Part Productions.

Worthy, J., & Prater, K. (2002). The intermediate grades: "I thought about it all night": Readers Theatre for reading fluency and motivation. *The Reading Teacher, 56*(3), 294–297.

Select Texts with the Child in Mind

Matching readers to texts involves many considerations including the specific purpose for reading a particular text, and the interests and background knowledge of the reader. The difficulty of the text for an individual student involves many factors; simply matching the student to a Lexile level or guided reading level is often insufficient. Just a few of the factors teachers need to take into account are the complexity of the ideas, the density of new concepts, the number of words unfamiliar to the student in their printed form, and whether the student has the decoding skills to figure out those words. In addition to all of those factors, particularly when working with older struggling readers, it is critical to locate texts the student finds engaging. These students' resistance can often be overcome by offering some choice to the student, and finding texts and tasks the student finds irresistible. When finding texts for young, advanced readers we need to consider their emotional maturity. Even though a second grader may have the reading skills to read books typically read by fifth and sixth graders, the subject matter may not be psychologically appropriate.

ACTIVITY 7.4
Racism and Sexism in Children's Books
NANCY A. PLACE

Activity Type: Homework and in-class activity.

Materials:
- *Ten Quick Ways to Analyze Children's Books for Racism and Sexism*, a publication of the Council on Interracial Books for

Standards Links

IRA Professional Standards:
4.2 Candidates use a literacy curriculum and engage in instructional practices that positively impact students' knowledge, beliefs, and engagement with the features of diversity.

Children (CIBC) adapted by the California State Department of Education in 1998 and available online at *www.chil-es.org/10ways.pdf.*

- A variety of children's books brought to class by the instructor and the teachers.

Common Core State Standards: Reading Anchor Standards
Craft and Structure
6. Assess how point of view or purpose shapes the content and style of a text.

Duration: In class: 45 minutes to 1.5 hours depending on the intensity of the discussion.

Professional Learning Focus:
Identification and appropriate use of children's books with racist and sexist elements.

K–8 Student Learning Focus:
Identification of racism and sexism in children's books.

Rationale

Although racism and sexism in children's books is not generally as blatant as it was when the CIBC initially published their groundbreaking guidelines for analyzing books for racism and sexism, elements of racism and sexism still are present in children's books. In discussing and putting a name to thoughts that may or may not be below the level of consciousness, teachers and children gain insight and power over the materials and attitudes that shape all of our lives.

Description

Prior to Class

Teachers read *Ten Quick Ways to Analyze Children's Books for Racism and Sexism*. They also bring to class books that they enjoyed as children and books that they are using in their teaching placements. I particularly ask them to bring materials that they believe are problematic, as well as materials that they think are good examples of nonstereotypical depictions of women or marginalized populations. I also bring books that meet these two criteria. The focus is on materials that could be used in K–8 classrooms.

During Class

As a class we review the course norms. These norms have previously been developed by the class (see Chapter 5) and include such items as active listening, valuing other's contributions, and respectful responses that forward the thinking of the group.

The teachers are then divided into groups of four. Each group has access to a variety of books including books that I have brought, as well as their own materials. I usually find that four to six books per table group is the right amount. I ask each group to sort the books into piles based on whether the book has racist and/or sexist elements and whether the book proactively works against stereotypical images. The teachers use the CIBC guidelines to justify their decisions.

Taking turns, each group shares out loud one book that they found problematic and why. This sharing frequently leads to longer discussions, particularly if the book is currently in popular use (*Skippyjon Jones* by Judy Schachner) or has been a popular childhood favorite (*The Five Chinese Brothers* by Claire Bishop). The discussions are usually thoughtful and intense and not everyone agrees with a group's decision. This is followed by groups sharing one book that they think works well to dispel stereotypes and why. My role is to maintain a neutral and respectful discourse so that all voices can be heard.

After the groups have shared we discuss whether any of the problematic books should be used with children and if yes, how they should be used. This conversation is grounded in the CIBC criteria. Some of the ideas for using books include teaching children to become "detectives" as they notice examples of stereotyping in a book, discussing the historical context of the book, and using text sets that show a variety of perspectives on a particular group (*The Paper Bag Princess* by Robert Munsch alongside a fairytale such as *Sleeping Beauty* by Walt Disney Productions).

A final aspect to this activity is a short assignment in which each teacher adds one book that could be used to support an increased understanding of diversity to a class bibliography. In addition to the usual bibliographic information, the entry includes a brief summary of the book and how the book will be used. Books with stereotypical elements can be included here with ideas about how they can be used to create teachable moments and learning opportunities for students.

Discussion

This activity never fails to elicit strong feelings on the part of the teachers, especially when the books being discussed have been childhood favorites. There is usually disagreement within the class, which I encourage. To examine previously held ideas people must feel free to put those ideas out for genuine consideration in a respectful environment.

I have found that this activity prompts teachers to choose and use their materials in a more thoughtful and nuanced way, with particular attention to balance and fairness toward children of color. The conversation leads to consideration of other kinds of diversity (physical and mental challenges and abilities, age, and class) and how celebration, empathy, and understanding may be taught in these areas using children's literature.

ACTIVITY 7.5
Illustrating the Importance of Independent-Level Text

JOANNE DURHAM

Activity Type: In-class activity.

Materials: A short paragraph of adult text with 10% of key content words omitted.

Duration: 30 minutes.

Professional Learning Focus:
- Matching text to readers and purpose.
- Differentiating instruction.

K–8 Student Learning Focus: Reading text with fluency and understanding.

Standards Links

IRA Professional Standards:
2.2 Differentiate instructional approaches to meet students' reading and writing needs.

3.3 Use assessment data to plan instruction systematically and to select appropriate traditional print, digital, and online reading resources.

Common Core State Standards Reading Anchor Standards
Range of Reading and Level of Text Complexity
10. Read and comprehend complex literary and informational texts independently and proficiently.

Reading Standards: Foundational Skills
Fluency
Read with sufficient accuracy and fluency to support comprehension.

Rationale

Teachers need to ensure that all students, including those children who are not yet independently reading on grade level, are exposed to complex texts that challenge their intellect and teach them to think inferentially and critically. Read-alouds, multiple readings, partner reading, and thematic inquiries help to scaffold entry into difficult texts. However, this important goal is often misinterpreted to mean that struggling readers should *only* read text that is very hard for them, even when they are reading independently.

It is important for teachers to understand that all readers need plenty of practice in reading texts on their own that are possible for them to decode and understand. *Reading* as I refer to it in this activity means both comprehension of printed language and accurate pronunciation of words. Many studies show that "lots of easy reading is absolutely critical to reading development and to the development of positive stances toward reading" (Allington, 2001, p. 44). While advanced readers spend much of their school day with texts that they can read fluently and understand, thus having opportunities to enjoy reading while consolidating their reading practices, struggling readers may never have this experience.

High-stakes testing adds pressure on teachers and administrators to ignore the need for appropriately leveled texts for children reading below grade level. The rationale is put forward that since children will encounter harder text on the test, they should be reading it all the time in the classroom. I have found that the simple exercise described below brings home the necessity of providing opportunities for all children to read independent-level texts, including those reading below grade level.

Description

I provide a paragraph or two of text from an adult source, often a paragraph from an SAT prep test. I substitute blanks for 10% of the key words in the original passage. I ask the participants to read the passage independently, and to be prepared to summarize it and explain the main ideas or the author's perspective.

Example:

The problem before a modern _____, hard pressed by the need of carrying on a thoroughly wholesome _____, is that of enlisting the interest of these _____ of people, and . . .

No one is ever able to explain the passage because they miss all the blank words. I then explain that if they were able to decode all the other words in the passage, they read it with 90% accuracy, the most difficult a text should be for guided reading. Then we discuss the implications for children of always being expected to make meaning from texts well above their reading levels. Finally, I provide a critical word in the passage—*newspaper*, the first omitted word—and we discuss the difference between guided and independent reading, and the purposes for a balance of reading opportunities.

Discussion

Teachers usually learn to identify frustration-, guided-, and independent-reading levels by the percentage of words read accurately. Anything below 90% is considered frustration level, and 95% or more is necessary for independent level.

However, these percentages remain abstract until one actually experiences what 90% accuracy is like for oneself as a reader. In the passage above, 3 of the 30 words in this part of the passage were eliminated; thus reading it correctly except for the blanks would be scored at 90% accuracy. Clearly, comprehension is totally compromised without the missing words. From experiencing their own failure in comprehension, participants realize that 90% accuracy is not as supportive to a reader as it sounds, particularly when the words missed carry a hefty portion of the meaning. (Miscues on function words like *the* or *of* will have far less effect upon comprehension.) We are used to the connotation of 90% as an *A*, but comprehension in this case is probably an *F*.

This experience demonstrates the futility of expecting students to do high-level thinking on their own without being able to read and/or understand the critical words. Furthermore, when struggling readers fail to answer comprehension questions about a passage that is too difficult for them to read, the remedy suggested is often to reteach the skill involved, such as identifying character traits or main ideas. This exercise helps teachers consider whether the problem is truly mastery of a comprehension skill, vocabulary knowledge, or being able to decode the words in the text. Sometimes students arrive at an accurate pronunciation, but when they do not know what the word means, they will still be unable to understand the passage. The experience encourages teachers not to waste valuable time reteaching skills unless they have more finely tuned data to support the need for such instruction.

The support offered through guided reading also becomes clear through this activity when I tell participants that the first blank word is *newspaper*. While the participants are still unable to fully comprehend the passage, they are able to make some sense from it. Providing this word is analogous to scaffolding in guided reading, when the teacher orients students to the topic to activate an appropriate schema for making meaning.

I always show the participants the complete passage after we discuss the implications. This is partly because they are curious and won't pay attention to anything else until they know what it was about! But I also use this as an opportunity to recognize that being able to read the words is just the first step in comprehension. The passage is still a bit obscure to some readers, even with being able to decode all the words. The need for various types of reading experiences becomes clearer through this demonstration. It is easier to recognize that reading aloud would be a beneficial place to show students how to handle difficult text, guided reading gives them practice with some support, and independent reading should be an opportunity to truly handle the challenges on their own.

Reference

Allington, R. L. (2001). *What really matters for struggling readers*. New York: Addison-Wesley.

Use Diagnostic and Classroom-Based Assessments to Inform Instruction

Reading and writing are both highly complex activities—not unitary processes—with many factors contributing to an individual's ease or difficulty in acquiring proficiency. Instruction at the right level of challenge for each child maintains student motivation and avoids wasting valuable instructional time with concepts already understood or too difficult for a child to master. Therefore, it is important for teachers to clearly understand the dimensions of reading and writing processes so that, in combination with their knowledge of individual children, they can provide targeted instruction to meet children's needs. Being able to provide appropriately targeted instruction is especially important for accelerating the literacy learning of underperforming children.

A widely held misconception is that reading difficulties are caused by poor phonics knowledge when, in fact, there are many reasons why children fail to reach age-level expectations in reading. For example, in reading, teachers need to consider the affective domain—a child's attitude toward reading, his or her interests, and his or her willingness to persist at difficulty. Teachers also need to think about a child's strategy use, vocabulary and background knowledge, the types and complexity of texts that he or she can comprehend, and his or her word identification skills and fluency. Similarly, in writing, a teacher needs to consider the same affective dimensions as applied to reading; the child's strategies for composition; his or her background knowledge of topics, texts, and vocabulary; and his or her proficiency in the foundational skills of spelling, handwriting, and grammar.

Classroom-based assessments (discussed in Chapter 8) can be used to determine students' strengths and weaknesses in each of these areas. When interpreted with appropriate caution, well-chosen standardized tests may also provide useful information. Once teachers understand the areas needing additional work, they can choose instructional approaches targeted to a particular area. Many books provide suggested activities targeted for specific areas of need.

Build Positive Dispositions

Variations in curiosity, persistence, and attitude toward challenge cause huge differences in literacy growth. Indeed, early differences in traits supporting academic resiliency are better predictors of reading development than early differences in phonological awareness (Niemi &

Poskiparta, 2002, as cited in McTigue, Washburn, & Liew, 2009). A "can-do" attitude, a willingness to persist in the face of difficulties, and a strong desire to learn new things provide the internal energy to learn and grow in all learning, not just literacy. Children who possess these positive dispositions can overcome minor learning difficulties with relative ease.

Success in literacy learning nurtures productive literacy dispositions. Children who succeed in literacy activities are engaged, and consequently experience enjoyment and satisfaction that help them persevere in challenging literacy situations, such as reading or writing complex text. On the other hand, interfering dispositions such as a low tolerance for frustration, avoidance of challenges, fear of being wrong, or a belief that innate ability matters more than individual effort prevent children from progressing at a desired rate. Interfering dispositions often develop when initial literacy instruction is not well matched to a child, and that child experiences repeated failure and frustration. Interfering dispositions may also be present in children who are experiencing family problems at home, fear for their safety at home or at school, or who are highly anxious about real or imagined problems. The ability to maintain focus and attention on literacy acts—another area in which children vary widely—also bears heavily on literacy acquisition and development.

Two effective tools to turn a discouraged, disaffected reader or writer into an engaged, persistent learner are student choice and planned success. As explained earlier, providing choice is motivating for the discouraged and/or disengaged literacy learner. Planning for success simply means that the teacher needs to carefully select texts and tasks that he or she is sure the student can successfully complete with minimal assistance to build in the child the belief that he or she can indeed complete the task. Opportunities to engage in more authentic tasks—those perceived as more like those pursued in the world outside the classroom—are often highly motivating for discouraged or disaffected students.

Curriculum Adaptation

Finally, many teachers use commercial or district-adopted curriculum materials to teach and assess reading and writing. By now it should be apparent that every child does not learn at the same pace, with the same techniques, or with the same materials as the "average" child. Teachers need to adapt and supplement the materials and curricula to truly meet the needs of all learners. Knowing students well enables teachers to make flexible and informed instructional decisions.

CHAPTER 8

Assessment

Assessment, the process and tools for evaluating student abilities, knowledge, or work, is a constant feature of most literacy classrooms today. There are four major purposes for assessment: (1) to provide information to teachers and students that helps teachers plan instruction and helps students understand what they need to learn, (2) to diagnose student difficulties, (3) to assess student expertise at the end of some period of time, and (4) to compare students' performance with other students (Taylor & Nolen, 2009). The purposes for assessment relate to the intended audiences. For example, diagnosing student difficulties can help teachers and schools provide targeted instruction for students who are struggling; comparisons of student performance often plays a role in school and district accountability.

Assessment plays a valuable role in guiding instruction. Therefore, in this chapter we focus on the first three purposes for assessments as they are developed and used by classroom teachers to influence instruction and improve student learning. In this chapter we discuss various aspects of assessment including the characteristics of quality assessment and types of literacy assessments, emphasizing classroom-based assessments.

CHARACTERISTICS OF QUALITY IN ASSESSMENT: VALIDITY AND RELIABILITY

What Is It?

The quality of an assessment is traditionally judged according to the two interrelated qualities of validity and reliability. Validity is the idea that an assessment should measure what it says it is measuring. Therefore, an assessment about reading comprehension should first define comprehension (the *construct*) and then ask students to perform a task that measures this definition—for example, reading a passage and then answering questions. Reliability is the notion that data from the assessment is a stable indication of the student's knowledge or ability in the construct. For example, the same assessment given again, or an assessment measuring the same construct, would get the same results. Reliability also refers to the idea that two assessors reading the same assessment will come to similar conclusions about the student's ability.

What Do Teachers Need to Know?

Teachers need to know that there are many threats to the validity and reliability of assessments. One possible threat (possibility for error) is developmental. Young children are used to making meaning in the context of real tasks. When test items are decontextualized they may not be reliable. For example, researchers found in one study that children tried to turn discrete items into a story, making the test results unreliable (Taylor & Nolen, 2008). The National Association for the Education of Young Children (NAEYC) recommends that "The methods of assessment are appropriate to the developmental status and experience of young children, and they recognize individual variation in learning and allow children to demonstrate their competence in different ways" (2009, p. 22). A second important threat related to reliability is "standard error of measurement." This is especially problematic when important decisions ("high stakes") are going to be based on one assessment. For example, a student who is sick on the day of the assessment will likely not perform to his or her real ability. This is one type of measurement error and an important reason why psychometricians (researchers who study tests and measurement) all agree that important decisions should not be made on the basis of one assessment. Measurement error is also related to validity. For example, measurement error is present when a student who can comprehend text, but does not write well, does not show his or her true comprehension on an assessment that requires him or her to write the answer to comprehension questions. Finally, fairness is also an important threat. If a student is asked to write a retelling as a measure of reading comprehension but has no experience with this task, the assessment will not be a good measure of his or her ability.

We believe that assessments should support student learning, not hinder it. Assessments have consequences ("consequential validity") and assessments, or the ways that they are used, that have negative impacts on students or instruction are inappropriate.

Accommodations and Modifications

When students have special needs that interfere with their ability to take an assessment in the way it is being offered, teachers may make accommodations for them. Accommodations involve changing the format or administration of the assessment but not the learning outcomes being measured. For example, allowing students more time to take an assessment and letting them dictate their answers to a reading test are all accommodations. Appropriate accommodations allow students to show what they know regarding the targeted learning outcomes and create more valid and reliable assessments for these students.

Assessment modifications, on the other hand, involve changing the learning objectives, expected performance levels, or curriculum on which the assessment is based. For example, a student who has a developmental disability and could not read a grade-level test could be assessed on a reading test at a lower reading level. Usually modifications occur in the context of an individual learning plan for students with special needs.

It is important to make a distinction between accommodations and modifications. A proctor reading a test aloud to a student would invalidate an assessment of reading comprehension. This would not be an appropriate accommodation because reading aloud to the student changes the targeted objectives from reading comprehension to listening comprehension.

ACTIVITY 8.1
First Grade Takes a Test
NANCY A. PLACE

Activity Type: In-class activity.

Materials: Book—*First Grade Takes a Test* by Miriam Cohen.

Duration: 45 minutes.

Professional Learning Focus: Validity and reliability considerations for assessments of young children.

K–8 Student Learning Focus: N/A.

Standards Links

IRA Professional Standards:
3.1 Candidates understand types of assessments and their purposes, strengths, and limitations.

Common Core Anchor Standards: N/A.

Rationale

In an era of increased testing for all children, I believe that it is especially important to step back and think about what assessments are actually showing us about children and their learning. The testing of young children is one particularly important area to consider because developmental issues may make some tests unreliable.

First Grade Takes a Test by Miriam Cohen is a short picture book that illustrates the conflict between the way that the children in first grade interpret a standardized, multiple-choice test, and the way that the "test people" have designed it. In the book, first grade is asked to take a test that will determine who moves from their class into a gifted classroom. The book shows the way that some of the children think about and answer the test questions and also what happens after they have completed the test.

I use this activity early in my course as a part of our discussions about issues of validity, reliability, and the purposes and audiences for various assessments.

Description

1. I introduce the book to the teachers simply by saying that it is a book about testing young children. I ask them to listen for the ways that the children respond to the test. I read the book straight through, being careful to show the corresponding pictures on the document camera. I then ask the teachers to talk among themselves, responding to the question "What did you notice?" We then share aloud briefly as a whole class.

2. I read the book again, this time asking the teachers to think about the purpose of the test and the intended audience for the test.

3. We debrief as a whole group, discussing the purpose and audience for the test, and whether or not the test was valid and reliable for the purpose. We also discuss the consequential validity of the test and other ways that teachers might collect information about children's cognitive development.

4. We finish the conversation by asking the key questions that we ask of all of the assessments we discuss:

- "What is being assessed?"
- "How is it being assessed?"
- "Who is being assessed?"
- "What is the purpose of the assessment?"
- "Who decides this?"

Discussion

I love this book. In ways that are recognizable and humorous to parents and teachers of young children, it provides clear examples of the thoughtful work that children are doing when they come to a testing situation—and how this meaningful work can create completely unreliable test results. For example, on one page we see that George is working on a multiple-choice reading test. The test has a sentence stem beginning "Rabbits eat . . ." George's choices are lettuce, dog food, and sandwiches. He raises his hand. "'Rabbits have to eat carrots or their teeth will get too long and stick into them' . . . George carefully drew in a carrot so the test people would know" (Cohen, 1980, unpaged).

This book never fails to get a laugh of recognition from the teachers in the class. The difference between the children's understandings of what the test people are asking and the intent of the test people are so graphically illustrated and true. Those teachers in the class with backgrounds in early childhood also recognize other markers of cognitive development that demonstrate that there are many ways to assess children's abilities and knowledge beside tests. I appreciate this book and the human face that it puts on standardized testing.

THE IMPORTANCE OF MULTIPLE ASSESSMENTS

What Is It?

There are many types of assessments, and each is useful for a specific purpose and a particular audience. Each type of assessment has limitations and will give a particular "slice" of a student's abilities. Not all assessments are tests, and not all tests do a valid and reliable job of evaluating student understanding or ability. Assessments can measure knowledge, ability, and disposition.

What Do Teachers Need to Know?

There are several important reasons for using multiple assessments. The first is that using multiple assessments helps teachers see students in a more holistic way, giving teachers an understanding of students' motivations and dispositions, as well as their abilities across a range of reading and writing behaviors. For example, six-trait analysis of a product cannot provide information on students' beliefs about and attitudes toward writing. For that you would have to use an interest inventory or conferencing with the student. Observation can also give information about students' engagement in processes. It is easy to make an assumption that just because students do well in writing or reading, they like to write or read. In actuality, this is not always the case.

The second reason for using multiple assessments relates to the idea that reading and writing processes are complex. Using multiple forms of assessment helps teachers understand reading and writing constructs with more depth. For example, a teacher who assesses his or her students' reading comprehension by listening to them read and talking to them about their reading, asking them to answer comprehension questions and do retellings, having them write book reviews, and observing them in book discussions will have a more accurate and deeper understanding of their comprehension than one who uses a single assessment. When teachers assess students in multiple ways over time the reliability of their claims is increased.

Formative and Summative Assessments

An important distinction in types of assessments is between formative and summative assessments. Summative assessments occur at the end of a unit of study and evaluate whether or not the student has mastered the learning outcomes of the unit. Formative assessment occurs in the process of learning and provides a way for students and their teachers to see students' progress toward learning outcomes. This type of assessment helps teachers and students identify what still needs to be learned. Most types of assessments (e.g., observation, portfolios, multiple-choice tests) can be used for either summative or formative purposes.

Summative assessment based on learning goals that match curriculum and instruction can give teachers a clear idea of the efficacy of their instruction. It can also give students an understanding of the level of their mastery toward clear learning targets. State or district assessments designed to measure students' abilities on grade-level learning standards are another type of summative assessment. A poor match between a teacher's learning goals and the learning goals of the assessment, whether the assessment is developed by the teacher or mandated by others, provides limited information about student learning and is frustrating to both teachers and students.

Formative assessment, along with student self-assessment, is recognized as a key factor for increasing student learning (Black & Wiliam, 1998). When students understand and care about what they need to learn and can set goals for making this learning happen, and when teachers are clear about the kinds of instruction students need to meet the learning outcomes, student learning is maximized.

Standardized Assessments

Standardized assessments are those assessments whose administration is the same across classrooms both in terms of content and administration. Standardized assessments come in a variety of formats including multiple choice, short and long answer, and performance. Some standardized assessments are used to provide diagnostic information for teachers, and others provide information across classes that can be collaboratively studied by teachers for the purpose of improving instruction. For example, teachers who administer the same writing prompt to their students under similar conditions can collaboratively assess the resulting student work. In doing so they can investigate the quality of student writing and the impact of their instruction. Mandated standardized state assessments may also be used by schools and districts to identify institutional strengths and weaknesses, but their main purpose is to provide information to audiences outside the classroom for accountability purposes. Increasingly it appears that these tests will also be used as a factor in teacher evaluation.

In the past 20 years states have shifted from primarily norm-referenced tests to standards-based tests. Norm-referenced tests are intended to compare students based on differences among students. Test items are designed to demonstrate a "spread" among students so there are some items that are very easy and some that are very difficult. These kinds of tests are designed so that some students will do well and other students will not. In contrast, standards-based assessments are built around district or state learning standards. The expectation is that all students will meet these standards.

Portfolios

Portfolios are composed of items purposely selected by a student, teacher, or parent. Items are often selected to show student progress toward learning outcomes, but they may also be chosen to reflect what the student feels is important or personally meaningful. Portfolios often include a variety of different kinds of assessments or student work.

There are several different types of portfolios. Showcase portfolios give evidence of students' best work; outcomes-based portfolios show students' mastery of stated learning objectives; process portfolios show the development of a particular piece of work, often artistic or literary; and personal portfolios are selected on the basis of what is particularly meaningful to a student (Valencia, 1998).

Portfolios are particularly useful for showing growth. Because of the range and personal nature of student work that can be collected over time, portfolios frequently offer a more reliable and valid portrait of growth in reading and writing for children who struggle in these areas, than information that is usually obtained from standardized tests (Place & English, 1998).

Important Classroom-Based Literacy Assessments

There are some classroom-based assessments that are particularly important for comprehensive literacy instruction. These assessments primarily help teachers assess student progress toward important learning outcomes or help teachers diagnose student literacy issues. A chart of some of these assessments, as well as the information that teachers can gain from informal assessments, can be found in Figure 8.1.

Several specific assessments are described in the activities that follow. In particular, we feel that assessing and developing case studies or profiles of actual students is a powerful activity, especially for preservice teachers who have little experience with assessment or its links to instruction.

Assessment	Dimensions of Reading/Writing Assessed
Running records *Example*: Fountas & Pinnell (1996)	Accuracy, word identification strategies, level of text complexity appropriate for child.
Miscue analysis *Example*: Goodman (1995)	Accuracy, word identification strengths and weaknesses, reading strategies.
IRI (informal reading inventory) *Examples*: DRA (Developmental Reading Inventory), QRI (Qualitative Reading Inventory), BAS (Benchmark Assessment System)	Accuracy, word identification strategies, fluency, rate, comprehension, level of text complexity appropriate for child.
Retellings *Example*: Koskinen, Gambrell, Kapinus, & Heathington (1988)	Comprehension, story structure, oral language.
DIBELS (Dynamic Indicators of Basic Early Literacy Skills)	Letter naming, decoding, phonological awareness, oral reading rate, comprehension.
Phonemic awareness inventories *Example*: Yopp–Singer Test (Yopp, 1995)	Phonemic awareness.
Sight-word inventories *Example*: New Instant Word List (Fry, 1980)	Word recognition in isolation (out of context).
Spelling assessments *Example*: Spelling inventories (Bear, Invernizzi, Templeton & Johnston, 2012)	Spelling development, phonics development, morphological knowledge.
Analysis of student writing *Examples:* Six trait rubrics (Culham, 2003) Writing process checklist assessment Tompkins (2011)	Six traits, concepts about print, phonics knowledge, assessment of writing processes (across drafts).
Interest inventories Selection available in *Assessment for Reading Instruction* (McKenna & Stahl, 2009) *Measuring Attitude Toward Writing* (Kear, Coffman, McKenna, & Ambrosio, 2000)	Student interests, motivations, perceptions.

(continued)

FIGURE 8.1. Possible sources of evidence: Dimensions of reading and writing.

Assessment	Dimensions of Reading/Writing Assessed
Informal conversations or reading conferences	Engagement, comprehension, perceptions of self as reader, understandings of reading and its purposes, motivation.
Observations of students reading	Fluency, reading strategies, concepts about print (CAP), attention/engagement.
Observations of students writing	Engagement, pencil grip, motivation.
Informal conversations or writing conferences	Engagement, six traits, perceptions of self as writer, understanding of students' writing processes, understanding of writing and its purposes, motivation.

FIGURE 8.1. *(continued).*

ACTIVITY 8.2
Case Study with Dialogic Inquiry Groups
CYNTHIA SCHMIDT, TRICIA DEGRAFF, and KAREN KINDLE

Activity Type: In-class component of field-based project.

Materials: Assessments and other artifacts of children's literacy learning collected during field work by teachers.

Duration: Groups meet every 2 weeks for about 30 minutes.

Professional Learning Focus:
• Reflective thinking.
• Problem-solving behaviors.
• Professional collaboration.
• Using assessment to inform instruction.

K–8 Student Learning Focus: N/A.

Standards Links

IRA Professional Standards:
2.2 Select and implement instructional approaches based on evidence-based rationale, student needs, and purposes for instruction.

Differentiate instructional approaches to meet students' reading and writing needs.

Implement and evaluate instruction in each of the following areas: concepts of print, phonemic awareness, phonics, vocabulary, comprehension, fluency, critical thinking, motivation, and writing.

3.3 Use assessment data to plan instruction systematically and to select appropriate traditional print, digital, and online reading resources.

Use assessment data to evaluate students' responses to instruction and to develop relevant next steps for teaching.

Collaborate with other reading professionals to modify instruction and to plan and evaluate interventions based on assessment data.

Common Core State Standards: N/A.

Rationale

Teacher educators must find ways to equip teachers to meet the needs of cognitively, culturally, and linguistically diverse students through differentiated instruction. In addition, teachers must learn to consider and reflect on their abilities to support all students in achieving high levels of literacy. Standards for the Preparation of Reading Professionals (International Reading Association, 2010) state that teachers should know how to plan literacy instruction for individual children based on assessments and focused observations of their literacy development. Instruction should be scaffolded to build on children's current strengths and move them forward toward more independent and thoughtful reading; however, developing the skills to observe, assess, and individualize instruction for children at different developmental levels is a complex task even for experienced teachers.

Novice teachers become quickly adept at administering the myriad of assessments that are used in their local education context, but often struggle with interpreting data in ways that lead to targeted, appropriate instruction for individual struggling readers within their classrooms. The variety of assessments adopted by local school districts makes it impractical, if not impossible, for teacher education programs to prepare teachers for analyzing specific tests. As teacher educators, what we can and should do is to initiate teachers into an inquiry process that demonstrates purposes and procedures for observation, interpretation, teaching, and reflection in a systematic way that will be applicable in all school settings.

We developed dialogic inquiry groups (DIGs) in our reading methods courses to provide an instructional space for inquiry into the cycle of continuous assessment to guide instruction for struggling readers. DIGs help teachers to enact different aspects of the assessment, analysis, and instruction cycle in a highly supportive, collaborative context that facilitates their transition from novice to more experienced teachers (see Figure 8.2). The peer discussions simulate the types of authentic conversations that practicing teachers use in planning groupings or interventions for children in their classrooms. The DIGs can be used to facilitate the types of approximations and decompositions of essential teaching practices suggested by researchers to support teaching and learning (Grossman, 2011).

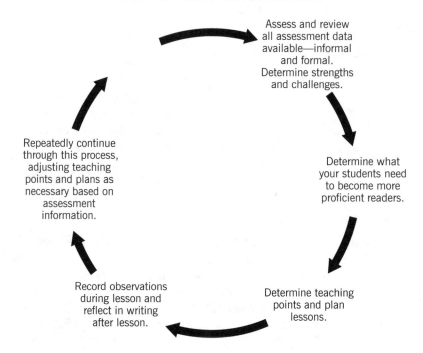

FIGURE 8.2. Inquiry cycle to guide continuous assessment and instruction.

Description

Reading education courses frequently involve "case study" assignments that require teachers to develop skills for continuous assessment and instruction by working with an individual struggling reader over the course of a semester and writing a report about their experiences. DIGs are small groups of four to six teachers who meet regularly throughout the semester to discuss their progress in this work.

The DIGs meet with the course instructor for about 20–30 minutes approximately every 2 weeks. Teachers bring personal learning logs, assessment records, and artifacts related to children's literacy performances to the DIG meetings. They take turns presenting evidence of each child's learning, explaining rationales for their teaching decisions, and seeking suggestions from their peers. Group members respond to each "case" as it is presented by posing questions or offering suggestions to the presenter. Teachers engage in discussion that simulates a professional meeting among those concerned about supporting a struggling reader.

It is essential that teachers bring artifacts that demonstrate some evidence of children's learning—for example, assessment results, running records, and audiotapes of children reading aloud. Concrete examples of children's performances improve the discussion by allowing everyone to comment and offer suggestions. In contrast, simply reporting events does not give enough information for peers or the instructor to offer alternative interpretations or suggestions.

The instructor should set the agenda for the DIG meetings and change the focus throughout the semester to keep pace with elements of the tutoring assignment. Early DIG meetings focus on considering results of initial interviews and assessments of children; later meetings focus more on the tutoring lesson and artifacts that demonstrate evidence of children's progress (see Figure 8.3 for examples of DIG agenda topics). The instructor facilitates the discussion and prompts members to ask questions or consider alternative interpretations that might extend learning.

Teachers are expected to prepare for dialogic inquiry group (DIG) meetings by answering questions and bringing evidence of children's reading and writing performances related to the topic of that meeting. Try to select topics that will encourage group members to compare and contrast evidence from different children. Encourage application of topics learned and discussed in class. Examples of agenda topics include the following:

1. What have you learned about the classroom environment related to literacy learning? What does it mean to be a good reader in this classroom? Bring some examples of literacy tasks and activities to the group meeting.

2. After interviewing and observing the child in the classroom for 2 weeks, what have you learned about the child's personal interests and attitudes that are related to literacy development? Bring a list of three strengths and two challenges that you have observed.

3. This week bring samples of running records and a miscue analysis chart to the DIG meeting. Be prepared to discuss the cueing systems your student is using. What can you do during tutoring to help your child become more independent in word recognition? Consider examples from our text.

4. Bring a 1-minute audiotape of your child reading an instructional-level text. Be prepared to discuss aspects of fluency you are observing with your peers. Also bring an example of text you are using for Readers Theater or repeated reading. We will share ideas for interesting texts to promote fluency.

5. Bring evidence of how your student responds to informational text: either a written response or an audiotaped discussion. Discuss your interpretation of your student's strengths and challenges and be prepared to discuss ways to extend your student's talk and writing related to texts.

FIGURE 8.3. Examples of dialogic inquiry group agenda topics.

In our experience, it is useful to group teachers who are working with children at similar grade levels and/or with similar literacy development needs—for example, early readers who need support in word recognition and fluency, or intermediate-grade readers who need support with fluency or comprehension. In this way, the DIGs develop a focus on particular developmental levels, and teachers can make comparisons among four to six different children at this level who demonstrate a range of literacy behaviors. In addition to the regularly scheduled meetings, group members are encouraged to meet informally, online or in person, to discuss common concerns with one another.

Instructors should scaffold so that teachers gradually assume more responsibilities for initiating and sustaining problem-solving discussions related to the assessment and teaching of particular struggling readers. The DIGs both support and challenge teachers to think more deeply about the work they do with struggling readers.

Discussion

We have been using the DIGs for 3 years and have regularly analyzed transcribed audiotapes and field notes to continually refine the process. These analyses have led to the following generalizations about the positive outcomes of participating in DIGs for teachers.

The DIGs provide opportunities for teachers to practice interpreting assessments and generating hypotheses about real students, while receiving guidance and feedback from a university professor. In some cases, we noticed teachers who displayed misconceptions about particular concepts or planned inappropriate instruction for students. The instructor was able to quickly intervene and scaffold better understanding through questioning and prompting, thus guiding the teachers to clarify misconceptions and build deeper understanding of a concept in a particular case.

Teachers have opportunities to practice using professional discourse to describe children's literacy development, as well as opportunities to clarify their understanding of specific reading behaviors and components of the reading process. Over the course of the semester, we have noted increased use of appropriate literacy terminology as they described student behaviors and discussed possible instructional strategies. In this way, our teachers developed a "shared understanding and common language about teaching" (Darling-Hammond & Baratz-Snowden, 2007, p. 127).

The DIGs can develop into learning communities where teachers collaborate as peers, while building confidence and experience in the complex tasks of assessing and teaching struggling readers (Wenger, 1998). We have documented an increase in peer interactions in some DIGs (Kindle & Schmidt, 2011). Early in the semester, teachers typically directed questions and comments to the instructor. Over time, some groups began talking more to one another and relied less on the instructor, building an authentic professional learning community through collaboration.

We are particularly interested in ways that DIGs can help teachers move from a concern about themselves, as novice teachers, toward a concern about their children's growth as readers. We know that this shift is significant in moving novices toward the goals of improving teacher education practices that impact learners. The DIGs are not an end in themselves, but a means toward deepening understanding and raising the level of professional discourse related to case study assignments.

Overall, we believe that the DIGs offer a flexible way for teacher educators to support teachers as they move from learning about assessment and instruction toward using assessment and instruction to support children in authentic contexts.

References

Darling-Hammond, L., & Baratz-Snowden, J. (2007). *A good teacher in every class-room: Preparing the highly qualified teachers our children deserve.* Retrieved November 16, 2009, from *www.eric.ed.gov/ERICDocs/data/ericdocs2sql/content_storage_01/0000019b/80/28/2e/7a.pdf.*

Kindle, K., & Schmidt, C. (2011). Outside in and inside out: Using a case study assignment in a reading methods course. *Teacher Education Quarterly, 3*(3), 133–149.

Grossman, P. (2011). Framework for teaching practice: A brief history of an idea. *Teachers College Record, 113*(12), 2836–2843.

Wenger, E. (1998). *Communities of practice: Learning, meaning, and identity.* New York: Cambridge University Press.

ACTIVITY 8.3
Developing Reading Comprehension Questions
LOTTA LARSON

Activity Type: Combination assignment and in-class activity.

Materials: N/A.

Duration: Three sessions, 45 minutes each.

Professional Learning Focus:
- Construct reading comprehension questions.
- Evaluate quality of comprehension questions.
- Assess students' reading comprehension.

Standards Links

IRA Professional Standards:
3.1 Candidates understand types of assessments and their purposes, strengths, and limitations.

3.2 Candidates select, develop, and interpret assessments, both traditional print and electronic, for specific purposes.

Common Core State Standards:
Reading Anchor Standards
Key Ideas and Details
1. Read closely to determine what the text says explicitly and to make

K–8 Student Learning Focus: Reading comprehension.

logical inferences from it; cite specified textual evidence when writing or speaking to support conclusions drawn from the text.

2. Determine central ideas or themes of a text and analyze their development; summarize the key supporting details and ideas.

3. Analyze how and why individuals, events, and ideas develop and interact over the course of a text.

Rationale

When asked how to monitor students' reading comprehension, most teachers will agree that posing high-quality reading comprehension questions can play an important role. The question, of course, becomes "How do you create a 'good' question?" Experienced teachers recognize that we never truly know whether a comprehension question (or any test question for that matter) is worthwhile until students have answered it and teachers have evaluated their responses. In addition to discussing how to create selected-response writing items and constructed-response items, I believe teachers benefit from hands-on practice in creating and grading reading comprehension questions. In this activity, they assume roles as both teachers and students as they consider reading comprehension questions from multiple perspectives.

Description

1. First I engage teachers in a class discussion about ways to assess reading comprehension. In particular, I introduce the idea of reading comprehension questions. At this point, I focus on selected-response questions (i.e., multiple-choice, binary-choice, and matching items), as constructed-response questions (short answer and essay) will be addressed at a later time. As part of the discussion, we explore advantages/disadvantages, characteristics, and format of each type of question.

2. As homework, teachers create a reading "quiz" on a nonfiction book or book chapter(s) that all class members have read or are currently reading. I explain that they should make their quiz look like an instrument they would actually give to students. I tell the teachers to print two copies of their quiz, reminding them *not* to put their name on either copy. I then ask them to leave one copy blank and to fill in the answers on the second copy. The purpose for filling out the second copy is twofold: It helps the quiz creator realize whether he or she made any mistakes,

and it will later serve as an answer key. Before dismissing class, I remind the teachers to bring the assessment instrument (quiz) and answer key to class (see Figure 8.4 for instructions to students).

3. During the next class period, I ask the teachers to sit in groups of six to eight. I assign each group a number (Group 1, Group 2, etc.). I ask them to keep the answer key tucked away but to take out the blank quiz. I remind them *not* to write their name on the quiz. Instead, to remain anonymous to their peers, I instruct the teachers to "code" their quizzes by recording, in the upper right-hand corner, their group number, followed by two random letters. For example, a member of Group 3 may code his or her paper 3GX. (To protect privacy, I suggest they avoid using their initials.) Once all quizzes are coded, I collect them and quickly sort into piles by group numbers. I then redistribute so all teachers get a quiz created by someone who is not a member of his or her group. In other words, the teachers "swap" papers but do not know with whom they exchange their assessment instruments.

4. Each teacher now assumes the role of a student. He or she completes the reading comprehension quiz, answering the reading questions to the best of his or her ability. In addition to answering the questions, each "student" also writes comments relating to the quality of each question. I always emphasize the importance of providing constructive feedback addressing strengths and weaknesses of all questions (based on the guidelines previously discussed in class), clarity of instructions, visual appearance of the quiz, and level of difficulty of the questions.

For tomorrow, please finish the Orbis Pictus Award winner [fill in title] that you have chosen. Create a reading "quiz" with six selected-response questions (multiple choice, true/false, and matching). Make sure you:

1. Number each question.
2. Include grade-level-appropriate directions.
3. Provide adequate space for students' answers.
4. Include point value for each question.
5. Add a line for the student's name.
6. Make the quiz visually appealing (e.g., use of appropriate font, images).

Print two copies of your quiz. Leave one copy blank. Fill in the second copy (circle the correct answers, etc.). Creating the second copy helps you catch potential errors, and you can later use it as an assessment key.

To protect your privacy, do not include your name on either copy.

FIGURE 8.4. Guidelines for creating comprehension questions.

5. Next, I collect all quizzes and, with the help of the codes, return them to the original quiz creator. The participants now assume the role of teachers. They grade the completed quizzes, referring to their answer keys, and provide feedback to their "student." The "teachers" also read the feedback (provided by their "students") regarding the quality of the questions and overall impressions of the quiz and instructions.

6. After the teachers have finished grading the quizzes and reading the feedback, I ask them to respond to the constructive feedback provided by their "student" regarding the quality and effectiveness of test items. I always encourage them to use a different pen/pencil color, to later help me keep track of which comments were written by the "student," and which were added by the "teacher." I then collect the quizzes.

7. Following this class session, I always review each assessment instrument and the feedback provided by both "students" and "teachers," to address any misconceptions or issues as needed during a subsequent session.

8. The following week, we repeat the activity. This time, however, the teachers create an assessment instrument with constructed-response questions (essay and short answer).

9. As a culminating activity, I ask the teachers to reflect upon the experience. This can either be done during class discussion, or individually in writing (see Figure 8.5).

Discussion

After incorporating this activity into my literacy methods course for several semesters, I have noticed a tremendous improvement in question-writing abilities. Often, teachers do not recognize a faulty, or unclear, question until they actually assume

---

- What did you learn from this activity?
- As a teacher, explain what it was like creating the quiz. What challenges did you encounter?
- In the role of student, how did you feel answering the questions? What did you notice about the quiz that you took?
- Did you agree/disagree with the "student's" feedback regarding the quality of your questions? Please explain.
- As a result of this activity, how can you create even better reading comprehension questions?

FIGURE 8.5. Reflection on creating comprehension questions.

the role of student and try to answer the question. The feedback opportunities provide the teachers with multiple ways to self-assess their own work and to learn from their peers. Diverse perspectives are provided, discussed, and appreciated among the class members. If time is limited, both selected-response and constructed-response items can be included on the same assessment (hence, eliminating the need to repeat the activity). This activity is most effective if used in conjunction with authentic children's or young adult nonfiction books or other forms of expository texts. In my literacy methods courses, teachers always read and discuss the most recent Orbis Pictus Award winner for outstanding nonfiction for children. However, I have also used this activity in conjunction with other expository texts, including articles from *Time for Kids* or *National Geographic Magazines for Kids*. The format of the quiz may, of course, need to be adjusted depending on the assigned reading.

Informal Classroom Observations

For classroom teachers, a powerful source of assessment information over time is informal observations and conversations with children. Many important features of reading and writing processes can be observed in the daily processes of instruction. However, teachers need to be aware of their own biases and perspectives in the process of observation (see Activity 8.4 on the role of perspective in observational assessment). Accurate descriptions and clear links to learning objectives support solid interpretations of observations.

Authentic Performance Assessments

Performance assessments are those in which students create a product or a live performance. When this work reflects scholarly activity or is related to everyday life outside of school, it offers students the opportunity to engage in authentic assessment. This type of assessment, based in work such as constructing websites, creating a poem, or writing a report, often has an audience beyond the teacher and is frequently motivating to students. An example of an assessment for scoring persuasive arguments is described in Activity 8.5.

The validity and reliability of performance assessments is increased when clear learning objectives and scoring criteria are understood by both the teacher and the students. Scoring rubrics, which delineate the learning objectives, criteria, and level of performance may be used to assess the work. Activity 8.6 shares an example of rubric development.

ACTIVITY 8.4
The Role of Perspective in Observational Assessments
NANCY A. PLACE

Activity Type: In-class activity.

Materials:
- Observation cards.
- Slide with an example of a poorly written student description.
- Optional: *Fish Is Fish* by Leo Leonni and "Why Does Joshua 'Hate' School . . . but Love Sunday School?" (McMillon & Edwards, 2000).

Duration: One hour with additional time for optional discussion of a book or professional article.

Professional Learning Focus: Importance of perspective and the potential for bias in observational assessments.

K–8 Student Learning Focus: N/A.

<u>Standards Links</u>

IRA Professional Standards:
3.1 Candidates understand types of assessments and their purposes, strengths, and limitations.

Common Core State Standards: N/A.

Rationale

Observation is perhaps the most common form of assessment used by teachers. Teachers observe students in many types of situations—in discussion, as they answer questions, as they participate in independent or group work—and then make assessments about students' knowledge, skills, and dispositions. The ability to gather information on student abilities in a wide range of situations over time adds reliability to teachers' classroom assessments, and yet there is the danger of bias. This activity is designed to help teachers become aware of the importance of the perspectives they bring to the observing process and to begin to build a case for the importance of being clear about the purposes for observation.

Description

Prior to the day of class I make arrangements with one of our staff or faculty members to come into class with a request for me to leave class immediately to finish a project. Just before class begins I hand out cards to some members of the class that say things such as "Pay attention to body language," "Pay attention to the emotional tone," "Pay attention to the time," and "Pay attention to the other teachers." I don't say anything to these teachers about why I am handing out the cards.

1. About 5 minutes after beginning class my staff confederate comes in and asks me to leave. We proceed to have an argument in front of the class for about 5 minutes.

2. My staff confederate leaves and I ask the class to do a quick write answering the questions "What just happened?" and "What did you notice?"

3. Following the quick writes people share what they wrote. We then discuss the differences between the quick writes. Topics that are covered in the following discussion include the difference between description and inference, and the idea that what you see is dependent on your frame for seeing. I ask people to note which parts of their quick writes are description and which are inferences. Always discussed is whether or not the incident was "real," which illustrates the role of previous experience in defining our inferences.

4. We follow this experience with examples of descriptions of two students (see Figure 8.6). One example is written using loaded language and draws unwarranted conclusions about the student. The other lacks specificity in description. We discuss the examples and revise them using language that is specific, descriptive, and neutral.

5. Finally, we discuss observational assessments and the importance of having a purpose for the observation. One purpose, for example, would be to learn more about the student as a person. For example, teachers might observe students on the playground to better understand the ways that they interact with other children. Or teachers might link specific descriptions of children's behaviors to learning objectives so that there is evidence to support inferences about academic growth.

6. If there is time, I will often read the book *Fish Is Fish* by Leo Leonni, about a fish who sees the world from his fish perspective. An article from *Language Arts*,

---

Jason

Jason (a seventh grader) is a smooth talker and a flirt. He is always stylishly dressed in the latest fashion. Jason participates in class, sometimes inappropriately acting like a clown. Although he comes to school regularly, he is unmotivated about completing schoolwork, most likely because of his background.

Megan

Megan (a kindergartner) happily sorted through the blocks on the table and picked out a large pile of them. She lined up the blocks using different colors and then made a remark about the work that expressed her satisfaction.

FIGURE 8.6. Student observations.

"Why Does Joshua 'Hate' School . . . but Love Sunday School?" by McMillon and Edwards (2000), also provokes strong discussion about the role that our perceptions and biases play in observation.

Discussion

I like this activity because it helps teachers think more deeply about an assessment technique they use every day, often unconsciously. In addition, the drama of the opening certainly wakes people up when they're tired after a long day at school. It becomes clear to teachers that the perspectives and background knowledge they bring to the experience influences their observations, as well as how easy it is to "leap to judgment." The discussion of the purposes for observation also helps teachers recognize the role that learning objectives can play in terms of limiting the tendency of teachers to focus on behavior when they observe as opposed to academics (Valencia, Martin, Place, & Grossman, 2009).

References

McMillon, G. T., & Edwards, P. A. (2000). Why does Joshua "hate" school . . . but love Sunday school? *Language Arts, 80*, 111–120.

Valencia, S., Martin, S., Place, N., & Grossman, P. (2009). Complex interactions in student teaching: Lost opportunities for learning. *Journal of Teacher Education 60*, 304–324.

ACTIVITY 8.5
Scoring a Persuasive Argument
Nancy A. Place

Activity Type: In-class activity.

Materials: Handout of scoring rubric for argument.

Duration: 1 hour.

Professional Learning Focus: Fairness in assessment: The importance of knowledge of scoring rules prior to engaging in task.

K–8 Student Learning Focus: N/A.

Standards Links

IRA Professional Standards:
3.1 Candidates understand types of assessments and their purposes, strengths, and limitations.

Common Core State Standards: N/A.

Note. This activity was developed by Catherine Taylor, University of Washington.

Rationale

This activity illustrates a key aspect in the development and use of performance assessments: Students who are being assessed should have a clear idea of the criteria on which they are being evaluated. I usually present this activity at the beginning of our course discussions on constructing performance assessments.

Description

1. Teachers are told that they will be experiencing a performance assessment. I divide the class into groups of six to eight students each and put the persuasive argument slide on the document camera (see Figure 8.7). I tell the teachers that each group will have 10 minutes to construct an argument for or against school uniforms that they will then present to the rest of the class. Their presentations to the class should each take no more than 3 minutes.

2. The groups present their arguments to the class.

3. After the presentations I hand out the scoring rubric (see Figure 8.8). I ask each group to self-assess their persuasive argument performance using the scoring rubric. The teachers are surprised, and some become upset, because they didn't know ahead of time the criteria on which their performance would be judged.

4. A discussion of the activity with a focus on fairness in assessment follows. Knowing and understanding the scoring criteria before the task is performed is crucial to students being able to reliably show what they know. Other aspects of fairness include teaching of the criteria (or knowing that the students already can perform them), and awareness of bias in the creation and scoring of the assessment.

Your task is to present a 3-minute persuasive speech. Your work will be worth 42 points.

Scenario
Your group is entering a speech contest. If your group wins, you will get new videotaping equipment for your school.

The topic of the speech
Take a position on whether school uniforms should be required in schools. As a team, prepare your position and present it to our class.

FIGURE 8.7. Performance assessment for persuasive argument.

Argument				
3 = Clear, effective 1 = Confusing, weak 2 = Understandable, believable 0 = Not done				
Criteria	**3**	**2**	**1**	**0**
The position is stated.				
Multiple arguments are given to support the position.				
Evidence is given to support each argument.				
The relationship between the evidence and the argument is described.				
Counterarguments are given.				
Evidence and examples are given to refute counterarguments.				

Group Presentation Skills				
3 = Balanced 1 = Very imbalanced 2 = Minor imbalance 0 = Not done				
Criteria	**3**	**2**	**1**	**0**
Each group member presented and supported one argument.				
Presenters took turns presenting ideas.				
Presenters' summary included all voices.				

Individual Presentation Skills				
3 = Effective, clear, consistent 1 = Difficult to understand 2 = Understandable; somewhat uneven 0 = Not done				
Criteria	**3**	**2**	**1**	**0**
Individual projected his or her voice.				
Individual made eye contact with the audience.				
Individual paced ideas.				

Visual Aid				
3 = Effective, clear, connected 1 = Difficult to understand 2 = Understandable and connected 0 = Not done				
Criteria	**3**	**2**	**1**	**0**
Visual aid conveys arguments and evidence.				
Visual aid uses words and pictures.				

FIGURE 8.8. Scoring rules for a persuasive argument.

Discussion

Even though the teachers have read materials about performance assessment before doing this activity, and they know that this is a role-playing activity, a surprising number are upset when they receive the scoring rubric. Our discussion reveals that some teachers are not used to receiving scoring rules prior to submitting assignments, and that all teachers have had this experience at some point in their careers. This activity leads to a good, and often personal, discussion about fairness in grading. Following this activity, the teachers have frequently questioned other professors about their grading practices.

ACTIVITY 8.6
Rubric Development: Let's Jump Rope
DEBORAH G. LITT

Activity Type: In-class activity.

Materials: Whiteboard, chalkboard, chart paper or LCD projector—any means of producing text a group can see.

Duration: 20–30 minutes.

Professional Learning Focus:
- How to develop an assessment rubric.
- Understanding of the strengths and limitations of rubrics.

K–8 Student Learning Focus: N/A.

Standards Links

IRA Professional Standards:
3.1 Candidates understand types of assessments and their purposes, strengths, and limitations.

Common Core State Standards: N/A.

Rationale

The inservice teachers I work with use rubrics for many aspects of literacy assessment; the preservice teachers use them as soon as they are placed in a classroom. However, these teachers are often using rubrics provided to them by their school or school district. I believe that if they learn how to develop their own rubrics they will have a flexible tool with which to guide student learning as well as assess it. In addition, they will have a deeper understanding of the strengths and limitations of rubric assessment if they work through the decisions required to create a rubric, and be better equipped to evaluate and modify ready-made rubrics. This in-class activity is preparation for another assignment in which the teachers develop their own rubric for assessing student performance.

Description

1. I introduce the activity by saying we are going to jointly create a rubric for jumping rope as practice for how one goes about developing a rubric. I explain my reasoning for why it is important to be able to create your own rubric when there are so many examples readily available. Just as with sewing a dress, baking your own bread, or singing in a choir, when you understand how something is created, you are better able to judge the premade product—and, in this case, to modify it.

2. I draw or project a 4" × 5" grid. I ask the teachers to suggest key criteria of skilled rope jumping to put in the left column. They typically suggest *duration*, *entry and exit*, and *speed*. These are the easy ones to agree on. Inevitably, someone suggests *tricks.* Another typical suggestion is *Double Dutch*. These two immediately raise the question of what constitutes acceptable skill versus advanced skill. How much should be required for a "meets expectation" and how much for "exceeds expectation" or "advanced performance"? What about rope turning? Should consistency in turning be "counted" as skill in jumping? These questions lead teachers to ask about the age range the rubric will be applied to. They recognize that what is "average" for an 11-year-old might be advanced for a 6-year-old.

3. Once the components of skilled jumping are established, we work together to fill in the specific criteria for *needs improvement*, *average*, and *advanced*. If the group shows confusion about how to begin, I share that I usually establish the middle level of my rubrics—*meets expectation* or *average* as a baseline and then proceed to establish the more advanced performance or unacceptable performance around that. With that piece of information, the teachers are ready to begin. I record what the teachers suggest, commenting on the options as they debate the merits of the suggestions. For example, one teacher might say that an average jumper must be able to jump 50 times before making an error. If we have established that the rubric is for 8- and 9-year-olds, I might ask if that is too high a standard. I point out that with a three-level rubric the middle range is often very large. For *duration* in this instance, fewer than 10 jumps might qualify for the *needs improvement* category, while a jumper might need over 50 jumps to be in the *advanced* category. The discussion turns to the merits of a four-level rubric if they want finer distinctions. We continue until most or all the boxes of the grid are complete.

4. I then lead a discussion about the challenges of creating a "fair" rubric.

Discussion

The debriefing discussion always raises many of the central issues related to rubric assessments, and assessment more generally. For example, for the purpose of completing this activity, we make decisions by quick consensus, but it is clear to everyone that not every participant fully agrees with every decision. Some people would establish more rigorous criteria for certain elements; others less. Thus, the arbitrary nature of the criteria become apparent. Another issue typically raised is whether the assessment would be based on a single jumping episode or determined by multiple observations. If multiple observations, over how long a time period? Teachers usually note that high-stakes assessments are based on a single observation, but that multiple observations give a more accurate picture of an individual child. Some teachers suggest very precise language, for example, jumps in without missing 9 out of 10 times; others offer more general language, for example, almost always jumps in without missing. Such differences provide an opportunity to discuss the advantages and disadvantages of each approach— while precise criteria may be more objective, in many cases they may be too rigid to provide a true picture of a child's proficiency. We discuss how a teacher might choose to give more weight to a particular category if it is deemed more essential to the overall skill. Should *duration* be worth more or less than *jumping in and out*? When rubric scoring is applied to written products, might you sometimes weight one element more than another depending on the type of product? Just about any issue related to rubric scoring can be elicited in a discussion about a rubric for jumping rope. The teachers in my classes can get quite excited about developing the criteria—especially those who were avid jumpers when younger. They invariably say that working through rubric development as a group helps them when they have to develop their own rubrics.

Conclusion

The months of drafting, talking, revising (and talking some more) that we spent writing this book have given us a renewed appreciation for the complexity of literacy teaching and learning—and for the challenges of preparing future literacy educators. In many ways the writing of this book mirrored the challenges of being literacy teacher educators.

The nature of teaching is complex—and literacy instruction especially so. Reflected in the chapters of our book are the dimensions of the content that literacy teachers must understand. Knowledge of literacy development at the word and text level, knowledge of how children learn and what motivates them to learn, reading processes, writing processes, creating literate environments, digital literacies, instructional differentiation, and assessment strategies are all a part of the corpus of content knowledge that literacy teachers need. In addition to this content knowledge, teachers need to know their children and have a repertoire of instructional strategies, all of which vary by the teaching context.

The complexity and interrelatedness of these ideas resulted in many long conversations about what to include, how to organize it, and the most challenging—what to omit. This is the dilemma each of us face as we plan our coursework. With limited time, what is most important for teachers to understand? How can we organize our content so that it makes the most sense for the teachers with whom we work? With learning separated into separate courses, assignments, and fieldwork, how can we help teachers understand the interrelatedness of the ideas and see the whole picture?

It is not possible for teachers to learn all they need to know in one university teacher education program or a set of professional development workshops. As a result, we want our teachers to become reflective practitioners, teachers who will continue to "learn in and from practice" (Ball & Cohen, 1999, p. 10). The ability to reflect on practice requires a base of theoretical and content-based understanding so that teachers can frame their observations and ground their analyses in knowledge of literacy instruction and learners. The ability to learn from practice is a key feature of the kind of analytic thinking that teachers need to grow as teachers, and one that we hope to nurture in our classes and through the resources in this book.

As one would expect, the adults with whom we work in our teacher education classes come to us with varying understandings of literacy development and instruction. This will also be true for the readers of this book. Some of our most intense conversations as authors, and some of our most difficult decisions as teacher educators, center around the issue of "grain size"—how much detail should be included in conceptual text or activities. We tried hard to strike the right balance here between oversimplifying a complex domain and overwhelming readers with detail. We made disrupting inaccurate or naïve assumptions commonly held by our students a key consideration in selecting the ideas and activities to include.

At a time of increasing curriculum and assessment mandates we are aware that we are preparing teachers for instructional contexts over which we have no control. We believe that our role is to help teachers be the best teachers they can be, whatever their situation. When teachers have a solid understanding of teaching and learning concepts and tools, they have the ability to serve all of their children well, both through the modification of curriculum materials and as advocates for their students. Our responsibility as constructivist teacher educators is to meet our teachers where they are both in terms of their conceptual understandings and their present or future teaching situations. It is imperative that we link our content instruction to actual practice in existing contexts.

Over the lifespan of their careers teachers, teacher educators, and professional developers who reflect on their instruction, particularly in concert with colleagues, will develop new insights about students and instructional strategies. This is rejuvenating and exciting work and should be supported at the policy level. It is our hope that the activities and stories in this book will help teachers find support and strength to continue to investigate their practices, even in difficult work situations. Joyful and effective teaching requires the integration of mind, hand—and heart.

References

Adams, M. J. (2011). The relation between alphabetic basics, word recognition, and reading. In S. J. Samuels & A. E. Farstrup (Eds.), *What research has to say about reading instruction* (4th ed., pp. 4–24). Newark, DE: International Reading Association.

Afflerbach, P., Pearson, P. D., & Paris, S. G. (2008). Clarifying differences between reading skills and reading strategies. *The Reading Teacher, 61*(5), 364–373.

Almasi, J. F. (1995). The nature of fourth graders' sociocognitive conflicts in peer-led and teacher-led discussions of literature. *Reading Research Quarterly, 30,* 314–351.

Almasi, J. F., Palmer, B. M., Madden, A., & Hart, S. (2011). Interventions to enhance narrative comprehension. In R. Allington & A. McGill-Franzen (Eds.), *Handbook of reading disability research* (pp. 329–344). New York: Routledge.

Anderson, R. C. (2004). Role of reader's schema in comprehension, learning, and memory. In R. B. Ruddell & N. J. Unrau (Eds.), *Theoretical processes and models of reading* (5th ed., pp. 594–606). Newark, DE: International Reading Association.

Anderson, R. C., & Nagy, W. E. (1992, Winter). The vocabulary conundrum. *American Educator, 16*(14-18), 44–47.

Anderson, R. C., & Pearson, P. D. (1984). A schema-theoretic view of basic processes in reading comprehension. In P. D. Pearson (Ed.), *Handbook of reading research* (pp. 255–291). New York: Longman.

Anderson, R. C., Wilson, P. T., & Fielding, L. G. (1988). Growth in reading and how children spend their time outside of school. *Reading Research Quarterly, 23*(3), 285–303.

Angelillo, J. (2005). *Writing to the prompt: When students don't have a choice.* Portsmouth, NH: Heinemann.

August, D. L., Flavell, J. H., & Clift, R. (1984). Comparison of comprehension monitoring of skilled and less skilled readers. *Reading Research Quarterly, 20,* 39–48.

Bakhtin, M. M. (1986). *Speech genres and other late essays* (C. Emerson & M. Holmquist, Eds.; V. W. McGee, Trans.). Austin: University of Texas Press.

Ball, D. L., & Cohen, D. K. (1999). Developing practice, developing practitioners: Toward a practice-based theory of professional education. In G. Sykes & L. Darling-Hammond (Eds.), *Teaching as the learning profession: Handbook of policy and practice* (pp. 3–32). San Francisco: Jossey-Bass.

Bear, D., Invernizzi, M., Templeton, S., & Johnston, F. (2012). *Words their way: Word study for phonics, vocabulary, and spelling instruction* (5th ed.). Boston: Pearson.

Berne, J. I., & Clark, K. F. (2008). Focusing literacy discussion groups on comprehension strategies. *The Reading Teacher, 62*(1), 74–79.

Berninger, V. W., & Swanson, H. L. (1994). Modifying Hayes and Flower's model of skilled writing to explain beginning and developing writing. *Advances in Cognition and Educational Practice, 2*, 57–81.

Biemiller, A., & Slonim, M. (2001). Estimating root vocabulary growth in normative and advantaged populations: Evidence for a common sequence of vocabulary acquisition. *Journal of Educational Psychology, 9*(3), 498–520.

Black, P., & Wiliam, D. (1998). Inside the black box: Raising standards through classroom assessment. *Phi Delta Kappan, 80*(2), 139–144.

Boscolo, P., & Gelati, C. (2007). Best practices in promoting motivation in writing. In S. Graham, C. S. MacArthur, & J. Fitzgerald (Eds.), *Best practices in writing instruction* (pp. 202–221). New York: Guilford Press.

Boulware-Gooden, R., Carreker, S., Thornhill, A., & Joshi, R. (2007). Instruction of metacognitive strategies enhances reading comprehension and vocabulary achievement of third-grade students. *The Reading Teacher, 61*(1), 70–77.

Bowers, P. (2010). Effects of morphological instruction on vocabulary acquisition. *Reading and Writing: An Interdisciplinary Journal, 23*, 515–537.

Bruning, R., & Horn, C. (2000). Developing motivation to write. *Educational Psychologist, 35*(1), 25–37.

Bus, A., & van IJzendoorn, M. (1999). Phonological awareness and early reading: A meta-analysis of experimental training studies. *Journal of Educational Psychology, 91*, 403–414.

Carlisle, J. F. (2011). Effects of instruction in morphological awareness: An integrative review. *Reading Research Quarterly, 45*(4), 464–487.

Chapman, M. (1997). *Weaving webs of meaning.* Toronto, Canada: Nelson.

Clay, M. M. (1975). *What did I write?: Beginning writing behavior.* Portsmouth, NH: Heinemann.

Clay, M. M. (2006). *An observation survey of early literacy achievement* (rev. 2nd ed.). Portsmouth, NH: Heinemann.

Coiro, J. (2005). Making sense of online text. *Educational Leadership, 30*–35.

Coiro, J. (2011a). Predicting reading comprehension on the Internet: Contributions of offline reading skills, online reading skills, and prior knowledge. *Journal of Literacy Research, 43*(4), 352–392.

Coiro, J. (2011b). Talking about reading as thinking: Modeling the hidden complexities of online reading comprehension. *Theory Into Practice, 50*, 107–115.

Coiro, J., & Dobler, E. (2007). Exploring the online reading comprehension strategies used by sixth-grade skilled readers to search for and locate information on the Internet. *Reading Research Quarterly, 42*(2), 214–257.

Coker, D. (2007). Writing instruction for young children: Methods targeting the multiple demands that writers face. In S. Graham, C. S. MacArthur, & J. Fitzgerald (Eds.), *Best practices in writing instruction* (pp. 101–118). New York: Guilford Press.

Culham, R. (2003). *6+1 traits of writing: The complete guide for grades 3 and up.* New York: Scholastic.

Cummins, J. (1981). The role of primary language development in promoting educational success for language minority students. In California State Department of Education (Ed.), *Schooling and language minority students: A theoretical framework.* Los Angeles: Evaluation, Dissemination and Assessment Center, California State University.

Cunningham, P. E. (1990). The Names Test: A quick assessment of decoding ability. *The Reading Teacher, 44,* 124–129.

Cunningham, P. M. (2013). *Phonics they use: Words for reading and writing* (6th ed.). Boston: Pearson.

Daniels, H. (2002). *Voice and choice in book clubs and reading groups.* Portland, ME: Stenhouse.

Delpit, L. (2002). No kinda sense. In L. Delpit & J. K. Dowdy (Eds.), *The skin that we speak: Thoughts and language and culture in the classroom* (pp. 31–48). New York: New Press.

Dewitz, P., Carr, E. M., & Patberg, J. P. (1987). Effects of inference training on comprehension and comprehension monitoring. *Reading Research Quarterly, 22*(1), 99–122.

Dowhower, S. L., & Beagle, K. G. (1998). The print environment in kindergartens: A study of conventional and holistic teachers and their classrooms in three settings. *Reading Research and Instruction, 37*(3), 161–190.

Duffelmeyer, F. A., Kruse, A. E., Merkley, D. J., & Fyfe, S. A. (1994). Further validation and enhancement of the Names Test. *The Reading Teacher, 48,* 118–128.

Duke, N. K., & Pearson, P. D. (2002). Effective practices for developing reading comprehension. In A. E. Farstrup, & S. J. Samuels (Eds.), *What research has to say about reading instruction* (3rd ed., pp. 205–242). Newark, DE: International Reading Association.

Dyson, A. H., & Freedman, S. W. (1991). Writing. In J. Flood, J. M. Jensen, D. Lapp, & J. R. Squire (Eds.), *Handbook of research on teaching the English language arts* (pp. 745–774). New York: Macmillan.

Edgerton, L. (2003). *Finding your voice: How to put your personality in your writing.* Cincinnati, OH: F&W Media.

Ehri, L. C. (1997). Sight word learning in normal readers and dyslexics. In B. A. Blachman (Ed.), *Foundations of reading acquisition and dyslexia* (pp. 163–189). Mahway, NJ: Erlbaum.

Ehri, L. C. (1998). Grapheme–phoneme knowledge is essential for learning to read words in English. In J. L. Metsala & L. C. Ehri (Eds.), *Word recognition in beginning literacy* (pp. 3–40). Mahwah, NJ: Erlbaum.

Ehri, L. C. (2005). Learning to read words: Theory, findings, and issues. *Scientific Studies of Reading, 9*(2), 167–188.

Evans, K. S. (2002). Fifth-grade students' perceptions of how they experience literature discussion groups. *Reading Research Quarterly, 37,* 46–69.

Farris, P., Fuhler, C., & Walther, M. (2004). *Teaching reading: A balanced approach for today's classroom.* Boston: McGraw-Hill.

Fountas, I., & Pinnell, G. (1996). *Guided reading: Good first teaching for all children.* Portsmouth, NH: Heinemann.

Freire, P. (1970). *Pedagogy of the oppressed.* New York: Seabury Press.

Fry, E. (1980). The new instant word list. *The Reading Teacher, 34*(3), 284–289.

Gabriel, T. (2010, August 1). Plagiarism lines blur for students in digital age. *New York Times.* Retrieved from *www.nytimes.com.*

Gambrell, L. (2011). Motivation in the school reading curriculum. *Journal of Reading Education, 37*(1), 5–14.

Garner, R., & Krauss, C. (1981). Good and poor comprehender differences in knowing and regulating reading behaviors. *Reading Research Quarterly, 16*(4), 569–582.

Gathercoal, F. (2004). *Judicious discipline.* San Francisco: Caddo Gap Press.

Gee, J. (1999). *An introduction to discourse analysis: Theory and method.* New York: Routledge.

Gersten, R., & Baker, S. (2000). What we know about effective instructional practices for English-language learners. *Exceptional Children, 66*(4), 454–470.

Goldenberg. C. (1993). Instructional conversations: Promoting comprehension through discussion. *The Reading Teacher, 46*(4), 316–326.

Goodman, Y. (1995). Miscue analysis for classroom teachers: Some history and some procedures. *Primary Voices K–6, 3*(4), 2–9.

Gough, P. B. (2004). One second of reading: Postscript. In R. R. Ruddell & N. J. Unrau (Eds.), *Theoretical models and processes of reading* (5th ed., pp. 17–28). Newark, DE: International Reading Association.

Graham, S. (2006). Strategy instruction and the teaching of writing: A meta-analysis. In S. Graham, C. S. MacArthur, & J. Fitzgerald (Eds.), *Handbook of writing research* (pp. 187–207). New York: Guilford Press.

Graham, S., MacArthur, C. A., & Fitzgerald, J. (2007). Best practices in writing instruction now. In S. Graham, C. S. MacArthur, & J. Fitzgerald (Eds.), *Best practices in writing instruction* (pp. 1–9). New York: Guilford Press.

Graves, M. F., & Watts-Taffe, S. (2008). For the love of words: Fostering word consciousness in young readers. *The Reading Teacher, 62*(3), 185–193.

Gunning, T. G. (2013). *Creating literacy instruction for all students* (8th ed.). New York: Pearson.

Hart, B., & Risley, T. R. (1995). *Meaningful differences in the everyday experience of young American children*. Baltimore: Brookes.

Hart, B., & Risley, T. R. (2003, Spring). The early catastrophe: The 30 million word gap by age 3. *American Educator*, pp. 3–4.

Hartman, D. K., Morsink, P. B., & Zheng, J. (2010). From print to pixels: The evolution of cognitive comprehension. In E. A. Baker (Ed.), *The new literacies: Multiple perspectives on research and practice* (pp. 131–164). New York: Guilford Press.

Haskell, C. (2012) *Design variables of attraction in quest-based learning*. Boise State University, Theses and Dissertations. Available at: *http://works.bepress.com/chris_haskell/14*.

Hayes, J. R. (1996). A new framework for understanding cognition and affect in writing. In C. M. Levy & S. Ransdell (Eds.), *The science of writing: Theories, methods, individual differences, and applications* (pp. 1–28). Mahwah, NJ: Erlbaum.

Hayes, J. R. (2006). New directions in writing theory. In S. Graham, C. S. MacArthur, & J. Fitzgerald (Eds.), *Handbook of writing research* (pp. 28–40). New York: Guilford Press.

Hayes, J. R., & Flower, L. (1980). Identifying the organization of writing processes. In L. W. Gregg & E. R. Steinberg (Eds.), *Cognitive processes in writing* (pp. 3–30). Hillsdale, NJ: Erlbaum.

Heath, S. B. (1983/1996). *Ways with words: Language, life and work in communities and classrooms*. Cambridge, UK: Cambridge University Press.

Hollings, E., & Guzman, M. T. (2010). Research on preparing teachers for diverse populations. In M. Cochran-Smith & K. Zeichner (Eds), *Studying teacher education: The report of the AERA panel on research and teacher education* (pp. 477–548). Mahwah, NJ: Erlbaum.

Hoover, W. A., & Gough, P. B. (1990). The simple view of reading. *Reading and Writing, 2*, 127–160.

International Reading Association. (2002). *Integrating literacy and technology into the curriculum: A position statement of the International Reading Association*. Newark, DE: Author.

International Reading Association. (2007). *Teaching reading well: A synthesis of the International Reading Association's research on teacher preparation for reading instruction*. Newark, DE: Author.

International Reading Association. (2010). *Standards for reading professionals: A reference for the preparation of educators in the United States.* Newark, DE: Author.

Johnson, D. (2011). *Train dreams.* New York: Farrar, Straus & Giroux.

Johnston, P. (2004). *Choice words: How our language affects children's learning.* Portand, ME: Stenhouse.

Johnston, P. (2012). *Opening minds: Using language to change lives.* Portland, ME: Stenhouse.

Kear, D. J., Coffman, G. A., McKenna, M. G., & Ambrosio, A. L. (2000). Measuring attitude toward writing: A new tool for teachers. *The Reading Teacher, 54*(1).

Kuhn, M. R., Schwanenflugel, P. J., & Meisinger, E. B. (2010). Review of research: Aligning theory and assessment of reading fluency: Automaticity, prosody, and definitions of fluency. *Reading Research Quarterly, 45*(2), 230–251.

Kuiper, E., & Volman, M. (2008). The web as a source of information for students in K–12 education. In J. Coiro, M. Knobel, C. Lankshear, & D. J. Leu (Eds.), *Handbook of research on new literacies* (pp. 241–266). New York: Erlbaum.

Lankshear, C., & Knobel, M. (2011). *New literacies: Everyday practices and classroom learning.* Maidenhead, UK: Open University Press.

Leu, D. J. (2002). The new literacies: Research on reading instruction with the internet. In A. E. Farstrup & S. J. Samuels (Eds.), *What research has to say about reading instruction* (3rd ed., pp. 310–336). Newark, DE: International Reading Association.

Leu, D. J. (2010). Foreword. In E. A. Baker (Ed.), *The new literacies: Multiple perspectives on research and practice* (pp. viii–xi). New York: Guilford Press.

Leu, D. J., Coiro, J., Castek, J., Hartman, D. K., Henry, L. A., & Reinking, D. (2008). Research on instruction and assessment in the new literacies of online reading comprehension. In C. C. Block & S. R. Parris (Eds.), *Comprehension instruction: Research-based best practices* (2nd ed., pp. 321–345). New York: Guilford Press.

Leu, D. J., Jr., Leu, D. D., & Coiro, J. (2004). *Teaching with the Internet: New literacies for new times* (4th ed.). Norwood, MA: Christopher-Gordon.

Leu, D. J., McVerry, G., O'Byrne, W. I., Zawilinski, L., Castek, J., & Hartman, D. K. (2009). The new literacies of online reading comprehension and the irony of No Child Left Behind: Students who require our assistance the most actually receive it the least. In L. M. Morrow, R. Rueda, & D. Lapp (Eds.), *Handbook of research on literacy and diversity* (pp. 173–194). New York: Guilford Press.

Locke, E., & Latham, G. (1990). *A theory of goal setting and task performance.* Englewood Cliffs, NJ: Prentice Hall.

Luke, A., & Woods, A. (2009). Critical literacies in schools: A primer. *Voices from the Middle, 17*(2), 9–18.

Lynch-Brown, C. (2007). *Essentials of young adult literature.* Upper Saddle River, NJ: Pearson Education.

Martin, S. D. (2002). *Fostering students' participation in writing activity in three urban classrooms.* Unpublished doctoral dissertation, University of Washington, Seattle, WA.

Martin, S. D. (2004). Finding balance: Impact of classroom management conceptions on developing teacher practice. *Teaching and Teacher Education, 20*(5), 405–422.

Martin, S. D. (2009, April). *How have they learned?: Preservice teachers' perspectives on pedagogical practices in a writing methods course.* Paper presented at the annual conference of the American Educational Research Association, San Diego, CA.

Martin, S. D., & Dismuke, S. (2013). Engaging teachers in digital products and processes: Interview feature articles. In K. E. Pytash, R. E. Ferdig, & T. V. Rasinski (Eds.), *Preparing teachers to teach writing using technology* (pp. 97–108). Pittsburgh, PA: ETC Press.

McCarrier, A., Fountas, I., & Pinnell, G. S. (1999). *Interactive writing: How language and literacy come together, K–2*. Portsmouth, NH: Heinemann.

McDaniel, C. (2004). Critical literacy: A questioning stance and the possibility for change. *The Reading Teacher, 57*(5), 472–481.

McKenna, M. C., & Stahl, S. A. (2009). *Assessment for reading instruction*. New York: Guilford Press.

McTigue, E. M., Washburn, E. K., & Liew, J. (2009). Academic resilience and reading: Building successful readers. *The Reading Teacher, 62*(5), 422–432.

Miller, D. (2009). *The book whisperer: Awakening the inner reader in every child*. San Francisco: Jossey-Bass.

Murray, D. (1982). *Learning by teaching: Selecting articles on writing and teaching*. Montclair, NJ: Boynton/Cook.

Nagy, W. E., Anderson, R. C., & Herman, P. A. (1987). Learning word meanings from context during normal reading. *American Educational Research Journal, 24*(2), 237–270.

National Association for the Education of Young Children. (2009). *Developmentally appropriate practice for children in early childhood programs serving children from birth through age eight*. Retrieved March 14, 2013, from *www.naeyc.org/files/naeyc/file/positions/PSDAP.pdf*.

National Council of Teachers of English. (2008). *NCTE framework for 21st century curriculum and assessment*. Retrieved from *www.ncte.org/library/NCTEFiles/Resources/Positions/Framework_21stCent_Curr_Assessment.pdf*.

National Reading Panel. (2000). *Teaching children to read: An evidence-based assessment of the scientific research literature on reading and its implications for reading instruction: Report of the subgroups*. Washington, DC: National Institute of Child Health and Human Development.

National Research Council. (2010). *Preparing teachers: Building evidence for sound policy*. Washington, DC: Committee on the Study of Teacher Preparation Programs in the United States, Center for Education. Division of Behavioral and Social Sciences and Education.

Paley, V. G. (2000). *White teacher*. Cambridge, MA: Harvard University Press.

Palincsar, A. S., & Brown, A. L. (1984). Reciprocal teaching of comprehension-fostering and comprehension-monitoring activities. *Cognition and Instruction, 1*(2), 117–175.

Paris, S. (2005). Reinterpreting the development of reading skills. *Reading Research Quarterly, 40*(2), 184–202.

Paris, S., & Myers, M. (1981). Comprehension monitoring, memory, and study strategies of good and poor readers. *Journal of Reading Behavior, 13*(1), 5–22.

Pearson, P. D., & Dole, J. A. (1987). Explicit comprehension instruction: A review of research and a new conceptualization of instruction. *Elementary School Journal, 88*(2), 151–165.

Pearson, P. D., Rohler, L. R., Dole, J. A., & Duffy, G. G. (1992). Developing expertise in reading comprehension. In S. J. Samuels & A. E. Farstrup (Eds.), *What research has to say about reading* (pp. 149–199). Newark, DE: International Reading Association.

Peck, C., Gallucci, C., & Staub, D. (2002). Vulnerability and the inclusion of children with severe disabilities in regular classrooms: Risk and opportunity. In G. Furman-Brown (Ed.), *Schools as communities: Promise to practice*. New York: State University of New York Press.

Peterson, R., & Eeds, M. (1990). *Grand conversations: Literature groups in action*. New York: Scholastic.

Piaget, J., & Inhelder, B. (1971). *The psychology of the child*. New York: Harper Torchbooks.

Pinker, S. (1994). *The language instinct: How the mind creates language*. New York: Morrow.

Place, N. A., & English, M. (1998). Examining growth over time. In S. W. Valencia (Ed.), *Literacy portfolios in action* (pp. 219–260). Fort Worth, TX: Harcourt Brace.

Pressley, M. (2000). What should comprehension instruction be the instruction of? In M. Kamil, P. Mosenthal, P. Pearson, & R. Barr, (Eds,), *Handbook of reading research: Vol. II* (pp. 545–561). Mahwah, NJ: Erlbaum.

Pressley, M., Mohan, L., Raphael, L., & Fingeret, L. (2007). How does Bennett Woods Elementary School produce such high reading and writing achievement? *Journal of Educational Psychology, 99*, 221–240.

Prior, P. (2006). A sociocultural theory of writing. In C. A. MacArthur, S. Graham, & J. Fitzgerald (Eds.), *The handbook of writing research* (pp. 54–66). New York: Guilford Press.

Pritchard, R., & Honeycutt, R. (2007). Best practices in implementing a process approach to teaching writing. In S. Graham, C. MacArthur, & J. Fitzgerald (Eds.), *Best practices in writing instruction* (pp. 28–49). New York: Guilford Press.

Raphael, T. E., & McMahon, S. I. (1994). Book club: An alternative framework for reading instruction. *The Reading Teacher, 48*, 102–116.

Rhodes, L. K. (1993). *Literacy assessment: A handbook of instruments.* Portsmouth, NH: Heinemann.

Richardson, J. (2009). *The next step in guided reading: Focused assessments and targeted lessons for helping every student become a better reader.* New York: Scholastic.

Rosenblatt, L. (1938/1983). *Literature as exploration.* New York: Modern Language Association of America.

Sadoski, M., & Paivio, A. (2004). A dual coding theoretical model for reading. In R. B. Ruddell & N. J. Unrau (Eds.), *Theoretical models and processes of reading* (4th ed., pp. 1329–1362). Newark, DE: International Reading Association.

Samuels, S. J., Rasinski, T. V., & Hiebert, E. (2011). Eye movements and reading: What teachers need to know. In S. J. Samuels & A. E. Farstrup (Eds.), *What research has to say about reading instruction* (4th ed., pp. 25–50). Newark, DE: International Reading Association.

Scarborough, H. (1998). Early identification of children at risk for reading disabilities. In B. K. Shapiro, P. J. Accardo, & A. J. Capute (Eds.), *Specific reading disability: A view of the spectrum* (pp. 75–119). Baltimore: York Press.

Scardamalia, M., & Bereiter, C. (1986). Research on written composition. In M. C. Wittrock (Ed.), *Handbook of research on teaching* (3rd ed., pp. 778–803). New York: Macmillan.

Scardamalia, M., & Bereiter, C. (1991). Literate expertise. In K. A. Ericsson & J. Smith (Eds.), *Toward a general theory of expertise: Prospects and limits* (pp. 172–194). Cambridge, UK: Cambridge University Press.

Schiefele, U., Schaffner, E., Moller, J., & Wigfield, A. (2012). Dimensions of reading motivation and their relation to reading behavior and competence (S. Nolen & L. Baker, Consulting Eds.). *Reading Research Quarterly, 47*(4), 427–463.

Sénéchal, M., Ouelette, G., & Rodney, D. (2006). The misunderstood giant: On the predictive role of early vocabulary to future reading. In S. B. Neuman & D. K. Dickenson (Eds.), *Handbook of early literacy research: Vol. 2* (pp. 173–182). New York: Guilford Press.

Share, D. L. (1999). Phonological recoding and orthographic learning: A direct test of the self-teaching hypothesis. *Journal of Experimental Child Psychology, 72*, 95–129.

Smith, F. (1988). *Joining the literacy club: Further essays into education.* Portsmouth, NH: Heinemann.

Snow, C. E., Griffin, P., & Burns, S. M. (2005). *Knowledge to support the teaching of reading: Preparing teachers for a changing world.* San Francisco: Jossey-Bass.

Spear-Swerling, L. (2004). A roadmap for understanding reading disability and other reading problems: Origins, prevention, and intervention. In R. B. Ruddell & N. J. Unrau (Eds.), *Theoretical models and processes of reading* (5th ed., pp. 517–573). Newark, DE: International Reading Association.

Stahl, S. A., & Murray, B. (1998). Issues involved in defining phonological awareness and its relation to early reading. In J. L. Metsala & L. C. Ehri (Eds.), *Word recognition in beginning literacy* (pp. 65–87). Mahwah, NJ: Erlbaum.

Sternberg, R. J. (2001). *Psychology: In search of the mind* (3rd ed.). New York: Harcourt College.

Taylor, C. S., & Nolen, S. B. (2008). *Classroom assessment: Supporting teaching and learning in real classrooms.* Upper Saddle River, NJ: Pearson.

Tompkins, G. (2011). *Teaching writing: Balancing process and product* (6th ed.). New York: Allyn & Bacon.

Tough, P. (2012). *How children succeed: Grit, curiosity, and the hidden power of character.* New York: Houghton Mifflin Harcourt.

Townsend, D. R., & Lapp, D. (2011). Academic language, discourse communities, and technology: Building students' linguistic resources [Special online edition]. *Teacher Education Quarterly.*

Troia, G., Lin, S., Cohen, S., & Monroe, B. (2011). A year in the writers' workshop: Linking writing instruction practices and teachers' epistemologies and beliefs about writing instruction. *Elementary School Journal, 112*(1), 155–182.

Tysseling, L. A. & McCulley, M. (2012). Going mobile: Reframing the classroom for 21st century: A self-study concerning digital class spaces in teacher education courses. In *Extending inquiry communities: Illuminating teacher education through self-study.* Proceedings of the ninth International Conference on Self-Study of Teacher Education Practices [Herstmonceux Castle, UK], Brigham Young University, Provo, UT.

Valencia, S. W. (1998). *Literacy portfolios in action.* Fort Worth, TX: Harcourt Brace.

Vygotsky, L. S. (1978). *Mind in society: The development of higher psychological processes* (M. Cole, V. John-Steiner, S. Scribner, & E. Souberman, Eds.). Boston: Harvard University Press.

Wheeler, R., & Swords, R. (2004). Codeswitching: Tools of language and culture transform the dialectally diverse classrooms. *Language Arts, 81*(6), 470–480.

Wheeler, R., & Swords, R. (2010). *Code-switching lessons: Grammar strategies for linguistically diverse writers, 3–6.* Portsmouth, NH: Heinemann.

Wolf, M., & Katzir-Cohen, T. (2001). Reading fluency and its intervention. *Scientific Studies of Reading, 5*(3), 211–239.

Wood, A., & Wood, D. (2000). *The napping house.* New York: Harcourt.

Yopp, H. (1995). A test for assessing phonemic awareness in young children. *The Reading Teacher, 49*(1), 20–29.

Index